MURDER & JUSTICE IN FRONTIER NEW MEXICO, 1821–1846

JILL MOCHO

Murder & Justice in Frontier New Mexico 1821–1846

✣ ✣ ✣

University of New Mexico Press Albuquerque

FIRST EDITION

Library of Congress Cataloging-in-Publication

Mocho, Jill, 1946–

Murder and justice in New Mexico, 1821–1846 / Jill Mocho. — 1st ed.

p. cm.

Includes bibliographical references and index.

Contents: New Mexico under Mexico, 1821–1846—Frontier justice—The bad life—Death before Christmas—The servant boy—Murder in the Bosque—Domestic Violence—Death at a Fandango—A matter of honor—Trouble in Tome—Murder within the community—Death in a mining camp—The missing peddler—Two Frenchmen—An acquittal—Conflict with foreigners.

ISBN 0-8263-1765-0 (cl) 0-8263-1800-2 (pbk.)

1. Murder—New Mexico—History—Case studies. 2. Trials (Murder)—New Mexico—History—Case studies. 3. Criminal justice, Administration of—New Mexico—History. 4. New Mexico—History—To 1848. I. Title.

HV6533.N4M63 1997

364.1'523'0978909034—dc20 96-10007

CIP

Contents

Acknowledgments

I wish to thank everyone who advised and encouraged me during the long process of researching and writing this work. I am grateful to Linda Hall and John Kessell for guiding me through the thesis that would eventually become this book. Special thanks go to Robert Himmerich y Valencia, whose encouragement and advice I sought on numerous occasions and who brought the manuscript to the attention of Durwood Ball at The University of New Mexico Press.

I am grateful to Robert Tórrez at the New Mexico State Records Center and Archives for his interest in the early stages of my research in the field of homicide and justice in Mexican- Era New Mexico and for sharing with me his own research in Spanish colonial and territorial New Mexican justice.

I wish to thank Charles R. Cutter for his careful reading of the manuscript. His expertise on Spanish colonial justice and Spanish legal terminology of this era was invaluable, and I appreciate all of his comments and recommendations.

I also appreciate the time spent by various people at campus computer labs (especially Paul and Cloe) who helped me with necessary technical support. My thanks go to Durwood Ball at the University of New Mexico Press and to the copyeditor Louise Cameron for her careful scrutiny of the manuscript.

Finally, I would like to thank my parents, husband and son, whose love and support made it possible for me to find the time necessary to pursue this interest.

Introduction

Criminal cases are an excellent source for the study of social history. They contain the voices of people who otherwise might not leave any written record of their lives. Homicides shed light on the conflicts, tensions, and values of the society in which they are perpetrated. Eleven homicide cases were adjudicated by local authorities in New Mexico during a twenty-five-year period when it was part of the Republic of Mexico. Most of the witnesses and suspects whose testimonies appear in these judicial cases were ordinary New Mexican *vecinos* (citizens); they were uneducated farmers, laborers, and artisans who could not read or write. Their statements offer a small glimpse into the personal lives of this silent segment of the population and an intimate look at the society in which these people lived.

The Mexican Era was ushered in by Mexico's independence from Spain in 1821, and it came to an abrupt end in 1846 when forces from the United States under Brigadier General Stephen Watts Kearny occupied New Mexico.[1] These were years of turbulence and change in New Mexico. The old order of Spanish colonialism gave way to the confusion of the Republican Era. Restrictions on trade were lifted, and *extranjeros* (foreigners) from the north found their way into New Mexico in increasing numbers. New economic opportunities brought more wealth into the area—a wealth that was not spread equally among the populace—and class distinctions became more pronounced. Life was often violent on the poorly defended frontier, where Indian depredations increased as military expenditure for the defense of the frontiers diminished. Mission churches that had been a source of comfort for vecinos on the frontier were secularized, and the few underpaid secular priests who were sent to replace the Franciscan fathers charged more for their services than the poor could afford. A local religious brotherhood, commonly called *Penitentes*, developed during this time to fill the spiritual void and to perform religious functions.

Obviously there was stress and conflict in this society. Was it reflected in the number of homicide cases that were adjudicated? Apparently not. Only eleven cases were found in the official records of this twenty-five-year period. Ten of these cases were located in the Mexican Archives of New Mexico (MANM), and one was found in the Sender Collection, a group of documents from the Río Arriba that had been missing since the early twentieth century.[2]

Is it possible that in this rough, frontier society there were no more than eleven homicides? Even taking into consideration that the population in New Mexico during this period was relatively small and scattered (42,000 in 1821, 65,000 in 1846), this is a very low figure.[3] Still, after commenting unfavorably on the state of legal affairs in New Mexico, Josiah Gregg did remark in his classic work, *Commerce of the Prairies*, that "there are few murders of any kind committed."[4]

Possibly some records were lost over the years due to neglect or outright destruction. In the capital, Santa Fe, Spanish and Mexican officials had maintained a repository of official government documents and correspondence. However, the Territorial Period under the United States was a disastrous time for the New Mexican Archives. The care or neglect of the archives usually depended on the whim of the current governor and his associates. At least one farsighted individual, Territorial Secretary Donaciano Vigil, recognized the value of the old documents, and from 1849 to 1851 he inventoried and indexed them for easier access.[5] On the other hand, one infamous territorial governor, attempting to create more space in the Palace of the Governors, threw boxes of old papers out into the streets.[6] It is safe to assume that some criminal cases, including perhaps a homicide, may have been lost over the years.

Another possibility is that some murders were never brought to the attention of the authorities, or if they were reported they were never brought to trial. From Taos, the merchant and trader Charles Bent wrote to U.S. Consul Manuel Alvarez asking that he forward a petition to the governor requesting the immediate trial of William Langford for the murder of Semon Nash.[7] In his 1842 report to U.S. Secretary of State Daniel Webster, Consul Alvarez mentioned two other murders that were never brought to trial, including that of a deaf mute, Frances Lacompte, clubbed to death by local authorities in Taos when he failed to respond to a summons.[8] In the same document, Alvarez mentioned that a Marcelino Pacheco had confessed to the murder of Juan Bautista Leal in Mora.[9] Matt Field, adventurer and journalist for the *New Orleans Picayune*, described a visit to the Santa Fe jail in 1839, in an article entitled "The Dying Murderer." Field described the misery of a prisoner dying of an unknown disease in the Santa Fe jail, where he was being held for the murder of his niece.[10] These four homicides do not appear in the archives; if they were ever tried in the alcalde courts, the records have since been lost.

The eleven cases presented here are only those homicides that came to trial and whose records survived in the official archives of the Mexican Era. The scarcity of homicide cases made it impractical for me to attempt any type of statistical analysis. Instead, each murder case is related separately in its own chapter. The cases make interesting stories that not only describe in detail the judicial proceedings, but also tell a great deal about how New Mexicans lived during this time.

The basis for these stories is comprised of records kept by local justices (either the *juez de paz* or the *alcalde*), who investigated the crimes. Thus, the investigative process and legal practices are described in some detail, depending on how complete the records are.

To flesh out the case histories, additional background information about New Mexican conditions and customs during the early nineteenth century was gleaned from various primary and secondary sources. Especially helpful were journals and diaries written during or shortly after the Mexican Era by foreigners who came across the Santa Fe Trail. These adventurers and merchants wrote detailed descriptions of New Mexican life and customs. Always colorful, but often prejudiced, these accounts are great sources of information on Mexican New Mexico.[11] Unfortunately, native New Mexicans seldom left such descriptive accounts of their society. However, a handful of New Mexicans, Mexicans from other parts of Mexico, and one Spaniard did write reports to government or church officials about conditions in New Mexico during the early nineteenth century. Although less descriptive than diaries and journals, such reports contain important and interesting background information on the social and economic history of this era.[12]

To make the cases more meaningful, the first chapter contains a brief historical background of the Mexican Era, emphasizing social and economic aspects of life in New Mexico at that time. Chapter 2 discusses the political organization of New Mexico and judicial procedures practiced on that remote frontier. These two introductory chapters are followed by a chapter on each of the eleven murders and the judicial investigations that followed. The cases have been organized into three sections according to patterns suggested by the relationship between the victim and accused murderer.

William Taylor, in his study on crime in eighteenth-century peasant villages of central Mexico and the valley of Oaxaca, described three patterns of homicides based on the relationship between victim and offender: (1) kinsmen, sex partners, or sex rivals, (2) townsmen, and (3) citizens of different communities.[13] The patterns distinguished in Taylor's study closely resemble the categories found in the New Mexico homicides: (1) domestic violence (*familia*), (2) neighbors or citizens (vecinos), and (3) foreigners or immigrants (extranjeros).

First, and most striking, was the pattern of domestic violence, covered in the section "Familia." Domestic violence, that which occurs between family members, is a recurrent theme in criminology. This form of violence is almost always perpetrated by the head of the family against its dependent and weaker members. Wives and children living at home are the most common victims of domestic abuse; however, in extended families victims might include servants, widowed female relatives, and other dependent persons living in the same household.[14] The four homicide cases in this section fit the category of domestic violence: three women murdered by their spouses and one servant boy who died as a result of a brutal beating by his master.

The next section contains three cases involving two unrelated Mexican men. Each murder was the result of a spontaneous outbreak of violence between friends or acquaintances, provoked by humiliation or injured pride. For lack of a more definitive name, this section is titled "Vecinos," a term which has several connotations. "Vecino" means neighbor, citizen, or resident; in Spanish colonial documents it often referred to a landowner, or taxpaying head-of-household. The term was used by nearly all of the Mexican witnesses and suspects in their testimonies, whether to specify residency or to imply landownership in a particular place is not certain; however, according to Cutter, the term was used loosely by New Mexicans to designate residency in a particular locale.[15] In this work, "vecino" is used in the most general sense, to signify a Mexican citizen or member of a Mexican community; this is to differentiate from crimes involving familia or extranjeros.

"Extranjeros," the final section, tells the stories of four homicide cases involving foreigners. The tension between extranjeros and local New Mexicans that developed throughout the Mexican Period sometimes led to violence. With good reasons, Anglos were often viewed as arrogant, racist, and disrespectful of Mexican culture.[16] Most contemporary accounts written by *norteamericanos* about New Mexico reveal an obvious cultural bias, and many exhibit outright racial prejudice.[17] That New Mexicans resented this invasion of foreigners who considered themselves culturally superior was only normal, and some violent encounters did occur. Two of the homicides were perpetrated by Mexican citizens against foreign merchants, and as a result they generated a great deal of publicity and anger among the foreign community living in New Mexico. One incident occurred between two Frenchmen. The final case involved a foreigner accused of murdering a local New Mexican.

A great deal of information about the lives of ordinary people is contained in these few murder cases. The motive for murder and the relationship between victim and attacker hold important clues to the tensions and values in a society. A concluding chapter to each of these sections ("Familia," "Vecinos," and "Extranjeros") discusses the possible social and cultural values and economic conditions that led to the conflict and violence described in the cases in that section.

Each case is prefaced with a "cast of characters," listing all of the persons mentioned in the court records and their significance in the case. The first characters mentioned—in the heading—are the suspect (*reo*), and the victim or deceased (*difunto*). They are followed by a list of the authorities involved in the trial: the justice (*alcalde* or *juez de paz*), the prosecutor (*promotor fiscal*), and the defender (*defensor*). Also included are the priest (*cura*), the doctor or surgeon (*cirujano*), witnesses (*testigos*), attending witnesses to the investigation (*testigos de asistencia*), and anyone else (*otros*) mentioned in the records.

The character sheet is headed by the location and date of the crime. The date may indicate the date of the murder, or the date when the investigation was first instigated, or, in the case of an incomplete file, the date of the first document. In one case the initial date is a guess at when the homicide occurred, since no body was found and the file is incomplete. The location of the crime is obvious in most cases, except where no body was found. In these cases, the place mentioned as the crime scene is an approximate location arrived at by using evidence brought out by witnesses.

Spelling of Spanish names and place-names generally follows the spelling found in the case files, hence, "Alburquerque" and "Del Bado." Most words follow modern spelling (extranjero was spelled "estrangero" in the files). Accents were rarely used in files; I have added them according to modern usage. Names that were difficult to decipher due to individual style of penmanship are approximate. Foreign names are given in both their Spanish equivalent and, if known, their actual English or French version.

Spanish words are usually defined the first time they appear in the text and are combined in a glossary at the end of the book.

The final chapter summarizes the workings of the Spanish judicial system as it was applied to homicide cases in post-colonial, pre-territorial New Mexico and makes some comparisons with crime and justice in other parts of Mexico during a similar time frame. By studying homicide cases we not only see how the judicial system functioned and how societies dealt with violent crime, but we also get a good insight into the values and beliefs of that society. The conclusion discusses what we know about this society based solely on information found in the murder cases.

MURDER & JUSTICE IN FRONTIER NEW MEXICO, 1821–1846

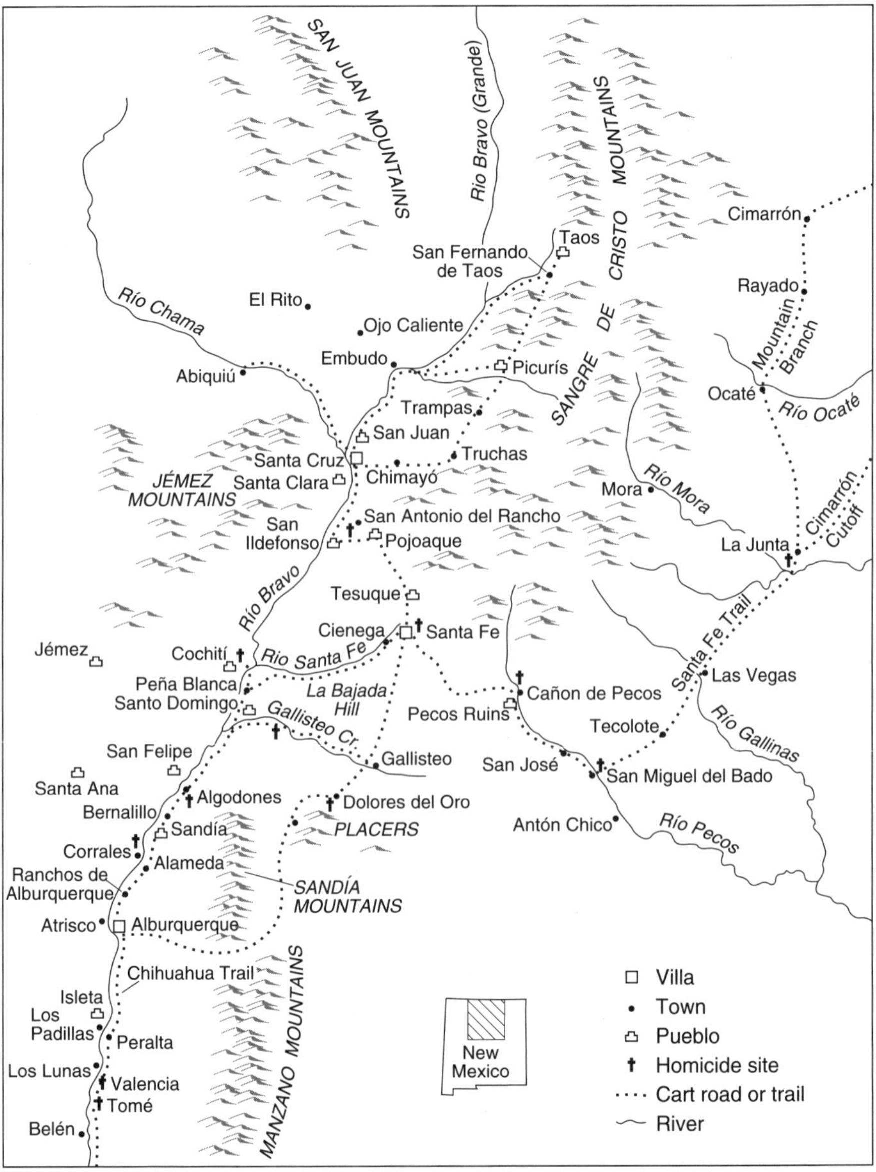
SAN JUAN MOUNTAINS
Rio Bravo (Grande)
SANGRE DE CRISTO MOUNTAINS
Cimarrón
Taos
San Fernando de Taos
Rayado
Mountain Branch
Río Chama
El Rito
Ojo Caliente
Embudo
Picurís
Abiquiú
Ocaté
Río Ocaté
Trampas
San Juan
Santa Cruz
Truchas
Chimayó
Santa Clara
JÉMEZ MOUNTAINS
Mora
Río Mora
San Antonio del Rancho
San Ildefonso
Pojoaque
La Junta
Cimarrón Cutoff
Río Bravo
Tesuque
Cienega
Santa Fe
Santa Fe Trail
Jémez
Cochití
Rio Santa Fe
Las Vegas
Peña Blanca
La Bajada Hill
Cañon de Pecos
Santo Domingo
Gallisteo Cr.
Pecos Ruins
Tecolote
Río Gallinas
San Felipe
Gallisteo
San José
San Miguel del Bado
Santa Ana
Algodones
Dolores del Oro
Bernalillo
Sandía
PLACERS
Antón Chico
Río Pecos
Corrales
Alameda
Ranchos de Alburquerque
SANDÍA MOUNTAINS
Atrisco
Alburquerque
Chihuahua Trail
MANZANO MOUNTAINS
Isleta
Los Padillas
Peralta
Los Lunas
Valencia
Tomé
Belén
New Mexico
Villa
Town
Pueblo
Homicide site
Cart road or trail
River

ONE

New Mexico Under Mexico, 1821–1846

For twenty-five years the flag of Mexico flew over the sparsely settled, remote, frontier region of New Mexico. That turbulent quarter-century began with Mexico's independence from Spain in 1821, and ended with the United States' annexation of the area in 1846. This brief interlude in New Mexico's long history is known as the Mexican Era. Sandwiched between more than two centuries of Spanish colonial rule and almost a century and a half under U.S. dominion, that brief twenty-five years under Mexico is a misunderstood and neglected part of New Mexico's history. Some have seen it as merely an extension of the long colonial period, and others view the Mexican Era as the beginning of the American occupation. The Mexican Period was both and neither; it was a time of transition and dramatic change, and a fascinating chapter in New Mexico history.[1]

Mexican independence from Spain brought a new government with more liberal policies. For the first time New Mexicans were allowed to trade with foreigners. The Santa Fe Trail was opened the same year, and eager extranjeros pushed across the prairies with wagonloads of merchandise to sell in the dusty plazas of New Mexico.[2] The foreigners were welcome and the exchange was mostly beneficial to all, but it soon became apparent that, once invited in, the extranjeros were there to stay. Inevitable conflicts and rivalries between local Mexicans and the aggressive Anglo and French merchants sometimes led to violence.

Many of these foreigners, mostly Anglo-Americans and French-Canadians, settled permanently in New Mexico. Taos became a favorite mecca of foreigners who built up a prosperous fur trade, established distilleries and mills, and engaged in various other mercantile enterprises.[3] In the capital, these North American traders set up shops on the plaza where they sold U.S. hardware and dry goods. To circumvent certain regulations against foreigners, many of these immigrants found it expedient to become naturalized citizens. Some converted to Catholicism and married local ladies, forging important social alliances with Hispanic families.[4] Towards the end of the Mexican Era, numbers of these foreigners, in partnership with Mexican friends and in-laws, acquired huge land grants.[5]

The Santa Fe traders continued on down the "Camino Real" into Chihuahua and Mexican cities farther south, breaking forever the monopoly of the Chihuahua merchants. This opened up new business opportunities for New Mexicans, who no longer had to rely solely on Mexico for trade. *Rico* families, many of whom ran huge flocks of sheep on immense acreages of land, had the opportunity to enter the Santa Fe trade and develop new mercantile interests. Further, they were able to afford the American goods that came across the trail. That small group of elite families, known as the *gente fina*, controlled the wealth, dominated society, and maintained power through intermarriage and politics.[6]

Manuel Armijo was perhaps the most notorious character of the Mexican Era; he was closely involved in all the major events that occurred in that turbulent quarter-century. Armijo was descended from two of the most prominent and wealthy landowning families of the Río Abajo region, the Armijos and the Chávezes, who were closely connected through generations of intermarriage.[7] He served as governor of New Mexico on three different occasions, for a combined total of close to ten years.[8] He was a trader and merchant in the prosperous Santa Fe trade. Armijo was a controversial figure, sometimes the hero and often the villain. He played a major role in the Rebellion of 1837 and the Texas Invasion of 1841. He was responsible for granting over sixteen and a half million acres of land to private individuals during the waning years of the Mexican Era.[9] Finally, Armijo has gone down in history as the governor who deserted New Mexico when conquering American troops marched into Santa Fe in the fall of 1846 at the start of the Mexican-American War.

Wealth created by new economic opportunities was not shared equally by all segments of the population, however, and New Mexican society became more stratified. The economic benefits of the Santa Fe trade were not so readily available to the poorer classes who continued to farm small plots of land or work as wage laborers for others. Many found themselves caught up in a system of peonage where they remained most of their lives indebted to a wealthy *patrón*.[10] The Rebellion of 1837 was a brief but bloody affair that hinted at class conflict between the gente fina of Río Abajo and the poorer Hispanic settlers and Pueblos of the Río Arriba.[11]

The terms Río Arriba and Río Abajo refer to two geographic areas that roughly divide New Mexico in half—north and south. The dividing point is a place called La Bajada (the descent) Mesa, where the Santa Fe Plateau drops fifteen hundred feet from the Río Arriba (upper river) to the Río Abajo (lower river). Historically, Río Abajo was the wealthier of the two areas; it was home of the *ricos* who raised sheep with the aid of *peones* on large tracts of land, in the broad valley of the Río del Norte (Río Grande). These wealthy families prospered during the Mexican Era, trading their sheep and fine U.S.-manufactured goods down the Chihuahua Trail. Generally, the Río Arriba was home to the poorer farmers and stockmen who worked small plots of land along the river valleys and mountain streams of northern New Mexico. The capital, Santa Fe, was about nineteen miles from La Bajada and not considered part of either Río Arriba or Río Abajo.[12]

In New Mexico, native people were classified into three general groups: (1) Pueblo Indians, so called because they were village (pueblo) dwellers, (2) nomadic tribes called *indios bárbaros* (wild Indians) or *gentiles*, and (3) detribalized Indians called *genízaros*. At the beginning of the Mexican Era, there were some nine thousand Pueblo Indians living in twenty pueblos in New Mexico. Although they could speak Spanish, professed Christianity, and had lived at relative peace with their Hispanic conquerors since the late seventeenth century, the Pueblos lived separately in their own villages where they spoke their native tongue and retained much of their preconquest way of life.[13]

Indios bárbaros was a generic term for the unsettled tribes of Apache, Comanche, Navajo, Ute, Pawnee, and other plains people who were never conquered and did not accept Spanish institutions or lifestyles. These nomadic tribes, armed with firearms supplied by unscrupulous American traders, roamed the outskirts of Mexican settlements awaiting an opportunity to raid for livestock and human captives.[14] Annual trade fairs had been established in Taos and Abiquiú during colonial times to allow the settlers and Pueblos to trade with nomadic tribes. Once the fairs were over, the usual hostilities resumed, but in the meantime Spanish-made blankets, iron implements, knives, and horses were traded to the indios bárbaros in exchange for buffalo hides, skins, meat, and captives.[15]

The human captives ransomed from indios bárbaros were taken into Spanish homes where they were made to pay for their ransom as *sirvientes* (servants). Indios sirvientes were schooled in Christianity, taught to speak

Spanish, and forced to give up their Indian culture and live as Hispanics. Supposedly when their servitude was over, they and their children were free to enter Hispanic society as *indios genízaros*. Not considered either Spanish or Indian, they suffered from lack of social status and found it difficult to be accepted in Pueblo or Hispanic societies. Throughout the eighteenth century genízaros were settled in towns in frontier areas that served as buffer zones between Spanish communities and the "wild" tribes. Towns settled by genízaros included Abiquiú and Ojo Caliente in the Río Arriba; Belén, Tomé, and Valencia in the Río Abajo; and San Miguel del Bado to the east.[16] Although by nationality genízaros were Indian, their lifestyle was essentially Hispanic, and consequently the Spanish considered them to be *gente de razón* (people of reason), a definition that excluded Pueblos who retained their Indian lifestyle.[17]

Following Independence, chaotic political conditions in Mexico allowed the frontier defenses to deteriorate. Presidio garrisons were undermanned, underfed, underpaid, and demoralized. As a result, the defense of New Mexico against indios bárbaros, civil uprisings, and possible invasions fell to the local people. Hispanic farmers and artisans and Pueblo Indians formed into militia units under officers chosen from the gente fina.[18]

Not only did the military defense of the northern frontier decline under Mexican administration, but spiritual leadership diminished as well. The Church attempted to secularize missions by replacing Franciscan *padres* with secular priests, but they were unable to send enough priests to administer to the growing population. The shortage of priests and the high fees they charged for performing basic religious services forced New Mexican vecinos to look for new ways to provide for their spiritual well-being.[19] La Cofradía de Nuestro Padre Jesús Nazareno, a penitential brotherhood, emerged to fill this spiritual vacuum. Although never sanctioned by the Roman Catholic Church, the brotherhood grew strong and spread throughout New Mexico. The Penitentes were a pious response to a spiritual need that the Catholic Church was no longer able to satisfy on the frontier.[20]

In this largely agricultural society, public education was sporadic and did not go beyond the primary level. Literacy was common only among the wealthy families who often educated their children at home or sent them to schools in other parts of Mexico.[21] These educated few were the ones who had access to public office; they became the governors, the alcaldes, and the jueces de paz.

Prior to Independence, New Mexico did not have a printing press, and the few books that were extant on the frontier were in private homes or owned by the church. In 1834, Josiah Gregg, adventurer, merchant, and author of *Commerce of the Prairies*, is credited with bringing 1,141 books (mostly school texts) and the first printing press over the Santa Fe Trail to the New Mexican frontier.[22] The press was used to print three separate and short-lived newspapers in Santa Fe, and the fiery native priest Antonio José Martínez used the press to publish some religious tracts and educational material for his students up in Taos.[23]

The frontier had few amenities to attract professional people. As a result, there were no doctors practicing in New Mexico throughout the Mexican Era. The only exception was the surgeon of the Santa Fe presidio and an occasional foreign doctor who might claim that distinguished title, with or without a medical degree. Sick and wounded persons had to depend on medicinal herbs, home remedies, *curanderos* (folk healers), and prayer to see them through their suffering. Some new drugs and a few foreign doctors arrived over the Santa Fe Trail, but most of these drugs proved more harmful than beneficial, and the doctors were often "quacks."[24]

Regardless of the warfare, violence, and lack of medical attention, the population of New Mexico did increase by 23,000 during the Mexican Era. Census reports indicate that shortly after Independence there were close to 42,000 New Mexicans, and by the end of the era some 65,000.[25] As the population increased, Hispanos spread out in every direction. Leaving the village of their birth behind, families pushed out into neighboring valleys and plains, where they established several new settlements before the American takeover.[26] The rise of population was due more to natural increase than to new immigration, which remained low during the Mexican Era.[27]

Even though the foreigners who settled in New Mexico prior to 1846 were few in number, the influence of the Anglos throughout the west by the mid-nineteenth century was strong, and there were those in the United States who had long felt that northern Mexico would be a nice addition to the country—a fulfillment of the "manifest destiny." With a flimsy pretext and the backing of the expansionist president, James K. Polk, the United States declared war on her southern neighbor.[28]

At the Palace of the Governors, Governor Armijo was visited by the eminent Santa Fe trader and acting U.S. emissary, James Magoffin. The meeting, on 12 August 1846, was secret, but it appears that Magoffin may have warned Armijo of the hopelessness of resistance.[29] As Kearny's force of sixteen hundred men and a battery of artillery advanced southward from Ratón Pass, through Las Vegas and San Miguel del Bado, Governor Armijo packed his trunks for the long journey south. Kearny entered Santa Fe unopposed on 18 August, and the exciting and turbulent Mexican Era came to an inglorious end.[30]

TWO

Frontier Justice

"Crime is never punished because there is absolutely no one who knows how to conduct an examining trial, to prepare a defense, or to prosecute a case."[1] This harsh appraisal of the state of the judiciary in New Mexico was made by Licenciado Antonio Barreiro, a government-appointed legal advisor sent to the territory in 1831. Barreiro, a professional lawyer formally educated in law, may well have been appalled by the judicial practices that he observed in that remote corner of the Republic where there were no lawyers and where officials acting in judicial capacities had no legal education.

It seems safe to assume that most local justices, although they had no formal legal education, were generally literate men, respected by their communities as competent and fair arbitrators. Certainly, justice in New Mexico was based more on common sense and tradition than on jurisprudence.[2] Nevertheless, homicide trials all conformed, more or less, to a certain pattern that indicates the justices had some sort of knowledge of what was expected of them in the performance of their judicial duties. Although an educated lawyer like Barreiro might have been shocked by this brand of justice, it appears to have worked fairly well, given the frontier conditions in which it operated.

To understand how the judiciary functioned and how criminal cases were adjudicated in New Mexico during the Mexican Era, it is necessary first to take a look at how the government was organized and changed during that chaotic twenty-five-year period. In New Mexico the various functions of government were not separated; executive, legislative, judicial, and often military duties were combined in a single office. Following Independence, the young Republic of Mexico continued to experience political turmoil:

the government changed hands and directions frequently in just a few years. On Mexico's northern frontier, New Mexico felt the effects of new political policies that restructured and reorganized her internal administration.

In the first few years after Independence, the province of New Mexico experienced a great deal of local autonomy under the government of Emperor Agustín I. The *diputación* (New Mexico's territorial legislation) operated throughout these years, even though it would not become a legal organization until the territory was established.

When the unstable and short-lived "empire" of Agustín de Iturbide collapsed in 1823, Mexico reorganized its internal political boundaries. In north-central Mexico, the Spanish *provincias internas* of Nuevo Mexico and Nuevo Viscaya were combined to form the Estado Interno del Norte. This huge state soon turned out to be unmanageable, unable even to determine the location of a capital. It was soon split up again, creating two separate states of Chihuahua and Durango and the territory of Nuevo Mexico. The *villa* of El Paso and its adjacent area, long a part of New Mexico, now fell under the jurisdiction of the state of Chihuahua. The following year these changes were confirmed by the liberal Constitution of 1824.[3]

In 1823, the diputación organized New Mexico into four *partidos*, each with a *cabecera* (head city) administered by an *ayuntamiento* (municipal council).[4] Cabeceras were established in each of the four villas (chartered cities) of New Mexico: the capital of Santa Fe, Santa Cruz de la Cañada in Río Arriba, Alburquerque in Río Abajo, and, far to the south, El Paso del Norte and its surrounding area.[5] Except for El Paso, which would be annexed to Chihuahua State, these administrative divisions would remain in force until 1836.

In the final days of 1836, a new conservative constitution was proclaimed, and Mexico was reorganized again under the centralist government of President Santa Anna. Attempting to gain more control for the central government, states and territories were abolished in favor of departments. Mexico was reorganized into twenty-four military departments whose governors were appointed by the president. Departments were further subdivided into divisions called *prefecturas* and *subprefecturas* or partidos.[6]

This arrangement lasted until 1844, when the department was divided into three districts: the northern district of Río Arriba, the central district (which included the capital), and the southern district of Río Abajo. Each district was ruled over by a prefect who kept administrative records in the villa of his jurisdiction.[7]

By Independence, most Spanish towns and Indian pueblos could boast an ayuntamiento to govern at the local level. Town councils acted as courts of first appeals, adopted local ordinances, and held elections. In theory, town councils were composed of one alcalde (magistrate), two *regidores* (councilmen), and a *procurador síndico* (attorney) elected by the community.[8] In reality, many towns could not muster a complete set of officials to serve on their councils, and the number of towns with ayuntamientos varied from one year to the next. The villas of Santa Fe, Santa Cruz de la Cañada, and Alburquerque maintained city halls throughout the Mexican Era.[9]

In towns that lacked ayuntamientos and in rural areas, alcaldes were often the only government officials. As such, they performed a variety of duties in the name of the governor. Alcaldes acted as judges in civil and criminal cases, gave possession of lands, collected taxes, and were sometimes called upon to lead the local militia against hostile Indians. The *alcaldes constitutionales* of territorial New Mexico were called jueces de paz under the department. Alcaldes were appointed by the governor, and jueces de paz were named by prefects.[10]

New Mexico was governed by a *jefe político* who administered civil affairs, and a *comandante principal* who was in charge of military matters. On occasion these offices were combined under one man. Territorial governors were usually from New Mexico, chosen by the National Congress from a *terna* (list) sent by the diputación. Under the departmental plan, the legislature (first called the *junta*, then the *asamblea*) lost much of its power, and governors were handpicked by the president from "outsiders," a policy which resulted in disaster in 1837.[11]

The political chief or governor in New Mexico served a multitude of legislative, executive, and judicial functions; consequently, he was a very powerful individual. New Mexico governors received orders from Mexico City, passed them on to local authorities, heard petitions from private citizens, and acted as a court of appeals in criminal and civil cases. As president of the legislature, the governor had the authority to grant lands and make policy. In the economic sphere, the governor kept a close eye on the local treasury and revenues received from Santa Fe trade.[12]

The workings of the judiciary altered very little under Mexican administration. Both the federalist government of the territory and the centralist government of the department realized the necessity of judicial reform in New Mexico, but neither was able to achieve any significant improvement over the colonial system.[13]

Under the Spanish crown New Mexico had been divided into *alcaldías*, jurisdictions presided over by *alcaldes mayores*, who functioned as justices in criminal and civil cases at the local level. More important cases were forwarded to the governor, who acted as judge of the first instance after the alcalde had made the initial investigations. Appeals were sent to the *audiencia* in Guadalajara, while the accused waited in the Santa Fe jail for final judgement and sentencing. The alcalde mayor who had originated the judicial proceedings was expected to execute the sentence when it was handed down from the higher court.[14]

The federalist government of the Mexican Republic attempted to make several judicial reforms. It hoped to create a separate judiciary, distinct from the executive and legislative branches of government. It was proposed that a district court with authority over the alcalde courts be established to handle the more serious crimes. In 1826, a law was passed creating a frontier judicial circuit that included New Mexico, Durango, and Chihuahua. This circuit was to be served by a court of appeals in Parral, Chihuahua. Unfortunately, the Mexican government was not strong enough to implement these reforms, and there remained no one in New Mexico with any legal training.[15] In 1829, Manuel de Jesús Rada, New Mexican deputy to the National Congress in Mexico City, urged that New Mexico have three *letrados* and a judicial court capable of completing cases within the territory.[16]

Rada's plan was never implemented. However, in 1831, the Mexican government did send New Mexico an *asesor* (legal advisor). Licenciado Antonio Barreiro, native of Chihuahua, was the only attorney ever to serve in New Mexico during the Mexican Era. Barreiro served two terms, in 1833 and again in 1834, as New Mexico's deputy to the National Congress in Mexico City. Given these terms in the capital, one could assume that his actual physical presence in the territory must have been minimal.[17]

While in New Mexico, Licenciado Barreiro wrote *Ojeada Sobre Nuevo Mexico*, a treatise on the territory according to his observations. Published in Puebla in 1832, the *Ojeada* is one of the few contemporary works written by a Mexican about New Mexico under the Republic. The *licenciado* was very critical of the judicial system in the territory. He spoke of the "doleful and deplorable condition of the administration of justice," and added that he could "fill many pages" on the problems of justice in New Mexico. He recommended restoring courts of the first instance.[18]

The Federalists were unable to correct the problems of the administration of justice in New Mexico, and the legal system remained little changed from colonial days. District courts were never established. Alcaldes who had no legal training continued to preside over local courts, and the governor still served as a court of appeals.[19]

The Centralists' attempt at judicial reform fared little better. With the new Constitution of 1836 and subsequent legislation, the conservative government in Mexico City endeavored to establish appellate courts and increase the number of justices in frontier areas. They met with the same problems as the Federalists; there was no one on the frontier who had the formal legal education required to fill judicial offices. Due to the lack of *jueces letrados* (judges with formal legal education), senior alcaldes of a district acted as *jueces de primera instancia* (judges of the first instance).[20] Then, in 1841, the court of the first instance was reconstituted in Santa Fe. Still, most cases continued to be referred to the local alcalde.[21] In June 1844, in an attempt to create a more efficient judiciary, Governor Mariano Martínez reorganized the department into three districts and called for more justices as well as district court judges.[22]

Despite all the attempted judicial reforms, frontier justice under the Republic continued to be in the hands of alcaldes and jueces de paz, who had no legal training. These local magistrates relied more on common sense and custom than on legal precepts, and, local politics aside, it seems likely that their judicial decisions were respected by the community they served.

Only a small group of people had the necessary education to aspire to political office in the upper levels of government. These positions were usually held by members of the same local families and often by foreigners.[23] Lesser positions, such as alcaldes or jueces de paz in small villages, were sometimes held by uneducated individuals.[24]

Gregg noted that there were no lawyers in New Mexico, a condition that he felt spoke "favorably of the state of litigation in that country."[25] The nearest attorneys were in Chihuahua, some six hundred miles to the south, over a rugged trail that traversed formidable desert terrain and hostile Indian territory. Although there were no attorneys, accused persons were expected to elect someone as a defensor to speak on their behalf, and alcaldes appointed an individual as *promotor fiscal* to prosecute the case against the defendant. Neither the defensor nor the promotor fiscal would have been trained lawyers, but both were generally chosen from one of the better educated elite families.[26]

Apart from the fact that New Mexico lacked formally trained legal personnel, those who did serve in that capacity were hampered by other deficiencies. A point made frequently in the homicide cases was the lack of notaries in New Mexico. In place of *escribanos públicos* (notaries public), two persons called *testigos de asistencia* would act as witnesses assisting the justice while he investigated the crime and took testimonies. At least two testigos de asistencia signed each document entered into a case.[27]

Another frequently mentioned problem in the administration of justice in frontier areas was the lack of official stamped paper. The paper came at some expense from Mexico, and its use was required for official documents. Although this was hardly the most important issue for frontier justices, it was not unusual for a presiding juez in an outlying area to apologize that he had written the case on *papel común* and to add that this would in no way reflect incompetency on his part.[28] *Papel sellado* contained various elements depending on its particular purpose. The paper was usually, but not always, stamped with an official seal and dated for a specific two-year period. For criminal cases it generally included a notice that the paper was "to be used only for criminal cases."[29]

Gregg speculated, "In judicial proceedings," no attention is paid to any code of laws; in fact, there is scarcely one alcalde in a dozen who knows what a law is, or who ever saw a law book."[30] Certainly there was limited access to legal works on the frontier. However, there is evidence that justices were kept informed of current legislation and could have had access to the major Spanish and Mexican laws through the governor in Santa Fe. In 1827, Governor Antonio Narbona prepared an inventory of the provincial archives for his successor Manuel Armijo. The archives included a copy of the *Recopilación de leyes de los Reynos de las Indias*, the major compendium of Spanish law, and the acts of the Spanish Cortes of 1812, along with other government decrees and legislation.[31] Provincial laws drafted by the legislature in Santa Fe were forwarded to local justices.[32] Further, alcaldes were kept informed of current laws coming from Mexico City and were expected to make them public in there jurisdiction. Public proclamations were read in town plazas after the citizens were summoned by the beat of drums. Afterwards the edicts or other announcements were tacked up in public places.[33]

In short, although justices in New Mexico had no formal legal education, they apparently did have access to laws and legal procedures. Further, local alcaldes and jueces de paz were generally literate men, prominent in their communities and respected as fair arbitrators of justice.[34] It appears from trial records that they made every attempt to follow accepted judicial methods in handling criminal cases.

Homicide trials adjudicated during the Mexican Era generally followed a set legal procedure that had changed little since colonial times.[35] There was no trial by jury. The local magistrate, alcalde, or juez de paz in the jurisdiction where the crime occurred served not only as the judge but as the chief investigator as well.

The suspect suffered numerous disadvantages under the Spanish legal system, especially as it was practiced on the frontier. The suspect was considered guilty and carried the burden of proving his innocence, a task made more difficult by the procedure known as *sumaria*. The sumaria was a preliminary investigation, the inquisitive first stage in the criminal procedure. During the sumaria, evidence was generally gathered against the suspect by the same magistrate who would act as judge in the case.[36]

The first step in the sumaria was the *auto de cabeza* or *auto cabeza de proceso*, the judicial act that initiated proceedings in a criminal case. It was generally a brief statement by the justice explaining that he had been informed of a murder and he was placing the matter under investigation. Once the justice had been advised of a crime in his jurisdiction, he called two persons to accompany him and act as witnesses during each stage of the proceedings. These testigos de asistencia were not necessarily the same individuals throughout the case.

In homicide cases, the next step in the judicial process was to examine the body in order to determine the cause of death. Theoretically, the *reconocimiento de heridas*, or *fe de heridas*, was to be accomplished by a doctor who would then make a signed statement regarding his findings. In New Mexico, the likelihood of finding a medical doctor was slim, except for the surgeon of the Santa Fe Company or the occasional foreign doctor.[37] Instead, the acting judge would often call on one or two ordinary citizens to perform this function. These people were sometimes designated as *peritos* (experts), but it is unlikely that they had any medical expertise. The body was to be examined carefully, taking note of the size and depth of wounds, what weapon had been used, and which wound had proven fatal. The victim was then pronounced dead, and the magistrate and his assistants continued to search for clues or evidence that might be found at the scene of the crime.[38] The justice would then make arrangements with the local parish priest to give the body proper burial.

Once these investigations were completed, the magistrate began taking testimonies from persons whom he believed may have some information about the crime. Other witnesses were called as the investigations proceeded. Testigos were brought before an alcalde or juez and sworn in before being questioned.[39] Witnesses were always asked to state general information about themselves, including name, age, place of residence, marital status, religion, and occupation. After the questioning was concluded, those witnesses who knew how to write signed their statements; others drew a simple cross.

Once the testimonies were completed, the alcalde or juez issued an *auto de prisión* (arrest warrant) *or auto de bien preso*, an act to insure that the prisoner was well secured. The latter seemed to imply the use of *grillos* (shackles or irons). The arrest warrant was generally a formality since the suspect was already in jail by the time it was issued. Occasionally a prisoner's possessions were confiscated by an *embargo de bienes* (attachment of goods) in order to pay for his expenses in the local jail.[40]

At some point during the sumaria, the defendant was questioned. This interrogation usually occurred after the other witnesses had testified and without the benefit of any defense consul. However, this pattern varied with different cases. When eighteen-year-old Andrés Márquez, accused killer of Juan Valdez, was called before Alcalde Baca for questioning, Baca abruptly discontinued the questioning and ordered the minor to name a *curador* (legal guardian) before he would proceed further.[41] Occasionally the justice in charge would question the suspect first, as in the trial of Manuel Gallego, accused of the murder of his wife, María Espíritu Santo Ruival.[42]

The sumaria, or fact-finding phase of the judicial proceedings, was now over. The second phase, known as the *plenario* or *juicio plenario*, was when the contest between the defense and prosecution unfolded. Cutter's description of plenario in colonial New Mexico is similar to what is found in homicide cases during the Mexican Era. The term plenario was rarely mentioned, but most of the same elements appear, albeit in a somewhat different order and with a different emphasis.[43] Cutter suggested that local authorities attempted to comply with regulations regarding the plenario, but due to lack of trained legal personnel this stage in the proceedings was often inconsistent with the norm or even absent. This was definitely the case with the Mexican Era homicides.[44]

Once the sumaria had been completed, local alcaldes and jueces sometimes packed up the prisoner and the proceedings, and sent them with an escort to the capital for the completion of the trial.[45] Whether the case was sent to the capital or completed in its original jurisdiction, the first step in the plenario was likely to be the ratification of witnesses. The alcalde instigated this process by issuing an *auto de prueba*, approving a certain period of time (possibly twenty or thirty days) in order to locate all the witnesses and bring them in to verify their testimonies. If a witness had since died or was absent from the department, another reputable citizen was called to verify that witness's character. *Ratificación* involved bringing the witnesses before the judge and reading them their previous statements. Under oath they were asked if their testimony was the truth and if they wanted to change or add anything. The statement was signed by those testigos who knew how to write their name. Many witnesses, unlike the testigos de asistencia, were uneducated vecinos, unable to write their names. They signed with a cross.

At some point in the proceedings, the justice might call a *careo*, an attempt to elicit the truth by a face-to-face confrontation between contending parties. According to Cutter, it was a fairly common judicial practice in Spanish colonial times.[46] In the Mexican homicide cases it occurred only once. When Manuel García de Lara refused to confess and witnesses for either side did not agree, Mariano Martínez ordered careos to take place following the ratification process. No one changed his or her testimony, and the careo was unsuccessful.[47]

Another judicial procedure that was available but rarely employed was the *tacha*, or disqualification of a witness. Disqualification of a potential witness due to close kinship ties, friendship, "interest," or anything that might affect the credibility of the witness was known as *generales de la ley* and was often carried out at the beginning of a testimony when the witness stated personal information about himself.[48] When Juez de Paz don José Salazar, an eyewitness to his brother's murder, disqualified himself as judge and witness in the case against the assailant, he demonstrated an awareness of the importance of this judicial safeguard.[49]

Homicide cases indicated that a formal confession, separate from any earlier statement made by the suspect, would be elicited during this stage of the procedure before a defender was appointed. The justice either asked that the defendant be brought to him, or he would go to the jail with testigos de asistencias in order to make charges and take the confession. The *confesión con cargos* was always referred to as a confession, even when the suspect denied the charges against him.

Following the formal confession, the justice appointed a promotor fiscal to prosecute the case against the suspect. Prosecutors often apologized for their limited knowledge of the law. They usually asked that the culprit (reo) be awarded the most severe penalty that the law allowed, to set an example for others and to assuage public outrage over violent crimes.[50]

The prisoner was notified that he should name a defensor to speak on his behalf. If he did not know anyone capable of performing this duty, the judge would appoint someone for him. A curador would be named for a minor (anyone aged under twenty-five).[51] In most cases the defendant chose his own defender. The defensor, after scrutinizing the file of papers in the case, would write his plea within the prescribed period of time and send it back to the justice. Defense pleas were often lengthy emotional appeals, begging that the court show mercy on the defendant and not inflict the *pena capital* (capital punishment).

The growing file of papers that comprised the case was sent back and forth between the two contending parties. If they could not reach a consensus, and they seldom could, the case might be referred to a legal advisor in far-off Chihuahua.[52] Proceedings had now reached the third and final phase: the *sentencia* (judgement). In civil cases or criminal cases of less magnitude, the justice who had tried the case would pass sentence. However, it appears that no one in New Mexico had the authority to pronounce a *sentencia difinitiva* in a homicide case without first consulting an individual educated in law. At least four homicide cases were sent to licenciados or asesores for consultation. The response of only one of them is available in the records; the others either did not answer, or the correspondence was lost. The Chihuahua lawyer who was consulted in the Andrew Daily case wrote a lengthy explanation of how a homicide case should have been handled according to prevailing laws.[53]

Of the eleven homicide cases on record, four remain incomplete, the judgement unknown, the proceedings having ended abruptly without any conclusion. The other seven cases ended with the release of the suspects. Three of these were let out on bond, two were released due to lack of evidence, one innocent man was acquitted, and the two suspects in the Daily case, who were confessed murderers, were eventually set free because it seemed no one knew what to do with them.

All of these suspects spent time in jail, yet it appears that the purpose of their incarceration was not punitive—rather a means to detain them until some final sentence could be passed.[54] With one notable exception, the presiding justices did not pass any sentences to punish the accused. Only in the Daily case was a sentence passed. The juez of Dolores del Oro, under pressure from the governor to conclude the case, ordered the two confessed murderers to be executed. Apparently realizing he did not have the authority to make this decision, he stipulated that it would not be carried out without first consulting a lawyer.[55]

Josiah Gregg was not far off when he commented, "I never heard of but one execution for murder in New Mexico, since the declaration of independence."[56] That one execution Gregg mentioned is not on record; however, it is apparent that the *pena del último suplicio* was not a common form of punishment in New Mexico. Prior to Independence, capital punishment was rare throughout Mexico.[57] In New Mexico between 1700 and 1821 there were only two documented cases where the death sentence was imposed and carried out: once in 1779, when a mother and daughter from Cochití were executed for the premeditated murder of the daughter's husband, and again in 1809, when two men were hanged for the murder of a Frenchman. Both death sentences had been handed down by the audiencia in Guadalajara.[58]

Capital punishment was never inflicted during the Mexican Era, even though it was frequently requested by prosecutors.[59] What other options were available as punishments for convicted murderers? During colonial times, there were fines, exile, public works, forced labor in *obrajes* or mines, and presidio service on the frontier.[60] None of these options was seriously considered for the homicides of the Mexican Era. One defensor did suggest that his client be sent off to a presidio for some years in lieu of execution. The disposition of the case was not on record.[61]

The only recorded executions that were carried out in New Mexico between Independence and the U.S. occupation occurred during the Rebellion of 1837. Under orders of Manuel Armijo, four rebels were beheaded and one shot for their part in the uprising in Río Arriba, which claimed the lives of the governor and several other prominent citizens. These executions were not punishment for murder but for insurrection, which was considered a threat to the established government.[62]

Ten years later in Taos, American authorities executed at least seven rebels who had taken part in the Rebellion of 1847. Possibly as many as twenty people were executed in New Mexico that year, mostly as a result of treason trials. This was a preview of what was to come. Americans had no qualms about inflicting the death penalty for convicted homicides. Territorial New Mexico under the United States, between 1849 and 1908 witnessed at least forty-nine and possibly fifty-three hanging executions, all but one for murder. These statistics highlight an interesting comparison between Spanish colonial/Mexican justice and American justice.[63]

The Mexican Era homicide suspects all spent time in the local *cárcel*, awaiting sentencing that could take months or even years. In most cases, the sumaria phase of the judicial proceeding was accomplished within a few days. However, the plenario took longer, as the case was sent back and forth between contesting parties and witnesses had to be located for ratification. The final phase, judgement and sentencing, could be the most difficult for the accused, who waited in jail while the case was forwarded to a legal advisor in Chihuahua.

Tardiness in the judicial process was not just a frontier problem. After reviewing numerous cases of homicide in central Mexico and Oaxaca, William Taylor noted that he saw "Few formal sentences of imprisonment as distinct from labor service, but it was not uncommon for men and women accused of homicide to wait two or three years for a verdict."[64]

Spending time awaiting sentencing could be worse than the punishment. A contemporary account of the Santa Fe jail in November 1838 described a filthy unsanitary place overrun with fleas, lice, bedbugs and other vermin, and a foulness that would destroy the health of the most robust individual.[65] A few years earlier, in 1832, Antonio Barreiro had commented in his *Ojeada*, "there are only a few filthy rooms in the capital which may be called jails."[66]

A royal *bando* (decree) on prison reform had been sent north from Comandante General García Conde in Chihuahua just prior to Independence in June 1821. It decreed an end to dark unhealthy subterranean prisons and ordered the destruction of all instruments of torture. Irons were not to be used to restrain prisoners, except on the order of the respective judge who deemed it necessary for security reasons, and then only the smaller *grilletes* were permissible.[67] Taking into consideration that the local cárcel was often only a room in some public building, it is understandable that a prisoner might need to be secured by shackles.

In the placer mines south of Santa Fe, Juez de Paz Manuel Delgado wrote up a list of rules to help govern the rough and unruly gold mining camps. He called for the construction of a secure public jail, and he asked that a separate jail be built for women criminals. He suggested that the women might earn their keep by cooking for the other prisoners.[68]

Certain classes of citizens were exempt from civil jurisdiction. From Spanish colonial times, New Mexico inherited the old military and religious *fueros*, privileges that allowed them to be tried in their own tribunals. The liberal Constitution of 1824, concerned with the equality of citizens before the law, let slip the opportunity to end these special privileges, and fueros remained intact throughout most of the Mexican Era.[69]

Only one homicide case involved military personnel. In 1843, Alférez Manuel García de Lara of the Second Regiment Cavalry was charged with the murder of civilian Antonio Moya in San Miguel del Bado. The original investigations were conducted by Juez de Paz Santiago Ulibarrí, who forwarded the case to Governor Armijo. Armijo sent the case on to Comandante General Mariano Martínez, and from then on it was handled by military authorities. Martínez appointed Captain don Damasio Salazar of the militia auxiliary to conduct the proceedings, after he learned that Colonel Pedro Muñoz of the Second Regiment was unavailable. The sumaria phase was completed by Captain Salazar and Comandante General Martínez. Alférez Lara named Captain Graduado Antonio Sena to defend him, but the outcome of the trial is missing.[70]

These three separate jurisdictions—regular citizens and the two groups protected by fueros—sometimes overlapped. For example, just prior to Independence a royal order from the Cortes (Spanish parliament) curbed ecclesiastical fueros in the area of crimes that merited corporal punishment. A cleric—secular or regular—guilty of a capital crime would be tried by a civil judge.[71] The Mexican homicides did not include any clerics.

In addition to military and clerical personnel, one other group of people had been given a special legal classification under Spanish colonial administration. Pueblo Indians were considered "legal minors" and provided with a *protector de indios*, an agent who acted as their legal representative in Spanish courts.[72] This office had been created in an attempt by the crown to incorporate native people into Spanish society and at the same time protect them as wards of the state. This special status was abolished in 1821 by a royal decree issued by the liberal Spanish Cortes for the purpose of eliminating special interests and making all citizens equal in the eyes of the law. Unfortunately it may also have been responsible for the loss of Indian communal lands that had been protected while Pueblo Indians still held privileged status.[73]

In summary, for all of its shortcomings, the judicial system in New Mexico functioned reasonably well. The most obvious problem was the lack of professionals with a legal education to fill judicial positions. Still, the magistrates who served in legal capacities were for the most part competent men whose judgements were respected in the communities they served. Although they were not educated jurists, alcaldes and jueces de paz were generally literate men, who acquired their knowledge through experience and had a practical approach to justice that reflected a strong sense of right and wrong. If definite sentences were never handed down in homicide cases and it appeared that "the most desperate and blood-stained criminals escape with impunity," as Josiah Gregg so vividly put it, it was not due to incompetent justices.[74]

Justice may have been hampered more by the system itself than by those who administered it. A great deal of power was vested in the hands of one magistrate. In order to guard against possible abuse of arbitrary justice, local magistrates without formal legal education were not allowed to pass judgement in homicide cases without first consulting a letrado. Capital punishment was rare in New Mexico, as it was in the rest of the country during both Spanish colonial and Mexican republican times. This seems to deny *la leyenda negra*, the "Black Legend" of supposed Spanish cruelty and makes an interesting counterpoint to the harshness of American justice in territorial New Mexico.[75]

Part One

Familia

✣ ✣ ✣

The Trial of Manuel Gallego for the Murder of his Wife María Espíritu Santo Ruival

SAN ANTONIO DEL RANCHO, 2 FEBRUARY 1834

✠

ALCALDE CONSTITUCIONAL, SANTA CRUZ: Juan Madrid
ALCALDE CONSTITUCIONAL, 1835: Juan Gallego y Martínez
ALCALDE, SAN ILDEFONSO: Juan Antonio Gomes
PROMOTOR FISCAL (PROSECUTOR): José Francisco Ortega
DEFENSOR (DEFENDER): Alonso Martín
LICENCIADO (LAWYER), CHIHUAHUA: don Agustín Abellano
TESTIGOS (WITNESSES): Joaquín Valdez; Juan Pablo Madrid
ALGUACIL (WARDEN): Ramón Fresques
FAMILIA DEL DIFUNTO, TESTIFIED: Madre, María Antonia de Herrera; hermano, Antonio Ruival
OTRO, MENTIONED: Polinar Lopes
TESTIGOS DE ASISTENCIA: Cipriano Olivas; José Cruz Rivera

✠

THREE

The Bad Life[1]

✠

Throughout most of Spanish colonial and Mexican times, Santa Cruz, now a small village just east of present-day Española on the road to Chimayó, was the administrative center for all of the communities of northern New Mexico. Founded by a charter under Governor don Diego de Vargas in 1695, it was christened with the lengthy and somewhat pompous title, La Villa Nueva de Santa Cruz de los Españoles Mexicanos del Rey Nuestro Carlos Segundo (the new villa of the holy cross of the Mexican Spaniards of our king Charles the Second). In the court documents the name was shortened to La Villa de Santa Cruz de la Cañada, and generally it was either called Santa Cruz or La Cañada.[2] The term "villa" meant that it was a chartered municipality, larger in size and having more status than the other frontier communities. This distinction it shared with only three other towns in New Mexico: Santa Fe, Alburquerque, and El Paso del Norte. In 1823, El Paso was annexed to Chihuahua, leaving only three villas in Nuevo Mexico.[3]

Santa Cruz was established as part of the reconquest and recolonization of New Mexico following the Pueblo Revolt of 1680. Two years after the reoccupation of Santa Fe in 1693, Governor Vargas settled forty-four families in the fertile Santa Cruz valley about twenty-five miles north of the capital. The area was not new to the Spanish; it had been settled earlier and abandoned along with the rest of New Mexico during the uprising.[4] This part of the Río Arriba was home to Tano-speaking natives living in San Juan, Santa Clara, Pojoaque, San Ildefonso, and Nambé pueblos. Numerous small Spanish communities grew up in close proximity to these Indian villages. The Barrio de San Antonio del Rancho, a tiny collection of dwellings in the neighborhood of the San Ildefonso Pueblo, was one of these Spanish settlements.

In 1834, Juan Madrid, alcalde constitucional of Santa Cruz, was advised by the alcalde of San Antonio del Rancho that a murder had been committed in that place. Madrid had been a common name in Santa Cruz since the first families settled there shortly after the reconquest, and Alcalde Madrid was most likely a descendant of one of these original settlers.[5] Madrid set out from Santa Cruz with two assistants to investigate the alleged crime in San Antonio del Rancho, twelve miles away. The road wound south next to the Río del Norte (Río Grande), passing a high basalt mesa known as La Mesilla (Black Mesa), a familiar landmark that would be the scene of a fierce battle in the Rebellion of 1837. Just two miles beyond this black mesa lay the San Ildefonso Pueblo; here the alcalde and his investigative party turned east.[6] A mile or so from the pueblo they reached San Antonio del Rancho, where they proceeded to the scene of the murder.

Madrid had been informed that Manuel Gallego, a 47-year-old farmer, had murdered his wife María Espíritu Santo Ruival, in their home some time during the previous night. When Madrid arrived at Gallego's home, grieving family members led him to the cadaver. The records don't indicate in what part of the house the body was found.[7] It was evident to Madrid that the woman had been strangled since a sinew cord (*cordón de nervio*) was found still wrapped around her neck; he did not look further to see if the victim had suffered any bruises or fractures. There was no doctor available to examine the body, and Madrid did not call any special "experts" (peritos) to assist him. When Ruival made no response to the alcalde's questions, he pronounced her dead in the presence of his two testigos de asistencia, and forwarded a letter to the parish priest of San Ildefonso asking that she be given ecclesiastical burial.

On 3 February, the day after the murder, the suspect had already been apprehended at his father's home in the Barrio de San Ildefonso, to where he had fled after strangling his wife. Gallego was arrested by Juan Antonio Gomes, alcalde of San Ildefonso, and incarcerated in the national jail of Santa Cruz in custody of the warden, Ramón Fresques. While in jail, Gallego confessed to Madrid and his two assistants, Cipriano Olivas and José Cruz Rivera, that he had strangled his wife with a sinew cord because she always argued with him. His testimony was repeated to him, and he verified it.

Between the time when the crime was committed and his imprisonment, Gallego had confessed the crime to several people, including his wife's mother and brother. These people became the witnesses in the case, and their testimonies and Gallego's confession would be the basis of the case against him, since there were no eyewitnesses to the deed. The records of the investigation indicate that these witnesses journeyed to Santa Cruz to give their testimonies.

María Antonia de Herrera was the first witness. Herrera said she was a widow, thirty years old, and mother of the deceased. Antonio Ruival testified next that he was single, twenty-two years old, and the full brother (*hermano carnal*) of the victim. Since there was only an eight-year difference in their ages, it is obvious that Herrera could not have been the biological mother of Antonio. If María was Antonio's full sister, as he testified, then Herrera could not have been her biological mother either. Herrera was probably María Ruival's stepmother. It also seems likely that Ruival was much younger than her husband, who had given his age as forty-seven. Unfortunately, case records do not give enough detail about the victims and their circumstances to piece together a complete story, and one can only speculate as to the rest.

Both mother and brother accused Manuel Gallego of killing his wife María. They were quite certain of this because Gallego had confessed the deed to them. Although neither one could say what Manuel's motive was, their statements indicate an unhappy marriage. Before her death, María had told her brother that she and her husband quarrelled often, and she admitted to her mother that Manuel had given her a *mala vida*. Exactly what she meant by a "bad life" is difficult to tell; no explanation was given. However, it is quite possible that she was the victim of domestic violence before she was murdered; Manuel apparently had a volatile temper, and, as he admitted later in his confession, he had been jailed on three previous occasions for fighting.

At the end of their testimonies, both mother and brother were asked how they thought Manuel should be punished. The victim's mother, María Antonia Herrera, wanted to see Manuel punished by being sent away, banished from the community—a punishment that was common under Spanish rule.[8] Antonio Ruival did not seek any punishment for the man who murdered his sister; he forgave Gallego and wanted to see him pardoned. Did Antonio feel that his brother-in-law had some justification in taking María's life? It was obvious that María had argued constantly with her husband. Perhaps Antonio considered his sister a nagging wife who deserved to be punished.

Two other witnesses were called to testify in this case. The first was 76-year-old Joaquín Valdez, a married man from the jurisdiction of San Ildefonso. Valdez listed his occupation as cantor, a religious song leader who may have sung at village festivities as well.[9] The second witness was Juan

Pablo Madrid, a 23-year-old farmer from Santa Cruz and most likely a relative of the alcalde. Both witnesses took an oath to tell the truth, and both testified that Manuel Gallego had told them that he had killed his wife by choking her with a sinew cord. Neither knew anything more about the incident, and neither was questioned about when or where Gallego reported his crime to them. Both witnesses signed their names to their statements. Following the testimonies, the alcalde made each witness appear before him to be ratified. Their statements were read to them, and they verified that they were true and they had nothing to add or change.

On 12 February, Madrid went to the jail to take Gallego's confession. The defendant's quarrelsome nature came to light when the alcalde questioned him about his previous arrests. Gallego admitted that he had been arrested and jailed on four occasions; the first three were a result of quarrels and fights that he had started. Gallego had been jailed first in Santa Cruz, but he was released by Alcalde Polinar Lopes after paying a seven-peso fine. The second arrest occurred in San Ildefonso, where he also secured his freedom with seven pesos. When he was arrested again on similar charges, the alcalde of Las Trampas, where the brawl occurred, charged him fourteen pesos to get out of jail. His fourth and most recent arrest had landed him once again in the Santa Cruz jail, this time for the murder of his wife, a crime to which he freely admitted.

Alcalde Madrid appointed citizen José Ortega as promotor fiscal, to prosecute the case against Manuel Gallego. Ortega accepted the appointment and swore to loyally and legally perform said job. After careful scrutiny of the files, Ortega concluded that there was no doubt that Gallego had murdered his wife, since he had freely admitted his guilt in both his statement and his confession, and the same story had been verified by the witnesses.

Prosecutor Ortega reviewed the few details of the case: the date, location, and murder weapon. Then he proposed that Gallego was disposed to kill his wife. By nightfall he was "alienated from all sentiments of humanity," and he had attacked María and achieved that "depraved and barbarous inclination." Later, his guilt led him to confess the deed. Apologizing for his limited knowledge of the law, Ortega went on to ask the tribunal to apply the *pena ordinaria*, the customary penalty, to Gallego as punishment for his crime and to satisfy public vengeance. This written prosecution was duly noted by the alcalde, who attached it to the growing bundle of folios that made up the case.

The prosecution completed, Madrid advised the prisoner to name someone who could speak on his behalf. It was common in these cases to allow the prosecution to have the first say, but even had the defense made its plea first, the odds were already stacked against the defendant.[10] The prisoner gave the alcalde permission to appoint a defensor; he could think of no one himself. Madrid named Alonso Martín, who promptly accepted and took an oath to perform the duties of the defense.

In the defense plea, Martín acknowledged that Gallego had murdered his wife, a crime that should not go unpunished, but he felt that capital punishment would be too severe if the culprit showed remorse. Much of Martín's defense was based on proving that Gallego was remorseful. Martín denied that the accused was "alienated from all human sentiments," as the prosecution had insisted, because after the crime was committed, he did not flee the scene of the crime until morning. Martín suggested that remaining with his dead wife, rather than making an escape, was a noble act on the part of Gallego—an indication that he regretted his actions. Gallego had freely confessed to the crime and incriminated himself, even before his capture. Martín pleaded for leniency, recalling that even the victim's brother had requested that Gallego be pardoned. The defense begged that Gallego be spared capital punishment.[11] Martín asked the court to excuse the defects in his defense, explaining that they were from lack of instruction and not from evil intent.

The written defense was attached to the legal file, and the alcalde forwarded the entire case to the prosecutor for his confirmation. Ortega confirmed the brief that he previously presented and asked that it be accepted. The case was then returned to Martín, who likewise reaffirmed what he had already written. On 22 April 1834, almost four months from when the crime occurred, the proceedings had come to a standstill. Alcalde Juan Madrid decided that inasmuch as the defense and the prosecution had not reached a consensus, the case must be sent to a juez letrado, a judge trained in law, who could advise on a final judgement. Madrid noted that he was remitting the case to the office of an *asesor* (legal advisor).

On 18 May of the following year, two final entries appeared in the case of Manuel Gallego.[12] Both were written by Juan Gallego y Martínez, the current alcalde constitucional of Santa Cruz de la Cañada. The first was a letter sent to Licenciado Agustín Abellano in Chihuahua, asking for his judgement in the criminal case against Manuel Gallego, which had come from the office of his predecessor, Juan Madrid. He concluded with "I have been impelled by necessity [to send the case] because in this territory there is no legal advisor nor lawyer." The second entry by the same alcalde explained that he had sent the Gallego case for legal advisement to the office of Licenciado don Agustín Abellano in Chihuahua, as directed by the

Supreme Court of Justice. There was no explanation as to why the case was not sent the year before by Alcalde Madrid, whose last entry indicated that he was "remitting" the case to an asesoría.

In May 1835, the same month and year that the Santa Cruz alcalde sent the Gallego homicide case to Chihuahua, Albino Pérez arrived in New Mexico to take over the office of governor from Francisco Sarracino. Poor economic conditions in northern New Mexico and Pérez's unpopular administration would trigger the Chimayó Rebellion that broke out in the Santa Cruz area two years later. The battle at La Mesilla in August 1837 was so fierce that Governor Pérez's Indian troops deserted to the other side, and the rest of his forces were obliged to retreat. Those who did not desert or escape were captured by the rebels, manacled, and marched off to the Santa Cruz jail.[13] Was Manuel Gallego there to greet them?

Like so many of these cases, this one has no definite conclusion. There was no letter from Licenciado Abellano advising the case, no notice that Gallego had been let out on bond, and no final verdict. We can only speculate as to when and how the prisoner got out of jail and where he went, but he probably did eventually find his way out of the Santa Cruz jail. One thing is certain: the mala vida of María Espíritu Santo Ruival had come to an abrupt end some time during the night of 2 February 1834, and her story is a part of the public record.

The Trial of Rafael Montoya for the Murder of his Wife María Albina Gonzales

CORRALES, 22 DECEMBER 1842

JUEZ DE PAZ, CORRALES, 1842: Juan José Lucero
JUEZ DE PAZ, CORRALES, 1843: Diego Antonio Montoya
PROMOTOR FISCAL (PROSECUTOR): Juan José Sánchez
DEFENSOR (DEFENDER): Agustín Durán
TESTIGOS (WITNESSES): None
PERITOS (EXPERTS): Fernando Aragón; Marcos Sánchez; José Gutiérrez; Rafael Lucero; Juan Montoya
CURA (PRIEST): Fernando Ortiz
OTROS: Lázaro Tórrez; don José Montoya; Uvaldo García
TESTIGOS DE ASISTENCIA: Juan Montoya; José Felís Benavídez; Juan Gutiérrez; Tomás Manuel Montoya; José Ramón Gutiérrez
FIADORES (BONDSMEN): Francisco Romero; José Antonio Romero

FOUR

Death Before Christmas[1]

✠

In late December 1842, María Albina Gonzales was traveling with her husband from Belén to their home in La Ciénega, a small community southwest of Santa Fe. Their journey took them north through the many small villages, *haciendas*, and *ranchos* that populated the stretch of the Río Grande Valley north and south of the Villa de Alburquerque. Perhaps María rode part of the way on the old sway-backed mare that was one of the couple's few possessions. As they trudged along the worn, rutted trail, the land looked brown and barren, with naked branches of cottonwoods outlined against a pale blue sky. The cold chill of winter bit through their clothing as they anticipated the warmth of home and the coming celebration of Christmas.

The entire journey was over eighty miles and would have taken three or four days to complete, but María was not destined to reach home nor to celebrate another Christmas. Arriving in Alameda, about ten miles north of Alburquerque and over half-way home, an incident occurred which may have triggered the violence that led to María's tragic death. At the Plaza de Alameda, María's husband, Rafael Montoya, a man of suspicious nature and volatile temper, recognized Lázaro Tórrez from nearby Ranchos de Alburquerque. Tórrez and two unidentified men threatened Montoya with pistols and insulted the couple with rude remarks. Insanely jealous, Montoya apparently assumed that his wife had encouraged Tórrez's advances and felt that his honor had been impugned.

Montoya and his wife left Alameda and crossed the river to the settlement of Los Corrales to report this incident to the local authorities. Los Corrales was part of the Alameda Land Grant, and tradition has it that it was named for the numerous corrals built by Alameda founder Juan Gonzales. Corrales actually consisted of two communities: Santa Rosalia de Corrales (or Upper Corrales) across the river from Sandía Pueblo, and the larger and more prosperous farming community of San Ysidro de Corrales (or Lower Corrales) directly to the south.[2] The juez de paz of Corrales that year was Juan José Lucero, and Rafael and María were directed to his home.

Public inns were rare in New Mexico until after the American occupation. In populated areas it was common for travelers to avail themselves of the hospitality of local residents, taking shelter for the night either in their homes or other outbuildings. When Rafael Montoya and his wife arrived at the home of Justice Lucero that cold December day, he offered them lodging for the night.

About an hour before midnight, Montoya and his wife awoke and went outside behind the judge's house to *aser agua* ("make water"). Early-nineteenth-century New Mexican homes were not equipped with either indoor or outdoor privies, and although chamber pots were available in many homes, most New Mexicans relieved themselves outside in the fields or woods.[3]

Outside in the cold dark night, Rafael, apparently without provocation, pulled a dagger and stabbed María in the back. Her scream broke the stillness of the night and awoke the occupants of the house. Startled from his sleep, Justice Lucero bolted from his bed and ran outside. In the pale moonlight, he could see the couple to whom he had given shelter. The woman started toward him crying that her husband had fatally stabbed her. The man, somber and resigned, standing with the bloodied knife still in his hand, admitted to Lucero that he had indeed committed the crime and surrendered himself without further comment.

While her husband was being escorted to the local jail, María was carried inside the judge's house and made as comfortable as possible. It seems likely that she was placed on the floor in a makeshift bed of sheepskins and blankets, the customary sleeping accommodation for most New Mexicans of the time.[4] The court records do not mention what kind of medical aid was given to the dying woman, if indeed there was any. According to contemporary accounts there were no local doctors of any kind in New Mexico, with the possible exception of a military surgeon at the Santa Fe presidio. During the Mexican Era a few foreign doctors found their way over the Santa Fe Trail, but generally the population relied on curanderos, folk healers with special knowledge of home remedies and herbs.[5] María was probably attended to by Lucero's wife or a household servant, but her wound was too grave for folk medicine to remedy.

The next day, Lucero summoned two citizens to act as medical experts, "since he could not find a surgeon in these parts." These peritos were to examine the victim and give a statement as to the type, depth, size, and seriousness of the wounds. Fernando Aragón and Marcos Sánchez were sworn in by the magistrate and proceeded to the place where María Albina Gonzales lay in agony. They examined María and signed a brief statement claiming that she had been stabbed once by a knife in the lower left side of the back. The wound was deep, and in their opinion the victim would soon die.

Lucero asked two other citizens to examine the murder weapon and to draw a likeness of it on paper for the record. He noted that their profession made them capable of such an undertaking, although he did not indicate what that profession was. The two men, José Gutiérrez and Rafael Lucero, carefully sketched a realistic image of the knife on official stamped paper. In addition, they signed a written statement that included a description of the knife, explaining that the handle was made from a foreign wood. The written description did not include dimensions, but if the drawing was life-size, the weapon was a total of ten inches in length, including a thin six-inch blade. The instrument was stained with blood, and the two men concurred that it was certainly the same weapon that had wounded the victim. The description and sketch were attached to the case, and the knife was kept as evidence.

From her deathbed, 26-year-old María Albina Gonzales was questioned by Lucero and his two assistants. Giving the sign of the cross and promising to tell the truth, she testified that her husband Rafael Montoya had done this to her behind the judge's house. She did not know why. That night they had gone outside to make water, and he had stabbed her, without warning or provocation. She was asked if they had quarreled on the journey from Belén, to which she answered no. She was also asked if her husband had ever found her with another man. María denied this but added that her husband was extremely jealous, even though she had never given him any reason.

In a final question, María was asked if she and her husband had talked or argued with anyone while coming from Belén. She replied that they had spoken only to the people in whose home they stayed. Was the incident in Alameda that had so aggravated her husband only an insignificant encounter that María had already forgotten?

It was Christmas Eve, a time of religious festivities when Hispanic New Mexicans lit small bonfires, known as *luminarias*, and performed the Las Posadas miracle play, reenacting Joseph and Mary's search for lodging on the first Christmas Eve. In communities that were large enough to have a resident priest, the villagers might have attended a midnight mass, but Corrales had neither church nor priest at this time.[6]

In the Lucero household, María Gonzales's condition had worsened, and there was no priest available to give the final sacrament or take her confession. At eight o'clock that evening, the judge was informed that the wounded woman had died. According to his records, Lucero immediately ordered two learned men (peritos) to examine the body and testify under oath whether or not the victim had died as a result of the knife wound. Juan Montoya and Rafael Lucero examined the cadaver and concurred that the knife injury had caused Gonzales's death.

Justice Lucero made arrangements for the body to be dressed for burial and sent word to the parish priest, asking that he see to the funeral and interment. Padre Fernando Ortiz was a member of the prodigious and wealthy Ortiz clan, whose twin brother Rafael and several cousins were also native clerics.[7] At this time, Ortiz was the provisional priest of the Villa de Alburquerque and the Sandía Parish, which included Alameda and Corrales. According to a copy of the death certificate, written by Ortiz several months later, María Gonzales was buried on 24 December, the same day that she died. It is more likely she was buried the following day. Her remains were interred in the *campo santo* (cemetery) of the Alameda chapel across the river from Corrales.

Father Ortiz wrote on the death certificate that Gonzales did not receive any sacraments because she died with violence. Here the padre was lamenting the shortage of priests, the long distances they had to travel to tend their scattered flock, and the resulting neglect of the spiritual needs of frontier folk. Given this sad state of affairs, it was not unusual for Catholic Hispanics to die without final sacraments. In his 1832 treatise on New Mexico, Licenciado Antonio Barreiro had written that "Nothing is more common than to see an infinite number of the sick die without confession or extreme unction."[8]

On Christmas Day, Rafael Montoya, the 28-year-old farmer and husband of the deceased, gave his deposition from the public jail. He showed no sign of remorse. He stated matter-of-factly that he had stabbed his wife behind the judge's house with a knife with a wooden handle; it was the same knife that he was shown. No one had actually witnessed the stabbing, but the judge had appeared immediately afterwards.

When questioned about why he killed his wife, Rafael gave several rather vague, unconvincing answers. He claimed that a certain Lázaro Tórrez of Ranchos de Alburquerque, accompanied by two other men with pistols, had threatened him, and he had deduced that this had something to do with his wife. Then Rafael stated that he had killed her because that same night she left the bed and did not want to return with him. After further questioning, he admitted that he had never caught her with another man, but he was suspicious. Twice he had found her with articles of clothing that he had not given her; these were shoes and stockings, which she claimed she had purchased for herself. The testimony ended here, and Rafael said he had nothing else to say. His statement was read to him, and he verified it.

In view of Montoya's statement, wherein he confessed to being the aggressor and principal perpetrator of this crime, the judge declared for bien preso. This was explained to the jailer so that he would take all precautions and secure the prisoner in *par de grillos* (a pair of fetters). A bando on prison reform, issued shortly before Mexican Independence, stated that these types of restraints were not allowed unless ordered by the acting judge for extra security.[9]

The following day, an act of embargo de bienes was issued by the judge to allow for the confiscation of the prisoner's property. The purpose of this procedure was twofold. First and most important, it was to provide for the prisoner's sustenance while he was incarcerated since there was no fund established for this need. Second, if the prisoner had anything of value, it was hoped this would provide insurance against his escape. The embargo de bienes was seldom used in New Mexico because few people had anything of value.[10] Montoya was a case in point; his only possession of any value was an old "saddle-back" mare that was promptly put up for public auction.

The new year brought with it a change of public officials. Diego Antonio Montoya became the new juez de paz of Corrales and inherited the unfinished murder case against Rafael Montoya. On 7 January 1843, Montoya made a note that he received the case from his predecessor, Juan José Lucero. The same day, the prisoner himself, still in shackles, was brought before the new judge. This formality completed, he was returned to jail.

At about nine o'clock the following evening, Rafael Montoya escaped from the Corrales jail. Apparently, security at the local cárcel had been lax, and Uvaldo García (probably the jailer) informed Justice Diego Montoya that the suspected murderer was on the loose. The justice sent messengers throughout the department with orders to capture the fugitive and return him to jail.

Rafael had headed north along the west bank of the Río del Norte. About fifteen miles north of Corrales, he passed the San Felipe Pueblo. He continued on to Cubero, a tiny settlement on a small land grant known as Santa Rosa de Cubero, about half-way between San Felipe and Santo Domingo.[11] Here, Rafael went to the home of don José Montoya, perhaps a relative of his, where the law caught up with him once again. After four days on the run, the fugitive was returned to the Corrales jail, where he was placed under tight security.

Two months later, the prisoner came before the tribunal, consisting of the judge and his two testigos de asistencia, to give his confession and be advised of all the charges made against him, in a proceeding called the confesión con cargos. The same questions were asked, and he reaffirmed his previous testimony. The judge seemed determined to find a motive for the killing, and he asked repeatedly about *riñas* (arguments), but Rafael continued to deny that he had any quarrel with his wife. Questioned about why he was carrying the knife, Rafael replied that when he traveled he carried the knife for his own protection. To the question why he had come to this jurisdiction, he replied that he came to ask for help from the judge, because *salteadores* (highwaymen) had threatened him. What was his motive for stabbing his wife? He repeated that it was because she had left his bed that night, and he added that it seemed to him that he had done well by taking her life for this reason! Obviously Rafael felt no remorse about killing his wife; indeed, he felt it was justified! In the concluding statements of his confession, he told the judge that he had fled from the jail to find someone to post bond for him.

Diego Montoya appointed Juan José Sánchez as promotor fiscal to prosecute the case against Rafael Montoya. Sánchez made several points in his rather lengthy written plea. María had told the truth in her testimony; she had done nothing to provoke this attack by her jealous husband. Although he made many accusations, he had never caught her in adultery—the only defensible motive for murdering one's wife. Each of the defendant's alleged motives for the killing were superficial, triggered by unfounded jealousy and faulty reasoning. The prosecutor then examined them one by one and found no reasonable excuse for Rafael's violent behavior.

First, Sánchez noted that the defendant had said he killed María because Lázaro Tórrez and two other men in the Plaza de Alameda had insulted him, and he believed that it was because of his wife. Later in his confession, when asked why he came to Corrales, he said that "highwaymen" had threatened him. The prosecutor suspected that Rafael was lying. How could he blame his wife for the actions of some impudent highwaymen? The prosecutor asked if this was the grievance that he kept in his heart that led him to murder María.

What about the articles of clothing that he had not given her? Were the stockings and shoes gifts from some unknown suitor? The prosecutor thought not. Certainly even poor men's wives were able to make such small purchases from money that their husbands or relatives gave them, or that they made from their spinning. Again, this was a poor excuse for such a deed. Rafael claimed that he killed his wife because she left the bed that night and refused to return. The promotor fiscal found it difficult to believe that a woman would venture out on such a cold night in a place unfamiliar to her and then refuse to return to the house. Even if this were true, it was a childish act on her part, and Rafael could have forced her to return without using violence.

The most damming evidence found in Rafael's confession may have been his total lack of remorse and his apparent belief that he had done well by taking his wife's life. In spite of his lack of training in jurisprudence, Sánchez concluded that Rafael Montoya deserved the último suplicio: execution would be a just punishment for his crime and would satisfy public vengeance.

On 3 April, the prisoner was brought before the juez de paz. The entire case was read to him, and he was asked to name someone to defend him. Rafael named Agustín Durán as his defensor. Durán had a long history as a public official in various positions, including territorial treasurer, Santa Fe alcalde, and member of the Departmental Assembly. A few years later, Durán would be involved in a plot against the American occupation.[12]

Two months lapsed before Diego Montoya actually forwarded the case to Agustín Durán in Santa Fe. He apologized for the delay, explaining that it was due to the recent problems with Tejanos and Navajos that had disrupted the department and interrupted work on the case. These were two very serious concerns in New Mexico that year. Marauding Navajo Indians on the western frontier, and the plots and raids of Texans along the eastern border kept New Mexico in turmoil throughout 1843.[13] Montoya hoped that Durán would make his defense plea with all possible speed.

Durán received the case and penned a reply from Santa Fe on 19 June, assuring Montoya that he would respond within ten days. Durán's written defense must have been misplaced; it does not appear with the rest of the proceedings.

This case, like most of the homicide cases, lacks a final judgement. On 16 January 1844, Corrales Justice Diego Antonio Montoya entered one last notice in the Rafael Montoya murder case. Two citizens, Francisco Romero of Cochití and José Antonio Romero of Corrales, had come forward as *fiadores* (bondsmen) to post bail for the prisoner. The two men promised to take full responsibility for Montoya and bear the obligation of returning him immediately to court whenever necessary.

Little more than a year after murdering his wife, Rafael Montoya was out on bail, and the case against him was closed. Montoya's short stay in jail hardly seems a sufficient punishment for his brutal crime, yet the meager sentence that he served must have reaffirmed his own belief that his actions were justified. Why did Montoya believe he had "done well" by taking his wife's life? Was there something in his society that led him to believe that the murder of one's wife was warranted? According to Spanish law, a man could legally "punish" his wife and her paramour; homicide was defensible in such circumstances.[14] However, Montoya admitted that he had never caught María in adultery, so what had triggered his violence and bolstered his belief that his actions might be construed as justifiable?

This case is revealing because the victim survived long enough to tell her side of the story. María Gonzales was questioned about her moral conduct to see if she had given her husband reason for the violent assault. Before she died, María was able to defend her virtue. She told the justice that her husband was extremely jealous, but he had never caught her with another man, nor had she given him any cause to distrust her.

María never mentioned that three men had threatened her and her husband on their journey, the incident that had apparently so upset Rafael. In any case, his jealous nature led him to believe that she had encouraged these men, and he perceived this encounter as a threat to his honor. In Hispanic society, an attack against a man's wife was perceived as an attack against his honor, and men who could not protect their women lost honor.[15] Montoya knew one of these men by name. Perhaps they had some feud, and Montoya feared this man would assault his wife to get at him. Although we will never know exactly what he was thinking, it is evident that Montoya's extreme jealous nature and his fear of having his honor tarnished led him to feel justified in murdering María.

The Trial of don Francisco Rael for the Murder of his Servant Juan José Montoya

ALGODONES, 26 AUGUST 1843

JUEZ DE PAZ, ALGODONES: José María Miera y Pino
JUEZ DE PAZ, BERNALILLO: Pedro José Perea
JUEZ DE PAZ, 1844: José María Gutiérrez
PROMOTOR FISCAL (PROSECUTOR): don José Alexandro Santiestevan
PROCURADOR (DEFENDER): Rumaldo Archibeque
TESTIGOS (WITNESSES): Salvador Barreras; José Antonio Encinas; Ramón Padilla; José María de Lara; Juan Cristóbal Gurulé
CURA (PRIEST), SAN FELIPE: Mariano de Jesús Lucero
CURA (PRIEST), SANDÍA: Fernando Ortiz
CIRUJANO (SURGEON): Autin Reina [?]
CARCELERO (JAILOR): Manuel Salazar
ALGUACIL (WARDEN): Vicente Chaves
CURADOR (GUARDIAN): Juan José Gutiérrez
PADRES DEL DIFUNTO (VICTIM'S PARENTS): Juan Montoya; María Chaves
ESPOSA DEL REO (REAL'S WIFE): Teresa Luna
OTROS, MENTIONED: Juan Archibeque's son, Miguel Serna; María de Jesús Baca; María de la Luz Cordova
TESTIGOS DE ASISTENCIA: Vicente Baca; Román Aragón; Juan Baca; Antonio Ramírez; Anastacio Lucero; José Ortega; Antonio Lucero; Felipe Castillo; Miguel Antonio Lovato; José Francisco Muñiz; Juan Trujillo; José Antonio Gerviso; Juan Arce; José M. Perea
FIADOR (BONDSMAN): Ignacio Miera

FIVE

The Servant Boy[1]

✠

It was late August 1843. In Corrales, Rafael Montoya was still in jail for murdering his wife. About fifteen miles up the river in the small farming community of Punto de los Algodones, life seemed peaceful. *Chicharras* (cicadas) were humming overhead in the huge old cottonwood trees that gave the town its name.[2] Corn and chilies were ripening in small irrigated plots, and apples were turning red in "orchards enclosed by cactus-crested mud walls."[3]

Algodones was not an old town; it had been settled only recently by farmers and stockmen from the surrounding area. Don Francisco Rael had come to Algodones from Alameda with his wife Teresa Luna. It appears that don Francisco was one of the wealthier residents of the village, possibly one of the patrón class: he owned stock, either cattle or sheep, and had at least one servant in his employ. Further, he was educated, socially well connected, and always referred to by the title "don."[4]

On this particular day, don Francisco was in a foul mood. His young servant, Juan José Montoya, had failed to return with the animals that he had been sent to fetch hours before. Rael grabbed his black *cabresto* (a thick, horsehair rope) and strode purposefully through the fields, intent on finding the culprit and giving him a beating he would not soon forget.[5]

Juan José was the son of Juan Montoya and María Chaves, of Tejón, a tiny community some seven or eight miles southeast of Algodones. Juan's exact age is unknown, but according to one of the witnesses in the case, he appeared to be twelve or thirteen years old. He was living as a sirviente in Rael's home. Servants often came from poorer families who hired themselves or their children out on a contractual basis. This practice was similar to the system of indentured servitude in the United States.[6]

Seething with anger, Rael searched his neighbors' fields and homes for the wayward lad. Juan José, unaware of the danger he was in, had slipped into the home of señor José Antonio Encinas. Juan was munching on a *tortilla* that Encinas's wife had given him when Rael burst into the house. Without asking any questions, don Francisco raged at the terrified youth, "Here you are genízaro malo," and he struck him with the cabresto.

Rael's use of the term "genízaro" may or may not have had any actual reference to the boy's heritage. As mentioned in chapter 1, the term was used to refer to detribalized Indians who had been forced to assimilate into Hispanic society. This class of people had originated from Indian captives (usually women and children) taken by indios bárbaros and ransomed to the Spanish, who kept them as sirvientes until such time as they could pay off the debt incurred by their ransom.[7] By the time this debt was paid, these people had been inducted into the Catholic faith, taught to speak Spanish, and otherwise prepared to live like Hispanics rather than Indians. Now considered indios genízaros, they were free to establish their own households, but their social status remained negligible and "genízaro" was often used in a derogatory manner.[8] Juan José and his family could have been of genízaro background—obviously his family was poor, and he and his wife found it necessary to hire their son out as a servant to don Francisco—but whether or not they were genízaros, Rael probably used the term as an insult.

The force of the first blow with the rope toppled Juan to the ground, where his master proceeded to beat him viciously. Holding him down with his left foot against the boy's neck, he savagely kicked Juan's chest with his other foot. Señor Encinas, in his seventieth year, stood by with his wife, unable or perhaps afraid to interfere, but their daughter cried out to don Francisco to stop. He warned her to keep out of it, but in the confusion Juan managed to free himself and flee towards the neighbor's house.

At Miguel Serna's, don Francisco caught up with the youth and began beating him again with the rope. Grabbing Juan by the hair, he threw him against a wall. When he staggered and fell, Rael continued to flail him.

Finally, Juan José managed to escape from his enraged master. While fleeing through a corn field, barefoot or perhaps in soft-soled moccasins, Juan ran a sharp stick deep into the instep of his left foot. Afraid and in excruciating pain, the youth spent the night hiding in the *bosque*. He was discovered the following day by a neighbor boy, the son of Juan Archibeque. Young Archibeque ran for help. At his home he found Salvador

Barreras, a friend of the family who had just arrived that day from El Tejón. The boy told Barreras that he had found don Francisco Rael's servant boy hiding in the bosque, where he had been "bitten by a snake."

Barreras was a resident of Algodones who had been one of the principal parties in the El Tejón Land Grant, a small grant made by Governor Armijo in 1840 for a town site.[9] Barreras owned a house in Tejón, where he was a neighbor of Juan José's family. Moved by compassion, Barreras headed for the bosque to help the injured boy. He found Juan José lying on the ground. His face was badly bruised, and he was unable to move his injured leg. Barreras hoisted Juan up on his back and carried him to don Francisco's house. When Barreras questioned Juan about his condition, he confessed that his face was black and blue as a result of a beating his master had given him. His leg was causing him the most pain, not as the result of a snake bite, but from having driven a sharp stick or a splinter of bone, the thickness of a finger, deep into his foot.[10]

Juan might have lived if he had received proper medical attention, but given the medical knowledge of the mid-nineteenth century he didn't have much of a chance. The deep puncture wound in his foot became infected, and his condition worsened. Three days after he witnessed the beating, José Antonio Encinas went to Rael's home to check on Juan's condition. He found the boy lying in bed spitting black blood into a rag. Juan was dying.

Juan José's father, Juan Montoya, had come from Tejón, probably learning of his son's plight from his neighbor Salvador Barreras. At eight in the evening on 30 August, Montoya went to José María Miera y Pino, the juez de paz of Algodones, in the Sandía jurisdiction, and reported that his son was near death as the result of a severe punishment meted out by his master don Francisco Rael.

Justice Miera y Pino immediately summoned two testigos de asistencia and the parish priest to accompany him to don Francisco's home, in order to verify the seriousness of the young servant's condition. Algodones, with a population of only several hundred inhabitants, had no church of its own. The nearest priest was Father Mariano de Jesús Lucero at the San Felipe Pueblo, just a few miles to the north on the opposite bank of the river. Lucero was a secular priest, one of fewer than a dozen who served the entire department of New Mexico at this time.[11]

With a heavy heart, Juan Montoya returned the following morning to inform the magistrate that his son Juan José had died during the night. Once again Miera y Pino summoned the witnesses and the priest to accompany him to Rael's home. This time his investigative party included an individual identified as a cirujano. It seems odd that there was a surgeon in the tiny town of Algodones. Why wasn't he called before the youth died? In any case, the doctor's identity remains a mystery, since, like that of many in this profession, his signature is barely legible. When mentioned in the prosecutor's report, the name appears to be Autin Reina, but this in no way resembles the doctor's signature.

At Rael's home, the cirujano first checked for a pulse. Finding none, he pronounced the boy officially dead and proceeded to examine the body. He noted that a stick had punctured the instep of the left foot and had gone into the flesh four *dedos* in the direction of the heel. (This probably meant the width of four fingers, which is the equivalent of three or four inches.) This leg was badly bruised and swollen from the foot to the hip and the doctor felt that death had been the result of this deep puncture wound. Encinas had not yet testified that Juan had been spitting up black blood, which may have indicated internal injuries received during the beating.

The justice ordered that the body be transferred to a public place, where the same four witnesses—Anastacio and Antonio Lucero and Vicente and Juan Baca—testified that it was the body they had seen in the house of don Francisco Rael. Miera advised the priest, Mariano de Jesús Lucero, to make arrangements for a speedy burial in order to "avoid the corruption of the cadaver," which was unavoidable in the late summer heat. That very afternoon at four o'clock, Juan José Montoya, the son of Juan Montoya and María Chaves of the Plaza de San Juan Nepomuceno del Tejón, was laid to rest in *tierra sagrada*. The actual location of this holy ground was not mentioned.

The following day Juan Montoya appeared before Justice José Miera y Pino and registered a complaint against Francisco Rael for beating his son and causing his untimely death. The justice ordered that Rael be imprisoned in the local jail and secured in par de grillos, to avoid his flight, until the case could be investigated.

On 3 September, three witnesses testified before Miera y Pino. José Antonio Encinas, José Ramón Padilla, and Salvador Barreras each told what he knew about the death of Juan José. Although Encinas and several members of his family had witnessed Rael beating the servant boy, only señor Encinas was called to testify. Encinas related the incident that took place in his home. He said that Rael had beaten Juan with the horsehair rope. He told how the youth ran to the neighbor's house, where Rael caught him and continued the whipping. He also described how Juan was coughing up blood as he lay dying at Rael's home three days after the beating.

Ramón Padilla, a 37-year-old farmer from Algodones, had been in the patio of María de Jesús Baca's home on the day in question. He had seen

Juan José run past, his master close on his heels. Padilla witnessed Rael lash out with his rope and saw it catch the boy's shoulder as he ran. Padilla did not lose sight of them. He saw Rael catch up to Juan José at Miguel Serna's home, where Juan succumbed to the beating and fell to the ground. Rael caught the boy up between his feet and continued to thrash him unmercifully. This was all that Padilla knew. He swore to it under oath and made the sign of the cross on his testimony before two witnesses.

Salvador Barreras told how he had been led to the bosque by the Archibeque boy, where he found Juan José Montoya badly bruised and unable to move his left leg, which had been injured when a stick punctured deep into his foot. Barreras reported how he carried Juan back to his master's house, and how Juan had told him that his master had beaten him and he had run away into the corn field, where a thick stick ran deep into his foot, causing him terrible pain. Barreras did not know why Rael beat his servant; the boy had not told him.

Almost three weeks later, Miera y Pino was replaced as the acting judge by Pedro José Perea, the juez de paz of Bernalillo. Don Pedro, in his early sixties, was the patriarch of the wealthy Perea family, whose home in Bernalillo was the headquarters for a vast sheep business and mercantile enterprise.[12]

When the case was turned over to Perea, Francisco Rael was brought to Bernalillo and given over to the custody of the jailer, Manuel Salazar. Bernalillo was only a short ride from Algodones and still within what was considered the jurisdiction of Sandía. One of Perea's first official acts was to ask the priest of San Felipe to send him a copy of the death certificate for his records. Lucero promptly complied with the request on official stamped paper, explaining in which book and on what folio the original could be found.

The prisoner was brought before Justice Perea and sworn in. Rael was a 36-year-old farmer, born in Alameda, baptized in the parish church of San Felipe de Alburquerque, now living in Algodones with his wife Teresa Luna. Rael had been at the home of Justice Miera y Pino early in the morning on the last day of August, when the *alguacil* (warden), Vicente Chaves, took him into custody. He knew that his servant boy, Juan José Montoya, was dead and that he was accused of killing him. He had beaten the *mozo* (young man, male servant) with his cabresto because he had taken too long bringing in the animals. After he beat him, the boy had tried to run home. On the way, José María de Lara had seen Juan and asked him where he was going. He responded that he had been beaten by his master and he was running away to his own home.

José María de Lara was called in for questioning. He was the nineteen-year-old son-in-law of señora María de la Luz Cordova and a farm worker from El Paso del Norte. Lara knew Francisco Rael and he knew that he was in jail for killing his servant boy José Montoya. The witness had seen the boy before he died. Lara testified that the servant had confessed to him that he was running away and had begged Lara not to tell his master. José María de Lara, a minor, penned in a cross at the bottom of his testimony, and Juan José Gutiérrez, acting as his legal guardian (curador), wrote his signature beneath the mark.

The victim's father, Juan Montoya, was asked to show his interest in the case. He came forth and pardoned the suspect. "Notwithstanding the grave offense that the aggressor had done to his son, he forgave him in all his heart because God our Lord pardoned him, and consequently, he [Montoya] renounced all laws or actions that would be imposed on him [Montoya] in order to proceed against him [Rael]."[13] This may have been a legal formality that allowed Montoya to step down as the *acusador* in the case. The accuser, or the party who brought charges against a suspect, was responsible for the burden of proof and also had an interest in seeing that the culprit was punished for his crime.[14]

On 11 October, Francisco Rael was ordered to hand over to the court 120 pesos. It is quite likely that this represented the embargo de bienes, goods which were confiscated from prisoners to pay for their maintenance in the local jail. This amount of money was guaranteed by don Ignacio Miera, who handed it over to Judge Pedro José Perea.

The witnesses were each asked to appear before Perea to have their previous testimonies ratified. The first to appear was Salvador Barreras, who was listed as the testigo acusador, which may indicate that he had taken over the role of accuser. Barreras had little to add to his first statement, although he was further questioned about whether the victim had been bitten by a snake and if he knew why Rael had beaten his servant boy. Barreras assured the justice that the Montoya boy had been wounded by a stick, not a snake, and he was not aware of Rael's motive for beating the boy. Antonio Encinas and Ramón Padilla appeared before the Bernalillo justice, Pedro Perea, to have their testimonies ratified. They had no more to tell and affirmed what they had told Miera y Pino some six weeks earlier in Algodones.

Perea called the suspect. He was first asked to tell the court in what parish he was baptized and to obtain proof of his baptism from the priest of that parish. Fernando Ortiz of Sandía Parish reported to the justice that after "scrupulous and minute review" of his baptismal books, he had not located a certificate of baptism for Francisco Rael. The following day, 17 October, Francisco Rael came forth to confess. He testified that he was a native of Alameda but had been baptized in the San Felipe Church in Alburquerque. Rael ratified his previous testimony, reaffirmed that he was Catholic, and named Juan Cristóbal Gurulé as another witness in the case.[15]

Perea suspended the confession to take the testimony of Gurulé, a 37-year-old farmer, born in nearby Las Huertas and living in Algodones. He had been to the Rael home and talked to the Montoya boy before he died. Juan José had showed Gurulé his injured leg and told him the whole story. Gurulé's statement reaffirmed what had already been stated, and did not add any new information.

After taking this final testimony, the justice called Francisco Rael to complete his confession. Once again he was asked to reaffirm that he was a Catholic. Rael had little to say about the death of his servant, except to repeat his earlier story. He emphasized the importance of the swollen leg and minimized the significance of the other less obvious bruises and injuries that were a result of the beating that he had administered.

Before the month was out, the justice appointed don José Alexandro Santiestevan to conduct the prosecution, and Rael named don Rumaldo Archibeque as procurador to defend him. The prosecution briefly recapped the entire case from beginning to end and concluded that Francisco Rael had killed Juan José Montoya. Santiestevan begged that in accordance with justice the most serious penalty be imposed on the culprit.

Don Rumaldo Archibeque wrote his defense of the prisoner from Algodones on 11 November. He asked that Francisco Rael be released from prison immediately, without penalty. His goods should be returned to him, and he should be set free on bond. The defense was mostly based on the examining doctor's statement that Montoya probably died as a result of the wound in his left leg, an injury that Archibeque described in some detail. The defense added that the doctor had mentioned some other things before concluding his testimony. (These "other things" that Archibeque neglected to report were the bruises that covered much of the boy's face!) He added that the doctor's testimony was to be given complete credence, whereas the testimonies of two of the witnesses should be considered useless and false.

The two testimonies that the defense defamed were those of Antonio Encinas and Ramón Padilla, the only eyewitnesses who testified to the severe beating that Rael gave to his servant—a beating that included violent blows to the chest that could well have resulted in serious internal injuries without leaving visible marks on the body. Furthermore, it was

Encinas who had reported in his testimony that he had seen Juan José spitting up black blood three days after he had been beaten by Rael. If the testimonies of these two witnesses were disregarded, the death of Juan José Montoya might be considered accidental.

At this point in the defense, Archibeque made reference to a work by Gutiérrez, citing a specific volume, chapter, and page numbers. This work must have been *Practica Criminal de España* by José Marcos Gutiérrez, which was published in Madrid in 1804. This would indicate that Archibeque actually had some legal training or at least access to legal works. Indeed, the records refer to Archibeque as a procurador, rather than a defensor. A procurador was a paid legal representative employed by the defendant.[16]

Archibeque ended his lengthy defense requesting that the defendant be set free on bond, without delay. The written defense was forwarded from Algodones by Justice Miera y Pino to Promotor Fiscal Alexandro Santiestevan in Bernalillo. Santiestevan wrote to the judge, informing him that he would not consent to the demands of the defense and that he was returning the case for the legal period of ninety days, at which time the evidence would be made public. The prosecutor was concerned that the defense was attempting to disqualify witnesses who had testified in the case, and he asked the judge to base his decision on the prosecution's proposal.

Almost six months passed before another entry was made in the case against Francisco Rael. On 7 May 1844, José María Gutiérrez, the current justice of the peace in Bernalillo, noted that he had sent a copy of the *publicación de probanzas* to Francisco Rael's procurador. The same day, Rumaldo Archibeque wrote to the judge to say that he was giving up the authority that Rael had conferred on him and that Rael should be notified that he needed to appoint someone else to defend him. The reason for this move is unclear, and it proved to be unnecessary. A little over a month later, on 19 June, Juez Actuante José María Miera y Pino, who had done the initial investigations in the case, allowed Francisco Rael to be set free on bond. Don Ignacio Miera, who had put up the 120 pesos for Rael back in October was named as bondsman.

One wonders if the Mieras were in cahoots with the defendant. After the crime was reported, Rael was found at Justice Miera y Pino's home. Ignacio Miera put up money for Rael's upkeep in jail and paid money for his bail when Miera y Pino allowed Rael out on bond barely eight months after his arrest.

The Rael case had some unusual qualities. Unlike the other murder suspects, don Francisco was educated and appeared to be a man of means. Although not necessarily a rich man, Rael was the only suspect who could afford to employ a procurador for his defense and the only suspect who was ordered to hand over a cash amount to the court for his "room and board" in jail.

Of the four suspects involved in cases of domestic violence, Rael was the only one who maintained his innocence. Rael's defense rested on the evidence of the examining "surgeon," who stated that the cause of death was a deep puncture wound in the boy's foot, caused by a sharp stick. The wound had not been a result of the beating. Further, the defense attempted to disqualify witnesses whose testimonies indicated that the beating itself was so violent it could have caused fatal internal injuries. Rael considered himself vindicated and expressed no sorrow over the youth's death.

The defendant was definitely favored in this case, either because of his social standing or because of the difficulty of proving it was the beating that had resulted in Juan José's death, rather than the accident that befell him in the bosque. Whatever the reason, Rael spent little time in jail and apparently even less time feeling any guilt over the boy's death. Rael went on about his business and was involved in several lawsuits following his arrest. In February 1844, even before he was released from jail, Rael was bringing suit against Juan Armijo for stealing his cattle. The following year, his wife Teresa de Luna brought a complaint against José María Valdez and Antonio Chaves for neglect of payment, and later the same year Rael made a complaint against José María Valdez and others for robbery.[17] It was business as usual for don Francisco Rael.

The Trial of Juan Antonio Chaves for the Murder of his Wife María Angelina Herrera

COCHITÍ, 19 JANUARY 1846

✣

ALCALDE, SANTA FE: Trinidad Barceló
ALCALDE ACTUANTE: don Tomás Rivera
ALCALDE: Anastacio Sandoval
JUEZ DE PAZ, COCHITÍ: Jesús María Cabesa de Baca
PROMOTOR FISCAL (PROSECUTOR): Miguel E. Pino
DEFENSOR (DEFENDER): Francisco Tomás Cabesa de Baca
LICENCIADO (LAWYER): Jesús María Palacio
TESTIGOS (WITNESSES): Juan José Cañijuebes; Manuel Suina; José Matalobos
PERITOS (EXPERTS): Juan Gervacio Aragón; Vicente Miera
SACRISTÁN (SEXTON): Felipe Herrera
OTRO: (witness to burial): Gerónimo Aguilar
TESTIGOS DE ASISTENCIA, SANTO DOMINGO: Francisco Tomás Cabesa de Baca; Juan Padilla; Fernando Armijo; Juan Paras; Juan Antonio Quintana; Albino Aragón
TESTIGOS DE ASISTENCIA, SANTA FE: Tomás Ortiz; Mauricio Durán; Antonio Ortiz; Domingo Fernández; Tomás López; Francisco Ortiz y Delgado; Manuel Sandoval

✣

SIX

Murder in the Bosque[1]

✣

The following homicide took place at the Cochití Pueblo in the last year of the Mexican Era. Cochití, one of the southern pueblos, is thirty miles southwest of Santa Fe, on the northern edge of the area known as the Río Abajo. The village is situated on the west bank of the Río del Norte, about six miles south of where that river emerges from the narrow White Rock Canyon that cuts between the Jémez Mountains on the west and the Caja del Río Plateau on the east.

Cochití is one of seven Keresan-speaking pueblos. Her nearest Keresan neighbors are Santo Domingo ten miles downriver, and San Felipe about five miles farther. Closer still is the Spanish settlement of Peña Blanca, where the Cabesa de Baca family lived. The Cabesa de Bacas were well-to-do landowners who had a long history of conflict with their Cochití and Santo Domingo neighbors.[2]

During Spanish colonial times, Indians were considered legal minors, and a protector de indios was hired to defend them in legal disputes. After Mexican Independence, this office was abolished, and the special legal status of natives was ended.[3] When a crime was committed on Pueblo lands, it was referred to authorities in that jurisdiction, and the accused was assigned a defensor to plead his case. Thus, this homicide case involving two Pueblo Indians was handled in the same way as other homicide cases involving Hispanics.

On a crisp winter day in 1846, three Cochití men were walking in the bosque (woods) upriver from their pueblo, when they discovered the body of a woman lying face-down among the cottonwood trees, her clothing stained with blood. The men recognized her as María Angelina Herrera, a

Cochití woman who had been missing for three days. Juan José Cañijuebes, Manuel Suina, and José Matalobos returned to Cochití to inform the governor of the pueblo of their grisly find. With the governor, they retraced their steps to the bosque and pointed out the woman's body.

The governor, whose name was not mentioned in the records, ordered them to examine the ground for possible clues regarding the murder. Noticing tracks leading away from the body, the men followed the footprints and came across Juan Antonio Chaves, the victim's husband. Chaves's shoes were examined to see if they matched the footprints found near the body. When it was realized that the suspect's shoes did not quite match the prints, the governor questioned Chaves to see if he had any other footwear. Chaves admitted he had another pair at home, and the party returned to the pueblo to discover his other pair of shoes stained with blood. Chaves then confessed that the blood was his wife's; he had killed her following an argument. Cañijuebes recalled that Chaves and his wife had often quarreled.

The governor of Cochití apparently did not keep any written record of his investigation; however, he immediately sent word to the local justice that a body had been found in his jurisdiction. Jesús María Cabesa de Baca of Peña Blanca was the juez constitucional of the Santo Domingo *demarcación*, which included the Cochití Pueblo. The justice filed a cabeza de proceso, initiating the investigation into the homicide of the Cochití woman. Cabesa de Baca stressed that the greatest care must be practiced in conducting the inquiry. In a *razón*, an explanation entered into the legal proceedings, he noted that the case that followed would be written on common paper, due to a lack of stamped official paper, and that this should not be taken as any indication of incompetence on his part.

Immediately, two peritos were appointed to accompany the justice to the bosque, where they would examine the body and attempt to discern the circumstances of death. Juan Gervacio Aragón and Vicente Miera agreed to perform the necessary duties. Neither knew how to sign his name to the statement each would be required to make as witnesses. Literacy was not a prerequisite for being an "expert," in a frontier society where illiteracy was common.

At three o'clock that afternoon, the investigative party, headed by Cabesa de Baca, arrived in the bosque north of Cochití. Here cottonwoods grew in profusion, and the dead dry branches were gathered for firewood. The men made their way silently through the woods. Only the crunch of dried leaves and twigs underfoot warned of their presence. A dark shape appeared ahead of them in the underbrush. As they grew near, the shape took the form of a woman's body dressed in typical pueblo style, wearing a black *manta* and hard-soled hide moccasins called *teguas*. A manta was a length of woven cotton or wool cloth that could serve many functions; it was often worn as a dress or wrap—usually over one shoulder, under the opposite arm, and belted about the waist.[4] A small bundle of firewood tied up in a cotton manta and a bloodied white handkerchief lay close by. Four *varas* (about eleven feet) from the body, the men discovered what appeared to be the murder weapon, a blood-stained rock weighing some five pounds.

The peritos, in the presence of the justice and two other witnesses, examined the body and confirmed that the woman was dead. They observed that there were no wounds on the victim's body; only her face showed signs of being severely battered. As far as they could determine, in their limited understanding of these things, the woman had been bludgeoned to death with the aforementioned rock. The blood-stained rock was kept as evidence, and the two experts, their task completed, drew the sign of the cross at the bottom of their statements.

The party returned to Cochití, accompanying the body of the deceased, and Cabesa de Baca made arrangements for an ecclesiastical burial the same afternoon. There was no priest present; the burial was conducted by the *sacristán* Felipe Herrera, probably a relative of the deceased. In preparation for the burial, family members would have carefully washed and dressed the body. A Pueblo medicine man might have placed corn pollen or cornmeal in the mouth of the corpse and performed certain rituals in accordance with native beliefs. Afterwards, he would have wrapped and sewed the body up in a blanket, and turned it over to the sacristán for Christian burial. The deceased was probably carried to the campo santo on a ladder and buried in a grave located and dug under the direction of the sacristán, who offered prayers at the grave site.[5] By half past six that evening, María Angelina Herrera was resting at peace in the cemetery of San Buenaventura Church at Cochití.

According to the case records, this whole scenario took place on 22 January 1846. It must have been a very long day. In Peña Blanca, Judge Cabesa de Baca received news of the homicide at eight o'clock in the morning; by three o'clock that afternoon he was in the bosque investigating the crime; at half past six the same evening, the victim was buried at Cochití Pueblo. At some time during this busy day, the justice made time to take the testimonies of the three men who had discovered the body. Their statements reveal that they had discovered the body and reported the crime to the Cochití governor that same morning. If this was true, they were walking in the bosque very early in the morning!

Cañijuebes, aged fifty, Suina, fifty-five, and Matalobos, thirty, were sworn in and questioned one at a time by Cabesa de Baca. Each told the same tale. All were farmers, married, natural citizens of Cochití, and professed Catholics. While walking together in the bosque, the three had discovered the body of María Angelina Herrera. They reported this to the governor of the pueblo, who returned with them to the spot where the body lay. Here they encountered footprints that led them to the husband of the victim, Juan Antonio Chaves. When a pair of bloodied shoes was found in his home, Chaves confessed that he had murdered his wife following an argument.

This was enough to convince Justice Cabesa de Baca that Juan Antonio Chaves had committed the murder, and he issued an auto de prisión, ordering the alguaciles (peace officers or sheriffs) of that jurisdiction to shackle Chaves and turn him over to the custody of the *alcaide* (warden) of the pueblo of Cochití. He ordered that charges be made and the prisoner's statement be taken.

One week later, the entire proceedings in the case, along with the murder weapon and the prisoner, were sent to Santa Fe. Cabesa de Baca included a note explaining that he had been unable to obtain the testimony of the prisoner due to the disposition of that court.

Trinidad Barceló was the alcalde segundo constitucional of Santa Fe who received the criminal case against Juan Antonio Chaves. It is quite possible that Trinidad Barceló was the brother of Gertrudis Barceló, better known as "doña Tules," one of the most notorious characters, and certainly the most notorious woman, of the Mexican Era.[6]

Alcalde Barceló acknowledged receipt of the homicide case and proceeded to take the testimony of the 26-year-old suspect. Juan Antonio Chaves admitted that he had killed his wife María Angelina Herrera, with a rock, in the bosque north of Cochití. Barceló questioned him about motive. Chaves replied that his wife had been missing for three days before he found her in the bosque, where he was gathering firewood. When he ordered her to go home and bring back rope to tie up the bundle of wood, she refused and a quarrel ensued.

Chaves claimed that his wife started the fight by hitting him with a rock. He was so enraged that he seized the rock from her hands and struck her full-force in the face with it. In a fury, he continued to bash her face and head until she died. The defendant was asked what he did after he killed his wife. Chaves responded that he left her lying on the ground where she had fallen, and returned home. The alcalde ordered the proceedings suspended for the time being. The statement was read to the prisoner, and he verified it and drew a cross next to his name.

Six days later, the prisoner was brought before the alcalde to continue his testimony, now called a confesión con cargos. Barceló read the entire case to Chaves, "clearly and expressly," and Chaves said he heard and understood it. Asked what he felt about the seriousness of the crime of murdering his wife, the prisoner responded that everything he had said was true, and he added in some bewilderment, "what do you want me to say *padrecito*?" Was "little father" a term of respect for an authority figure of the dominant class or an ironic form of derision? Whatever Chaves's intent, the alcalde was still searching for a more plausible motive. What had María Angelina done to deserve this?

The suspect repeated once again that his only reason for killing his wife was fury with her for striking him with a rock. Frustrated, Barceló admonished Chaves that this was not a sufficient motive for murdering one's wife; he could have used other means to correct her behavior. Alcalde Barceló charged Chaves with the murder of his wife, "the worst crime that a man could commit," and asked the suspect to respond. Chaves confessed to the murder but had no further comments and showed no sign of remorse.

The prisoner was then questioned about details of the crime. Chaves acknowledged that the blood-stained shoes were the ones he wore when he murdered his wife. He was shown the "murder weapon," and he identified it as the rock he had used to beat María to death; the blood stains that covered it were hers. The confession was suspended, and Chaves signed with a cross next to his name, confirming his statement. The confession was witnessed by two testigos de asistencia, Tomás Ortiz and Mauricio Durán.

Barceló named Miguel E. Pino as promotor fiscal to prosecute the case against Chaves. This was probably Miguel Estanislao Pino, son of Pedro Bautista Pino who was the New Mexican deputy to the Spanish Cortes back in 1810 and author of the *Exposición*, an important source on early-nineteenth-century New Mexico history published in 1812. Pino had been married three times, and Miguel, born in 1821, was the son of his third wife María Baca. The Pinos were among the rico families of New Mexico, involved in the very profitable sheep raising industry and trade with central Mexico.[7]

Within two days after his appointment, Pino delivered his written plea to the judge. He referred back to the testimony and the confession of the prisoner, and concluded that Juan Antonio Chaves, without any sufficient cause, moved by passion, and lacking humanity and the bonds of love that all husbands should possess for their wives, had murdered María Angelina Herrera. Furthermore, Chaves had freely admitted his guilt, in both his testimony and his confession, and at no time had he shown any regrets for committing this atrocious crime. To punish such a terrible deed and to satisfy public vengeance, the prisoner should be given the penalty indicated for a crime of this nature.[8]

Echoing the sentiments of other New Mexicans who found themselves in similar judicial positions, Miguel Pino apologized for his limited understanding of the law and remarked "you must not hold it against me, if in discharging my duties, I do not meet the formal methods to which men learned and instructed in the law are surely inclined."[9] New Mexicans called to perform legal services realized their limitations and relied more on common sense and community norms than on precepts of the law.

The case, in twelve folios, was sent to Peña Blanca to Juez de Paz Jesús María Cabesa de Baca, who had carried out the original investigations. He was instructed to forward it to Francisco Tomás Cabesa de Baca and inform him that he had been named defensor for the criminal Juan Chaves. Francisco Tomás was the son of Juan Antonio Cabesa de Baca and the grandson of Luis María Cabesa de Baca, both of whom had been involved in land disputes with the Cochití Pueblo. Jesús María Cabesa de Baca, the justice of Peña Blanca, was either the newly appointed defensor's brother or cousin.[10]

After swearing to defend the prisoner to the best of his abilities under the law, Francisco Tomás Cabesa de Baca sat down to write a lengthy defense of some three and a half folios (seven pages), a task he completed in the record time of one day. He returned it promptly to the justice of that jurisdiction, who forwarded it to the alcalde in Santa Fe.

There is no doubt that Francisco Tomás Cabesa de Baca took his duties seriously. He began his well-prepared and eloquent defense by stating that "if life is man's most precious possession, then to deprive him of it is also the greatest outrage, because it violates one of the principal social pacts."[11] He went on to say that in this act of taking a life there are degrees of malice that merit punishment according to the law. In order to apply the punishment that the crime deserved, one must determine the degree of deceit or malice with which the crime was committed.

The plan of the defense was to determine what the character of this homicide was and whether it deserved the ultimate punishment. Cabesa de Baca believed that public opinion would no doubt find Chaves guilty of a treacherous murder, deserving of execution; however, the powerful voice of the public was often fallible. Don Francisco hoped to bring out evidence in favor of the suspect to prove that he was not deserving of the death sentence. The defense pointed out that there were no eyewitnesses to the murder. Chaves's confession was the sole evidence against him, and the defendant's confession alone should not be allowed to determine his guilt.

The core of Cabesa de Baca's defense was that Chaves, by virtue of being a native, was innocent. He claimed that natives were so ignorant of Spanish law, politics, and religion that they could not know the gravity or the consequences of homicide. Further, the defensor asserted that native beliefs, "antiquated customs which they have conserved from their primitive beginnings," allowed vengeance killings. He claimed that in this jurisdiction, homicides among the Pueblos were not uncommon and rarely punished. The defensor felt that this would explain why his client had confessed such a reprehensible deed without the slightest concern.

Today, Cabesa de Baca's remarks would be considered racist, but for his time his attitude toward Pueblo society and his limited understanding of native culture were not unusual. Through centuries of Spanish dominance, the Pueblos had not integrated with their conquerors; they lived apart in their own towns, and continued to practice their own culture and speak their native tongue. Even though they could speak Spanish and practiced Christianity, their way of life was essentially Indian, not Hispanic. For this reason, the Mexican population did not consider them to be gente de razón.[12] This might explain Cabesa de Baca's rather odd defense: Chaves was innocent because he was a native, and natives did not have the same regard for human life that gente de razón possessed.

In conclusion, Cabesa de Baca insisted that the murder was not premeditated or treacherous. Rather, it was a spontaneous act provoked by the argument with his wife, whose whereabouts for the previous three days had been unknown to him. Therefore, the defense asked that Chaves be sentenced to some years in the presidio rather than receive capital punishment. This would "correct" the criminal and serve as a warning to others.

Within the week, the case was returned to Trinidad Barceló in Santa Fe, who forwarded a copy to the prosecutor, Miguel Pino. Pino was not so prompt; it took him three months to reply. On 5 June, he wrote to the alcalde segundo, excusing his negligence by saying he had been gravely ill and overloaded with work, but now he was returning the case for its completion. By the time it reached his office, Trinidad Barceló was no longer handling the case. Instead, Anastacio Sandoval received the letter from the prosecutor and sent the case on to the defense.

The defender, Cabesa de Baca, wrote a shorter plea, wherein he reiterated what he had stated in his earlier defense. He added that the tardiness of the prosecution was in his client's favor. Criminal cases were to be handled promptly, within a specific period of time prescribed by the law, yet it was now five months since he had sent his defense to the alcalde in Santa Fe, and no steps had been taken to conclude the case. Furthermore, he wanted to know the whereabouts of the letter from the prosecution that Anastacio Sandoval had ordered attached to the case? Anastacio Sandoval read the defense and realized, to his embarrassment, that he had inadvertently forgotten to attach the prosecutor's note to the case.

On 5 August 1846, Sandoval wrote that he was handing the case over for consultation to Licenciado Jesús María Palacio, who could be found visiting in La Peralta in the department of New Mexico. Palacio was a Mexican merchant and lawyer who was apparently doing business in New Mexico and had offered his assistance in this matter.[13] This was the final entry in the case; there was no written answer from Licenciado Palacio, and the final judgement and sentencing are not in the records.

One pertinent question was never brought out in the case: when did the murder take place? Obviously, Chaves had not just murdered his wife on 22 January, when he was found near the body; otherwise, he would still have been wearing the bloodied shoes that he had worn when he committed the crime. Instead, Chaves must have been returning to the scene of the murder he had perpetrated earlier.

One brief notice in the proceedings mentioned a possible date of death (a date that was never referred to again) as 19 January.[14] The body was discovered and the investigation initiated three days later, on 22 January. Is it not interesting that the suspect and the defense both claimed that María had been missing for three days before Chaves found and killed her? They seemed to imply that María's unexplained absence may have triggered her husband's sudden violence against her. If she had been murdered on 19 January, as that one brief entry indicated, then María's three-day absence was because her husband had already killed her and then spread the rumor that she was "missing."

What happened to the prisoner? There is no record of him being let out on bond. It seems likely that Juan Antonio Chaves was still sitting in the Santa Fe jail when General Stephen Watts Kearny and the Army of the West marched into Santa Fe on 18 August 1846 and raised the Stars and Stripes over the dusty plaza, claiming New Mexico for the United States.

SEVEN

Domestic Violence

✠

The family has always been considered one of the greatest strengths of Spanish society. Within the basic institution of the family, children learned the values and traditions of their culture. "Familia" meant not only the nuclear family, but often extended to include elderly parents, unmarried or widowed female relatives, orphans, and servants—all living in the same household. In a larger sense, family meant cousins, in-laws, and godparents, because intermarriage and *compadrazgo* (the intimate relationship between parents and godparents of a child) linked families together in social and economic alliances.[1]

If domestic violence seems inconsistent with this strong family tradition, it is important to realize that other cultural forces were at work as well. Society was dominated by males and a strong patriarchal family was the expected norm. Patriarchs were very concerned with maintaining family honor, and this was closely tied to the behavior of the women in their families. Men were expected to be able to control "their" women (wives, unmarried sisters, daughters, and female servants) and maintain authority within the family. If the male head-of-household perceived any threat to his power or felt his honor had been impugned by the conduct of his wife or other female family member, he might resort to extreme measures.[2]

Marriage was an alliance, an essential connection in a network of social and economic relationships. A marriage contract was forged by the parents of the bride and groom for the benefit of the family; it was not generally a love match. Marriage was sanctioned by the church after the lineage and background of the partners had been carefully scrutinized in *diligencias matrimoniales* (marital investigations) to see that there were no impediments to the union.[3]

Women had no political power — they could not vote or hold office — but they did have access to the legal system, and court records show that many made good use of this privilege. Women had control over their own property and sued frequently to protect their possessions.[4] However, in the realm of domestic violence, the law courts were less favorable to women. Society was dominated by men. Alcaldes and jueces that presided over the courts were all men and, although these magistrates often showed a high degree of understanding and compassion in their judgements, when it came to domestic problems their usual response was to call for a reconciliation and send the woman home to her husband.[5] It was generally assumed that if the woman was beaten by her husband, she probably deserved it. As evidenced by the María Gonzales case, the victim's moral character was questioned to see if she had given her husband just cause to "punish" her. Even minor misconduct on the part of the wife could be used as evidence against her.[6] Husbands had authority over their wives to discipline and punish them as they saw fit. Women were expected to be submissive and obedient to their spouses.

Men tended to side with each other to protect these male prerogatives. This is evident in the Ruival case, where the brother of the victim asked that his brother-in-law be pardoned, rather than punished, for the murder of his wife. In this male-dominated society, the judicial system bolstered the patriarchal system, which expected men to maintain order within their families. Expecting little support from the judicial system, and fearing increased violence against them, women who were beaten rarely reported the abuse.[7]

Incidences of domestic violence were probably higher than available documentation indicates, since many women were afraid to bring charges against their spouses. It is also likely that some cases of abuse were arbitrated by the local justice before charges were ever filed. A cursory glance at the calendars of the Mexican Archives of New Mexico and the Sender Collection reveals that approximately thirty-six cases of assault were reported to the alcalde courts during the Mexican Era. Of these, at least eleven were committed against women, and six of these eleven were husband-wife attacks. In one of these six cases the victim's father brought charges against the son-in-law, and in another the priest reported the crime.[8] Wives brought charges against their spouses in two cases, indicating that at least some women had faith that the judicial system would protect them.[9]

If most cases of wife abuse went unrecorded, child abuse cases were almost unheard of, although one case of attempted assault by a man on his wife and stepson appears in the Mexican Archives.[10] The Juan Montoya case was the only homicide involving a minor as the victim. This case showed that domestic violence was not always directed at the wife, but that children and servants could also be subjected to extreme brutality in the name of discipline. Montoya, a young mozo of don Francisco Rael (a prosperous sheep raiser and cattleman), was severely beaten by his master. Although he lived at his master's home, the Montoyas kept themselves informed of their son's well-being, and it was his father who reported Rael to the authorities. When Juan escaped from his master, he had attempted to run home to his own family for protection, and it is likely that his death would have gone unchallenged if it had not been for the intervention of his father.

Servants had access to the legal system and could bring their grievances to the courts, but in the case of a child it was usually up to the family to bring suit. Servants who were disobedient or lazy could expect to be slapped or beaten if it did not cause injury.[11] Obviously, Rael overstepped the bounds of acceptable behavior, and it was well within the rights of the Montoya family to bring charges against him for the brutal beating he dealt their son.

Domestic violence was seldom punished, and if it was, the penalty was very lenient.[12] Even in the case of murder, it seems that justices were reluctant to come to any final decision on sentencing.[13] The Ruival and Herrera cases were turned over to licenciados for advisement, but the final outcome is not in the records. The assailants in the other two cases, Rafael Montoya and Francisco Rael, were released on bail.

Murder was considered more serious than wife beating; however, if the husband actually caught his wife *en fragante* (in the very act) this was considered adequate provocation to take her life and (at least according to one promotor fiscal in New Mexico) the only defensible excuse for wife murder.[14]

None of these cases of wife murder was considered excusable, and the justices, prosecutors, and even the defenders expressed outrage over the crimes. Nevertheless, the idea that there was any defensible excuse for murdering one's wife is proof that the Spanish legal system upheld the patriarchal family structure and allocated authority to the husband to control his wife and punish her as he saw fit.

The belief that women needed to be "controlled and corrected" is very evident in the case records. Prosecutor Sánchez suggested that, instead of stabbing his wife, Rafael Montoya might have used his strength to force her to return to the judge's house that night in Corrales.[15] Alcalde Barceló, in charge of conducting the investigation into the murder of the Cochití woman by her husband, rebuked the defendant for not using other means to "correct" his wife's behavior.[16]

Pueblo culture did not share the same family structure as Hispanic culture. Unfortunately, the case of the Cochití couple illustrates more about Hispanic society and beliefs than it does about Native American views. Pueblo views on women and marriage were not as authoritarian as traditional Spanish ones. Cochití women shared more privilege and power within their communities than their Hispanic counterparts.

Although not a matriarchal society, which is extremely rare, most Pueblos were matrilineal, tracing descent through the mother. Children were born into the mother's clan and were expected to marry outside of her clan (clan exogamy). For at least a short period after marriage the couple lived with the wife's family, a practice known as matrilocal residency. Homes, and even the produce of the fields once they came into the home, were the property of the women. Men held the high public offices, but women were dominant in the home and clan councils.[17]

Although Pueblo families were not patriarchal and women had more authority within the family than in typical Hispanic homes, this did not rule out the possibility of domestic discord. As the Herrera/Chaves case indicates, unhappy domestic situations within Pueblo culture could turn violent.

What lead to the violent confrontations described in these four murder cases? Motive was always difficult to ascertain. In most cases the suspect claimed a particular incident had triggered the sudden violence, but the real reason was probably much more complex.[18]

Manuel Gallego told the alcalde that he strangled his wife because she constantly argued with him. Rafael Montoya had suspicions about his wife's fidelity, although he had never caught her with another man. He felt that he was justified in stabbing her when she refused to return to the judges house with him. Juan Antonio Chaves claimed that his wife had left home and had been missing for three days without telling him of her whereabouts. When he found her in the bosque, she further infuriated him by her disobedience and outright defiance of his authority. Francisco Rael told the investigating judge that he had beaten his servant boy because he had taken too long bringing in the animals.

None of these reasons seems significant enough to kill for; however, they all have one thing in common. In each case, the aggressor, who was the head of the household, felt that his authority had been defied. The husbands believed that they had the right to correct their wives for any stubbornness or misconduct. Rael felt that it was his right to beat his servant as punishment for disobedience. In any case, neither the statements nor the confessions of the defendants indicated that they felt any guilt or remorse about the violent deaths they had perpetrated, and it appears that for the most part they felt that their actions were justified. At least one of the suspects, Rafael Montoya, seemed to feel that the murder of his wife was necessary to defend his honor.

The concept of honor came from Spain; its importance is evident in several of the homicide cases. To preserve honor could be a motive, often not vocalized, for murder. The Spanish male's honor was tied to the concept of *vergüenza* (literally, shame; figuratively, it meant the importance placed on having a good reputation with one's fellow citizens). For women, honor was tied to a high standard of modesty and purity. Failing to uphold that standard would render them *sin* vergüenza, and the male members of their familia would lose honor. In this sense, honor for men was dependent on the deportment of their wives and daughters, and men were expected to see that women did not do anything to bring dishonor to the familia. Among men, honor was reflected in the respect and dignity that they showed to each other. In case of insult or humiliation, a man might find it necessary to use force in order to redeem his honor.[19]

In addition to conflicts within the family, these trials revealed an undercurrent of racial tension and prejudice between various ethnic groups living in New Mexico. The Rael case indicated the contempt held for genízaros, the displaced Indians from various tribes who lived like Hispanics. When Francisco Rael caught up with his young servant and began lashing him with a whip, he called him "genízaro malo." Although Juan may or may not have been a genízaro, his status as a servant relegated him to a similar inferior category. In the Herrera/Chaves case, the defensor Cabesa de Baca's remarks showed his obvious racial prejudice and lack of understanding of Pueblo culture. Most assuredly prejudice and class hatred cut both ways, but the documents were written by the Spanish, and the native perspective is left silent.

SANTA CRUZ DE LA CAÑADA

The barrio of San Antonio del Rancho, where Maria Espíritu Santo Ruival was murdered, fell within the jurisdiction of the villa of Santa Cruz.

(Photograph courtesy Museum of New Mexico, Santa Fe, negative no. 102247.)

PEDRO JOSÉ PEREA

Perea was the *juez de paz* of Bernalillo in 1843 who tried Francisco Rael for the murder of his young servant boy. *(Photograph courtesy Museum of New Mexico, Santa Fe, negative no. 7755.)*

ALAMEDA CHAPEL

María Albina Gonzales was buried in the cemetery of the Alameda chapel after she was stabbed to death by her husband across the river in Corrales. *(Photograph courtesy Museum of New Mexico, Santa Fe, negative no. 104662.)*

MISSION OF SAN BUENAVENTURA OF COCHITÍ PUEBLO

Murder victim María Angelina Herrera was buried in the cemetery of San Buenaventura in 1846.

(Photograph by Carter Harrison courtesy Southwest Museum, Los Angeles, negative no. 35214.)

Auto cabeza de proceso

This legal document, signed by Santa Fe Alcalde José Francisco Baca and two *testigos de aistencia*, initiated the investigation into the death of Juan Valdez in 1826. This document was written on *papel sellado* (official stamped paper) dated for the years 1810 and 1811 and carries the seal of Spanish king Carlos IV. The seals of King Fernando VII dated 1814–1815 and 1816–1817 were added later to update the validity of the document. Lacking official paper for the years of his office, Alcalde Baca added in writing that the paper was valid for the years 1826 and 1827.

(Mexican Archives of New Mexico, roll 5, frame 1016.)

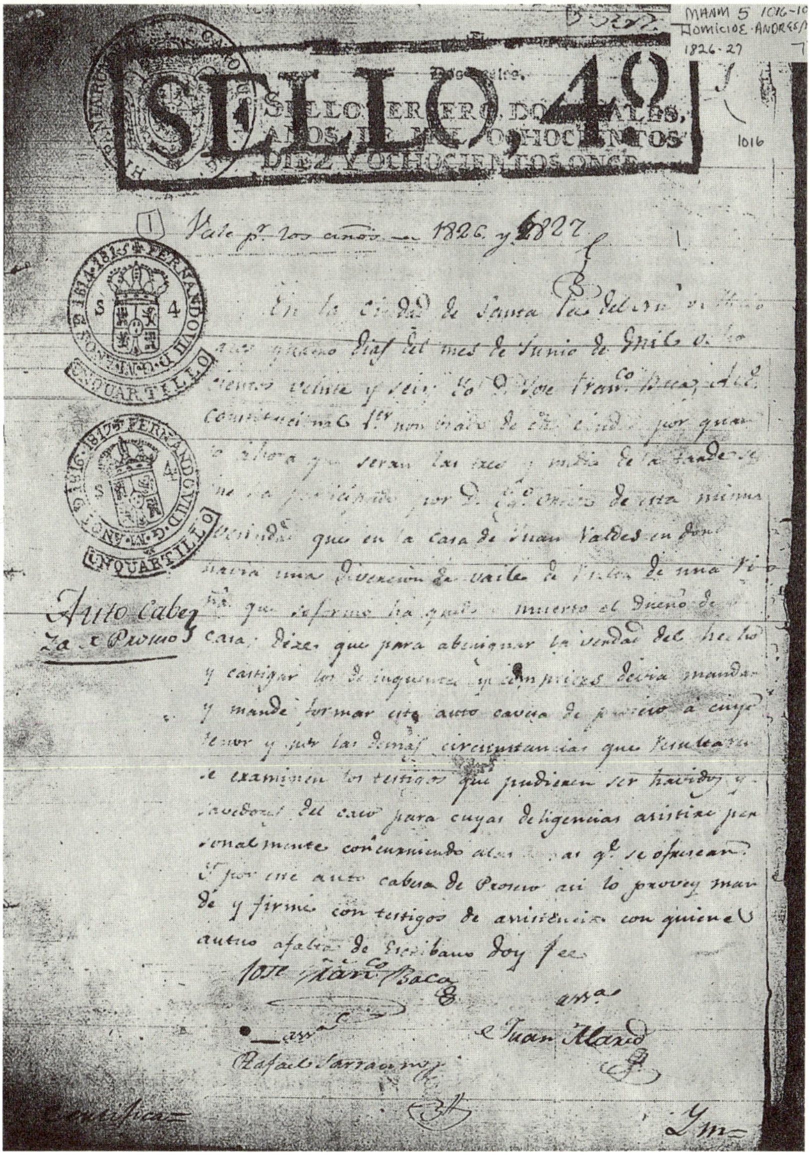

SELLO 4º

Vale p.r los años de 1826 y 1827

Auto Cabeza d Proceso

En la Ciudad de Santa Fee del Nuevo Mexico a los quatro dias del mes de Junio de mil ocho cientos veinte y seis, Yo D. Jose Fran.co Baca, Alc.e Constitucional 1.ro nombrado de esta Ciudad, por quanto ahora que serian las seis y media de la tarde se me ha participado por D. [illegible] de esta misma vecindad que en la casa de Juan Valdes en donde havia una diversion de baile [illegible] ha quedado muerto el Dueño de la casa; dize que para averiguar la verdad del hecho y castigar los delinquentes y complices devia mandar y mande formar este auto cabeza de proceso a cuyo tenor y por las demas circunstancias que resultaren se examinen los testigos que pudieren ser havidos y savedores del caso para cuyas deligencias asistire personalmente concurriendo [illegible] que se ofrescan. Y por este auto cabeza de Proceso asi lo provey mande y firme con testigos de asistencia con quienes actuo a falta de Escribano doy fee.

Jose Fran.co Baca

asist.a Juan Alarid

asist.a Rafael Sarracino

Fandango

Called either *fandangos* or *bailes*, these festive occasions were a major form of entertainment during the Mexican Era. They were occasionally the scene of violent encounters as witnessed by the Valdez and Lara murder trials.

(Colonel Frank Triplett, Conquering the Wilderness, *New York & St. Louis, 1885.)*

SAN MIGUEL DEL BADO

Only three years before this sketch was made in 1846, San Miguel del Bado, on New Mexico's eastern frontier, was the scene of a tragic encounter between a Mexican military officer and a local New Mexican.

(Sketch by Lieutenant J. W. Abert, U.S.A.; Photograph courtesy Museum of New Mexico, Santa Fe, negative no. 147360.)

Acequia

This photograph of an Albuquerque irrigation ditch, taken in 1881, probably resembles the one in Tomé that led to the fatal dispute between José Maria Sebada and Pablo Salazar. The one story adobe dwelling in the background might also be typical of New Mexico homes during the Mexican era.

(Photograph by Ben Wittick courtesy Museum of New Mexico, Santa Fe, negative no. 15754.)

CERRO DE TOMÉ AND THE VILLAGE OF VALENCIA

This sketch was made shortly after the American takeover and is close to the village of Tomé where Pablo Salazar was murdered.

(W. H. Emory, Notes on a Military Reconnaissance from Fort Leavenworth to San Diego, *Washington, 1848.)*

Part Two

Vecinos

The Trial of Andrés Márquez for the Murder of Juan Valdez

SANTA FE, 4 JUNE 1826

ALCALDE, SANTA FE: don José Francisco Baca
ALCALDE SEGUNDO, 1829: don Francisco Trujillo
PROMOTOR FISCAL (PROSECUTOR): Ramón Abréu
DEFENSOR (DEFENDER): Juan Bautista Alarid
LICENCIADOS (LAWYERS): don Rafael Bracho; don Ignacio Sariñana
TESTIGOS (WITNESSES): Tomás Segura; José María Márquez; Francisco Varela; Esquípula Pacheco; Juan Vigil; Francisco Esteban Valdez; Miguel Rodríguez; Miguel Rodríguez, Sr.
CURA (PRIEST): don José Tomás Terrasas
CIRUJANO (SURGEON): Mariano Larrañaga
OTRO (REPORTED CRIME): don Ignacio Ortiz
TESTIGOS DE ASISTENCIA: Rafael Sarracino; Juan García; Juan Alarid; Juan Vigil; Atanasio Bolíbar; Ignacio Ortiz; Rafael Sarracino; Domingo Fernández; Antonio Benavídez
FIADORES (BONDSMEN): Bartolo Márquez; don Felipe Sena

EIGHT

Death at a Fandango[1]

✠

New Mexicans were a gregarious people, fond of music, dancing, gambling, and gossip. *Bailes* and *fandangos* were social gatherings where these favorite pastimes were pursued with great enthusiasm, both in large towns and small isolated villages. According to Santa Fe merchant and author, Josiah Gregg, the term "fandango" was used to describe those "ordinary assemblies where dancing and frolicking are carried on," whereas "baile" was "generally applied to those [dances] of a higher grade."[2] This distinction between (what we might call) a shindig and a ball hardly seems evident in court records, where the two words appear to be interchangeable.

Early accounts of New Mexico by Americans seldom fail to mention the frequent occurrence of these events where friends and neighbors met and danced to tunes strummed on the violin (fiddle) and guitar (using the same instruments and often the same music that accompanied Sunday mass). The musicians, *violinistas* and *guitarristas*, were respected members of the community who played at all important functions, including dances, weddings, fiestas, and church services. According to Josiah Gregg, these fandangos were almost nightly affairs attended by all classes of people, from the most wealthy and prominent to the poorest peon.[3] Anyone who had a house large enough to accommodate a large gathering of people could host one of these events. New Mexican homes seldom consisted of more than three or four rooms. The main room, or *sala*, often served several purposes: a parlor during the day and sleeping quarters at night. (The simple bedding was rolled up against the walls to form sofas.)[4] Since New Mexican homes were so sparsely furnished, it wouldn't have taken long to clear the sala in preparation for a dance.

When Juan Valdez made preparations to host a baile at his home in Santa Fe, he certainly had no reason to believe that the festivities would end in a terrible tragedy. Although whiskey and wine were available for purchase on these occasions, most accounts indicate that bailes and fandangos were generally not rowdy affairs.[5]

A Santa Fe census taken in 1823 listed a Juan Baldes as an eighteen-year-old laborer living in the *barrio* (neighborhood) of San Miguel with his widowed mother, doña Dolores Carrillo, and two brothers—Francisco, fifteen, and Gregorio, three.[6] This is most likely the same Juan Valdez who was killed at a fandango given in his home three years later.

It was Sunday, 4 June 1826. The day was hot and apparently so were tempers. Some time between three and half past three in the afternoon, while the merrymakers were dancing in the house, a scuffle broke out in the patio. An unidentified voice was heard to cry out above the noise of the party, exclaiming that Juan Valdez had fallen dead. In the confusion that followed, Juan's body was carried immediately into an adjoining room, where friends gathered, hoping to revive him. José María Márquez, close friend of the dead man, had pulled his brother Andrés from the fray, beaten him, and sent him running for home. Word spread quickly through the crowd that Andrés Márquez had killed Valdez.

Don Ignacio Ortiz hurried to inform the authorities. When Alcalde Constitucional Primero don José Francisco Baca heard the news, he immediately ordered an auto cabeza de proceso and proceeded to Valdez's home, accompanied by four men to witness the investigation.

Valdez was found in a room in his home, wrapped in a *sarape*, in the arm's of his friend José María Márquez. Grieving family and friends surrounded the deceased. Perhaps not truly believing him dead, they made futile attempts to revive him. He had died so suddenly. There had been one blow with a fist, and Juan had fallen to the ground. No weapon was used: no knife, no sword, no pistol. There were no wounds, no blood, and no marks on his body that would indicate that he had suffered any injuries. He was still dressed as he had been at the dance, wearing a white jerkin over his cotton shirt, a pair of blue trousers, and wool stockings.

Don José called Juan Valdez by name three times in the presence of witnesses. When Valdez showed no sign of life, the alcalde declared that he was dead and proceeded with the investigation. Finding no marks of any kind on the body, the alcalde sent for José Mariano Larrañaga, the cirujano of the Santa Fe Company, to examine the cadaver and give a statement as to the cause of death.

Mariano Larrañaga, in his mid-forties, was the son of the army surgeon

Dr. Cristóbal Larrañaga who had the distinction of bringing the smallpox vaccine to New Mexico two decades earlier.[7] Under the directions of Commandant General Salcedo, Larrañaga took a group of New Mexican children to Chihuahua in 1804 to bring the live vaccine back to New Mexico, where the disease periodically ravaged frontier settlements. The vaccine was transferred from arm to arm on the journey home. By 20 November 1805, Larrañaga reported that he had vaccinated 3,610 New Mexican children. This was certainly a contributing factor to New Mexico's increase in population in the first half of the nineteenth century, but it was not the end of epidemic diseases.[8]

The younger Dr. Larrañaga faced another dreaded disease that had scourged New Mexico settlements: measles. Unfortunately, there was no vaccine against this killer, and George Champlin Sibley, surveyor of the Santa Fe Trail, recorded in his journal numerous deaths in Santa Fe due to measles early in the spring of 1826. On 1 January, Sibley noted in his diary that there had been nine deaths in town since the previous day, and later in the month he mentioned several deaths and funerals of children who had died as a result of measles. Perhaps Larrañaga was called on to attend those stricken with the disease, but Sibley mentioned only a "quack doctor" who had recently arrived from Kentucky.[9]

In the home of Juan Valdez, Mariano Larrañaga was sworn in and proceeded with the examination of the deceased. He found no broken bones nor any wounds of any kind, and he concluded that Valdez had died as the result of a blow he had received in a vital place somewhere between the mouth and the stomach. This may sound rather vague for a doctor's statement, but a more accurate diagnosis would have required an autopsy. The surgeon's report was attached to the file after it had been witnessed by two testigos de asistencia, Rafael Sarracino and Atanasio Bolíbar.

Atanasio Bolíbar was a *peninsulare* (a Spaniard born in Spain but living in the Americas). Spain did not recognize Mexican Independence in 1821, and Mexico feared a possible invasion, so Spaniards still living in Mexico were viewed with suspicion. In the later part of the decade following Independence, the Mexican government passed several decrees prohibiting Spaniards from holding civil, military, or ecclesiastical offices, and finally it called for them to be expelled from the Republic. New Mexican governor, Manuel Armijo, took the legislation seriously and proceeded against Spaniards living in his domain. Among the Spaniards forced to leave New Mexico were several Franciscan priests, a school teacher, and the merchant Atanasio Bolíbar.[10]

Alcalde Baca went about the business of questioning the witnesses.

Tomás Segura was first to testify. He said he was married and listed his age as thirty, more or less, and his occupation as *criador* (stock raiser). He was present at the fandango at Valdez's home at about three that afternoon, when he heard a rumor that there had been a quarrel between Miguel Rodríguez and Francisco Esteban Valdez, brother of the deceased. Rodríguez and others had been standing in the doorway when Juan Valdez reproached them for blocking the entrance. Rodríguez made some reply that Esteban took badly, and they argued. They apparently resolved the disagreement, but shortly afterwards the two started up again in the patio. After that everything happened quickly. Segura saw Andrés Márquez move as if to hit Juan Valdez; Segura rushed forward and grabbed Andrés from behind, but not before Andrés had struck Valdez in the stomach. As Segura's arms encircled Andrés, his captive's brother José María Márquez jerked Andrés by the hair and began slapping him. Segura heard a voice cry out that Valdez had fallen, and soon he saw the host being carried unconscious from the patio.

Segura was questioned about who else was present at the time of the argument, and he named Francisco Varela. Segura was dancing when the first argument broke out, and there were many people and much confusion. Segura had definitely seen Márquez hit Valdez, and he was sure that Márquez was not armed. There was no weapon, only his bare hand.

José María Márquez, brother of the suspect, came forward and took the oath in the presence of the same testigos de asistencia. He promised to tell the truth in everything he knew regarding the death of Juan Valdez. He stated that at about three o'clock that day he arrived at the dance at Juan Valdez's house. There were people gathered in the doorway, and Valdez spoke to them saying, "Gentlemen, stand aside or come inside and cool off, it is very hot." To this Márquez answered, "Juan speaks well. Let us go inside or get out of the doorway," and he walked past the others and entered the house. The host remained, urging Miguel Rodríguez to come inside. Márquez noticed that Juan's brother Francisco Esteban Valdez was speaking with Rodríguez, but it was impossible to hear what words passed between them because of the noise of the crowd. Márquez lost track of them, and when he saw them again they had moved into the patio and were throwing punches at each other. A crowd gathered. Attempting to break up the fight, José María Márquez grabbed Rodríguez from behind and others seized Francisco Esteban Valdez.

After that, José María Márquez noticed that Tomás Segura had moved up behind his brother Andrés Márquez, and it looked as if Andrés was trying to get into the fight. Segura seized Andrés from behind, and José

María grabbed his brother by the hair and began slapping him. Next, he noticed that Juan Valdez had stopped in front of them; he took two steps and fell to the floor dead. A voice cried out. Already people were saying that his brother Andrés had struck the fatal blow that killed Juan.

Francisco Varela, a twenty-year-old tailor, was called to testify because he had been named in Segura's statement. Varela was dancing when the disturbance broke out and did not actually witness the fight. He did see Valdez wrapped in a sarape after the incident occurred, and he did hear the rumor that Andrés Márquez had killed him, but he could not say for sure who told him this.

A fourth witness, 26-year-old Esquípula Pacheco, was also at the party, but he knew no more than the previous witness because he too was dancing the waltz. Pacheco was enjoying himself and had not paid any attention to the ruckus until he noticed the group gathering in the patio. Moved by curiosity, he went outside where he saw Valdez lying dead on the ground. He learned from Tomás Segura that Andrés Márquez was the culprit of the deed. Pacheco also mentioned that Juan Vigil was present when Valdez fell.

Vigil was questioned next. He remembered that he heard a commotion and saw people gathering in the patio. He went outside to investigate and arrived in time to see Andrés Márquez hit Juan Valdez in the belly. Tomás Segura seized Márquez from behind and Valdez remained standing for a moment before he fell to the ground. Vigil also heard a voice shout out that Valdez was dead. Someone, he did not see who, picked up Juan and carried him into the house. Vigil did recall that no weapon had been used. No one in the group was armed. Juan Vigil attested that he was thirty-three, single, an artisan, and a resident of Santa Fe. He signed his name next to the alcalde and his two assistants.

It must have been getting late by the time Alcalde Baca made his final judicial act that day. In view of the statements of the various witnesses, Baca declared that Andrés Márquez stood accused of the crime under investigation, and he ordered Márquez to be imprisoned in the national jail, *sin comunicado* (incommunicado), in the custody of the *cabo* (corporal).

The following day, 5 June, at half past three in the afternoon, just twenty-four hours after he had died, Juan Valdez was laid to rest in the cemetery of Santa Fe. The body, dressed in shirt and trousers, had been wrapped in a simple shroud, and the parochial priest of the capital, don Juan Tomás Terrasas, was paid ten *reales* to officiate. According to Josiah Gregg, "in New Mexico lower classes seldom made use of coffins: the body was wrapped in a simple blanket and laid in the ground, and the earth was tamped down rigorously as the grave was filled in." This offended Gregg's sensibilities, as did what he called "the ruinous cost of the burial fee charged by the priests.[11]

Later that year, Agustín Fernández de San Vicente was appointed vicar general of New Mexico and journeyed to that remote Mexican territory on a *santa visita* with instructions to root out clerical abuse and institute reform where necessary. Fernández was disgusted by the sorry conditions of New Mexican churches, the lack of religious materials necessary to conduct mass, the shortage of priests, and general clerical abuse. In the capital, Father Terrasas came under attack for neglect of the parochial church and his poor record keeping.[12] Terrasas, who would have been forty-five in 1826, died toward the end of that year, and his estate was settled by don José Francisco Baca, the same alcalde who handled the Valdez homicide case.[13]

On 6 June 1826, Baca continued taking testimonies in the Valdez murder trial. The sixth witness was Francisco Esteban Valdez, eighteen-year-old brother of the victim. He was present at the fandango at his brother's home when a group of people gathered in the doorway. Juan asked them to disperse because they were blocking the entrance. Miguel Rodríguez apparently took offense and began to argue with Juan. Esteban stepped towards them and attempted to soothe Miguel's feelings, and Juan walked away. In a short while, Miguel returned to the door and once again Juan asked him to move. Rodríguez stubbornly refused and took a swing at Juan. Esteban came between them, and an angry fight ensued as Esteban and Miguel began punching each other. They broke through the doorway and into the patio, where they were pulled apart by others in the crowd. Suddenly, out of the confusion, Esteban saw his brother being carried out of the patio. It was said that Andrés Márquez had killed him.

Questioned further about motive and possible quarrels that the participants may have had, Francisco Esteban Valdez denied that either he or his brother had ever had any disagreement with Andrés Márquez or Miguel Rodríguez. Although it is never mentioned in the records, it seems likely that alcohol was a contributing factor in this tragic affair.

Miguel Rodríguez gave a slightly different version of the same story. He was standing in the doorway with a group of people at the Valdez house, where a fandango was in progress. The host, Juan Valdez, approached and asked them to come in or go out, but not to block the doorway. Rodríguez apparently thought this was humorous and made a smart retort to Valdez. Valdez, laughing, told him to come inside, and seizing Miguel by his jerkin he pushed him into the house. Suddenly the joke turned sour, and Rodríguez pulled away from Valdez, replying that he was offended and would not enter his house. Juan's brother, Esteban, took this as an insult, and he had words with Rodríguez. Juan left momentarily, only to return and again insist that Miguel come inside. Juan and Miguel began to scuffle, but Esteban broke in between them. Esteban and Miguel burst into the patio, throwing punches at each other. In the midst of the fight, Miguel saw someone carrying Juan Valdez into the house; he heard a voice say that Valdez was dead. Miguel Rodríguez knew nothing else. He did not see who killed Valdez. There had been no quarrels between any of them until that day. They had all been friends since childhood.

The prisoner, Andrés Márquez, was brought in to give his testimony. When the alcalde realized that Andrés was only eighteen, he suspended the questioning and informed him that he needed a legal guardian before they could proceed. Márquez asked don Juan Bautista Alarid to serve as his curador, and Alarid accepted the appointment, swearing to defend the minor to the best of his abilities.

Márquez was sworn in and questioned in the presence of his legal guardian. He stated that he had been taken prisoner by two soldiers of the Santa Fe Company by order of Alcalde Baca as a result of a fight with Juan Valdez at a fandango in Valdez's home. Márquez related that Miguel Rodríguez and Francisco Esteban Valdez had been fighting, and that he had attempted to separate them by grabbing Esteban from behind. Esteban's brother, Juan Valdez, came up from behind and hit Andrés three times in the back. Andrés released Esteban and turned and faced Juan with anger. Juan took two steps backwards, Márquez hit him, and he fell to the ground. Meanwhile, Tomás Segura grabbed Andrés from behind and his brother José María Márquez began beating him and sent him off home. Andrés repeated what earlier participants in the fight had reported: they had not had any argument prior to that date, and they had all been good friends since childhood.

Márquez mentioned that Miguel Rodríguez primero, Miguel Rodríguez's father, was present when the fight broke out in the patio. The elder Rodríguez, a fifty-year-old farmer from Santa Fe, was questioned, but he denied being present in the patio until after the fight was over.

Three of the witnesses were questioned regarding Márquez's testimony. None of them saw Juan Valdez assail Andrés Márquez. Tomás Segura could not verify the reason for the fight; the first thing that he saw was Andrés turning on Juan Valdez. Miguel Rodríguez segundo explained that he was fighting with Esteban Valdez, and he did not see Andrés Márquez and Juan Valdez come to blows. When he first heard the voice cry out that Valdez was dead, he was afraid that it was Esteban Valdez, not his brother Juan. Next, Esteban was questioned about Márquez's testimony. Esteban claimed that when he was scuffling with Rodríguez someone grabbed him from behind, but he didn't know who it was. Esteban did not see Juan Valdez hit Andrés Márquez either; this also had occurred behind his back. No one had witnessed Juan's attack on Andrés.

Andrés Márquez repeated his earlier testimony and confessed to having given the fatal blow that ended the life of Juan Valdez. At this point in the proceedings, the alcalde named don Ramón Abréu as the promotor fiscal to prosecute the case against Márquez. Ramón Abréu was an active public servant who would have the misfortune of being appointed prefect of the first district by the unpopular Governor Pérez in 1835. When the bloody uprising against Pérez broke out two years later, Ramón Abréu and his two equally distinguished brothers were among the casualties.[14]

Baca notified the suspect that he must name a defender. Márquez asked his legal guardian, don Juan Bautista Alarid, to defend him, and he accepted. Baca signed an auto de prueba, which allowed for a period of thirty days in which to ratify everyone who had testified in the case. The two assistants who attested to the death of Valdez, the surgeon who examined the body, and all seven witnesses were read their previous testimonies, which they verified as true and signed in the presence of witnesses. This was all accomplished within a few days, and the case, in thirty-one folios, was given to Juan Bautista Alarid in order to prepare the defense.

Alarid did not deny that the defendant, Andrés Márquez, had killed Juan Valdez, nor that this crime was one that deserved the full attention of the law; however, in Márquez's defense he noted that the two had been lifelong friends, that there was no motive, no quarrel, no intent to kill, and no weapon. Márquez had not instigated the fight, rather he was attempting to stop one when he seized Esteban Valdez from behind. Juan Valdez mistook Márquez's intention, and believing that he was attacking his brother, Juan began punching Andrés in the back. Andrés angrily turned on his assailant and struck him one blow with his fist. Here the defense implied that Juan Valdez may have had some medical problem that would explain why one blow with a bare hand would be sufficient to kill him. In any case, Andrés had certainly not intended to kill his friend but had hit him in a moment of anger. For these reasons, the defense begged the court not to sentence Márquez to the pena capital. A less severe penalty would be more fitting for this crime.

The written defense was attached to the case, and it was forwarded to the prosecutor on 4 July 1826, one month after the incident had occurred. The promotor fiscal, Ramón Abréu, answered promptly. He stated that Márquez entered the quarrel that caused the death of Valdez, not to prevent a fight, but rather as a malicious act designed to hold Esteban Valdez while his antagonist, Rodríguez, beat him. He questioned the defense's implication that Valdez had died suddenly due to some possible illness or infirmity; certainly, if Valdez did have such an illness, Márquez, who claimed to be a lifelong friend, would have been aware of it. Abréu concluded that the deed was committed with enough premeditation that it was deserving of severe punishment. He asked the court to punish Márquez for this crime in order to discourage others from attempting similar deeds.

The alcalde and judge of the case now signed the publicación de probanzas, a judicial act to make known the evidence in the case, and he made all involved parties aware of this act. Further, he asked both the defense and the prosecution to write up a second brief, complete in one folio, to be attached to the case. Both parties complied with a short note explaining that one should refer to their previous writs. The case was now complete enough to be forwarded to a lawyer for legal advice.

On 17 July, Baca forwarded the case, complete in forty-one folios, to Licenciado don Rafael Bracho in Chihuahua.[15] Due to illness, Bracho was unable to handle the matter and referred the case to a fellow lawyer, Ignacio Sariñana. There is nothing in the records to indicate that Sariñana ever replied.

The New Mexico officials had done their part in the judicial process; Márquez waited in jail for some reply from Chihuahua. No reply was forthcoming, and finally, on 9 March 1829, the citizens don Felipe Sena and Bartolo Márquez came before Santa Fe alcalde segundo, Francisco Trujillo, to post bond for the 21-year-old prisoner.[16]

Andrés Márquez spent three long years in the Santa Fe jail, where he had plenty of time to contemplate the meaningless brawl that ended his friend's life. Certainly, the young man had never intended to kill Valdez; his sudden death from a single blow to the stomach was an accident. When Valdez, suddenly and it seemed without provocation, punched him in the back, Andrés's quick anger and his sense of honor led to a swift and fatal reaction.

The Trial of Alférez Manuel García de Lara for the Murder of Antonio Moya

SAN MIGUEL DEL BADO, 27 OCTOBER 1843

✠

JUEZ DE PAZ, VADO: Santiago Ulibarrí
JUEZ DE PAZ, VADO: Manuel Antonio Baca
JUEZ DE PAZ, DOLORES: Juan Aragón
JUEZ SUPLENTE: Capitán don Damasio Salazar
DEFENSOR (DEFENDER): Capitán don Antonio Sena
TESTIGOS (WITNESSES): Manuel Sena; Miguel Gerónimo Baca; Felix Montoya; Pedro Roxas; Ramón López; Julio García; Francisco Sena
PERITOS: (EXPERTS): Nepomuceno Archuleta; José Miguel Sánchez
SUMMONED WITNESS: Colonel don Pedro Muñoz
CURA (PRIEST): José Francisco Leyba
GOBERNADOR (GOVERNOR): Manuel Armijo
COMANDANTE GENERAL: Mariano Martínez
PRACTICANTE: Francisco Ferrales
VICTIM'S EMPLOYER: don Antonio José Otero
OTROS, MENTIONED: Colonel don Juan Andrés Archuleta; Pablo
TESTIGOS DE ASISTENCIA: Francisco Vasto; Juan Francisco Sena; José Felís Zubia; Bernardo Vásquez Franco; Rafael Aragón; José Antonio Casaus; Remigio Ribera; José Felís Sánchez y Rael; Domingo Gutiérrez

✠

NINE

A Matter of Honor[1]

✠

San Miguel del Bado was a frontier settlement on the eastern edge of New Mexico, the first of any size encountered by travelers on the Santa Fe Trail. When Susan Shelby Magoffin passed through San Miguel in 1846, she described it as "both larger and cleaner" than any village she had seen so far, and she was impressed that San Miguel had both a church and a public square.[2] San Miguel del Bado (St. Michael of the ford) was situated at a river crossing where the Santa Fe Trail forded the Río Pecos, almost equidistant from the abandoned pueblo of Pecos, twenty some miles to the northwest, and the young settlement of Las Vegas, twenty some miles to the northeast. Josiah Gregg described the Río Pecos as a "silvery little river" whose waters rippled from the snowy Santa Fe Mountains, and San Miguel as "irregular clusters of mud-wall huts."[3] In 1846, Lieutenant J. W. Abert sketched a panorama of the village, showing the twin towers of the San Miguel Church dominant above a collection of one-story adobe dwellings, with mesas and low hills on the horizon.[4]

The land had been granted to a group of settlers back in 1794, and as its neighbor (the Pecos Pueblo) declined in population, San Miguel grew in size.[5] A census, signed by Manuel Antonio Baca in 1845, listed the population of the San Miguel area as just a little over fifteen hundred persons.[6]

San Miguel became an important stop on the Santa Fe Trail. It was considered a port of entry. Both a customs house and a military garrison were established there (although apparently the customs house never operated as such, and duties continued to be collected in Santa Fe until after the American occupation).[7]

Until the mid-1830s, Santa Fe had the only military garrison in New Mexico, but throughout the Mexican years only a small group of soldiers was housed in the dilapidated presidio buildings just off the plaza, directly behind the *casas reales*. By 1836, two other garrisons had been established: one to the north in Taos, and one on the eastern frontier in San Miguel del Bado. Due to lack of funds, all three garrisons remained undermanned, and the ill-equipped underpaid soldiers suffered from low moral.[8] Since Mexican Independence, the defense of the frontier against constant Indian raids and real or imagined threats of foreign invasion had been neglected by the central government.[9] New Mexico had to rely on its own resources to defend her settlements from the many tribes of indios bárbaros that became more and more bold during the Mexican Period. Since the garrisons were so weak, the job of defense usually fell to the militia, untrained and unpaid civilians who had to supply their own arms and munitions.

The ranks of the militia were filled by poor farmers and Pueblo Indians; officers usually came from the wealthy and powerful classes who could afford arms and horses. Militia service was a terrible hardship for the poor in northern New Mexico, and their misery and frustration was a major contribution to the Rebellion of 1837 in Río Arriba.[10]

The Texas Rebellion and subsequent independence from Mexico in 1836 shocked the government of Santa Anna, and when the revolt against Governor Pérez broke out in Río Arriba the following year, federal troops were sent to aid Armijo in putting down the rebellion. The Veracruz Dragoons combined forces with Armijo's militia to put down the insurrection, but by 1838, the Dragoons were forced to leave New Mexico for lack of funds to sustain them. After the Texas "Invasion" of New Mexico in 1841, the central government finally paid heed to Armijo's pleading and sent troops back to New Mexico to help defend the frontier. By 1842, New Mexico sported a permanent artillery unit manned by Mexican nationals and armed partially by artillery pieces taken from the hapless Texans captured the previous year.[11] Also, there were two Mexican national cavalry regiments stationed in New Mexico: the Third Regimental Cavalry, and the Second Regimental Calvary (which was stationed in del Bado).[12]

One Friday night in late October 1843, young Manuel García de Lara, an officer with the Second Regimental Cavalry in San Miguel del Bado, was out on the town looking for some excitement. García de Lara was an *alférez*, a field-grade officer in the army ranked somewhere between second lieutenant and colonel.[13] Alférez Lara, perhaps in the market for a new pair of boots, left the shoemaker's house at about half past eight that evening. As he walked along the streets he could probably make out the outline of the church against the darkening sky. There, in the vicinity of San Miguel's, he encountered a civilian with whom he struck up a conversation.

The civilian's name was Antonio Moya, and he was from Tomé where he worked as a servant for don Antonio José Otero, a sheep baron, merchant, and one of the wealthiest citizens of New Mexico.[14] Although Moya was not from Bado (a Badeño), he had local friends and acquaintances, and he offered to accompany the officer to a fandango at the house of Ramón López.

The two made their way to the dance where they were seen chatting amiably. Within a few short hours and just minutes before his death, Antonio Moya would accuse Alférez Lara of stabbing him through the heart.

Julio García, Ramón López's 22-year-old son-in-law, was present at the baile at López's home. He saw Moya come in from outside, cry out that Alférez Lara had stabbed him, and slump over dead. García was stunned. He turned and ran from the house to notify the authorities.

The justice, Santiago Ulibarrí, went immediately to the López home where he found a man's body lying on the floor, his clothing drenched with blood from a stab wound near the heart. Those who were present informed him that this was Antonio Moya, a resident of Tomé. The man was not breathing and did not respond to questioning; Ulibarrí pronounced him dead. Two responsible citizens were called upon to examine the body and determine the cause of death. Nepomuceno Archuleta and José Miguel Sánchez signed a statement saying that they believed the victim had died as a result of a *puñalada* (dagger wound) to the heart.

Commander General Mariano Martínez was notified immediately of this fatal incident involving the military officer. Mariano Martínez had been appointed by Armijo as the comandante general in October that year. This appointment separated the civil office of governor from the military office of commander general. When Martínez became governor the following May, the two offices were again united under one man.[15]

The comandante ordered Colonel Pedro Muñoz of the Second Regimental Calvary to take Alférez Lara into custody. Muñoz had come to New Mexico with the Veracruz Dragoons in 1837. As a young captain, he distinguished himself in the Battle of Pojoaque, which ended the insurrection in Río Arriba. Following in the wake of the Texas Invasion, he returned to New Mexico in the spring of 1842 in charge of national troops sent to defend the frontier.[16]

Ulibarrí sent a notice to the parish priest, José Francisco Leyba, to attend to the burial of the deceased. Father Leyba had been the parish priest in Alburquerque from 1817 to 1829, and in 1821 he wrote to the bishop of

Durango about the poor conditions of the churches in New Mexico. Leyba was in Alburquerque when Agustín Fernández de San Vicente conducted his santa visita to New Mexico in 1826.[17] Leyba himself was not always the best example of priestly virtues. A year after the santa visita he was accused of gambling. He was the parish priest at San Miguel on two different occasions after he left the Alburquerque parish: from 1829 until 1832, and again from 1839 until 1851. If we can believe the American trader, James Josiah Webb, who met Leyba when he was the priest at San Miguel in 1844, the padre was an earthy character who enjoyed his whiskey.[18]

Once the burial arrangements had been seen to, the juez began taking the testimonies of those who were present at the baile and who might have information about the murder. The first witness was Manuel Sena, a forty-year-old farmer and resident of San Miguel who was at the baile the previous evening and saw Moya moments before he died. Like most of those questioned in this case, he did not actually witness the crime. Sena saw Moya stagger in from outside and approach Miguel Gerónimo Baca, who was seated with others watching the dance. Moya had the strength to announce to the startled group, "Look at me. They have killed me." Sena heard Baca ask Moya who had done this to him, to which the dying man replied, "Lara." After taking a few faltering steps, he collapsed and fell to the floor.

Manuel Sena did not know the motive for the murder. He did say that Alférez Lara had been accompanied by a soldier of his own regiment of the squadron of dragoons whose name he did not know. He also knew that Lara had been taken into custody by Pedro Muñoz on the orders of the comandante. Sena believed that the wound had been made by a sword. This was the extent of Sena's knowledge of the incident.

Miguel Gerónimo Baca, a 41-year-old widowed farmer of the same jurisdiction, had been mentioned in Sena's testimony. Consequently, Baca was sworn in and asked to recall what he knew about the incident. His testimony verified the statement of the first witness. Baca remembered that after Moya fell to the floor, those persons who had witnessed his death and heard his final words condemning the alférez, cried out that Alférez Lara had killed Moya. Baca knew no more about the matter, and he signed his name to the statement along with the juez de paz and his two assistants.

Justice Ulibarrí asked Colonel don Pedro Muñoz to bring Felix Montoya in for questioning. Montoya was thirty-eight, married, a native of El Paso, and had lived in San Miguel del Bado for ten years. He was present at the dance and heard Alférez Lara order a soldier to call Antonio Moya outside. He saw Moya leave the house and accompany the soldier to where Lara was waiting. They exchanged a few words but did not quarrel; afterwards Alférez Lara drew his sword and thrust it into the unsuspecting victim. Moya managed to make his way inside the house and incriminate his murderer before he died.

Montoya noticed that earlier in the evening the two had been quite friendly. Moya had befriended Lara and given him a peso so that he might enjoy himself dancing the *panaderos*, and he told him not to be embarrassed because he (Moya) had money.

By the middle of the nineteenth century, the latest European dances had reached New Mexico, and the musicians' repertoire would have included the popular waltz (*valse*), and possibly polkas, schottisches, the two-step, and quadrille, along with more traditional Mexican steps.[19] At the baile at Ramón López's home, it appears that the musicians were especially fond of a dance called los panaderos (the baker's dance), so named because the upper body movements imitated the movement of bakers as they kneaded dough and baked bread. There were several variations of los panaderos, which had been a favorite dance in eighteenth- and nineteenth-century Spain, but the literature available on New Mexican folk dances does not mention them.[20]

The prisoner was brought forward to tell his side of the story. His full name was Manuel García de Lara, he was nineteen, single, an alférez of the Second Regiment of the cavalry, and a Mexican citizen. García de Lara said that he had not known Moya until he saw him near the church and asked him if he knew where there was a fandango that night. Moya took him to the dance and they sat talking together. When the party-goers began to dance to los panaderos, Moya gave him a peso to treat a female companion with whom he danced.

After the dance was finished, the alférez sat down and continued conversing with Moya about a girl that he knew in Las Peraltas. Las Peraltas, situated about nine miles north of Moya's home town of Tomé, was the residence of Moya's employer, the wealthy Otero family. When the dance began again, Lara told Moya that he would do all right, that it wasn't necessary to treat the Badeños, and he continued dancing.

Alférez Lara stated that Moya sat out another dance and bragged about how wealthy the Oteros were, and how they were going to be one of the richest families in the department. After this remark, he gave Pablo, whose last name was never mentioned, a slap (on the back) and walked outside. Lara remained seated, speaking with another man (perhaps Pablo?) who was drinking *aguardiente*, a popular local alcoholic beverage, and telling Lara how he wished he had money to entertain the señoritas.

At fandangos and bailes there was either a special table or a separate room set aside where whiskey and brandy were served. These alcoholic beverages and other refreshments could be purchased to help pay for the dance. It was common for the gentlemen to treat their dance partners to a drink between sets.[21]

The panaderos had started up again when Moya returned to the room and sat down in the same chair where the alférez was already seated.[22] Lara hastily withdrew. He saw people entering the room and was embarrassed by what he perceived as Moya's shameless and impudent act. García de Lara claimed that he was so humiliated that he seized his sarape, sombrero, and sword, and left immediately for home.

Lara's recollections were duly noted in his testimony, and he was further questioned by Justice Ulibarrí. No, he did not see who killed Moya. No, he was not accompanied to the dance by anyone from his company. Yes, there was a soldier present at the baile, but he was not with Lara. He left Moya in good humor. They had had no argument, and as far as he knew, Moya had not offended anyone else. Lara knew no more; his testimony was completed.

Pedro Roxas, a soldier of the Second Regiment, was called to testify. He was single, thirty, more or less, and a vecino of Aguascalientes in central Mexico. On the night of 27 October, he went, unaccompanied, to a baile at the home of someone whose name he did not know. He arrived early and left for home, alone, about ten that night. Roxas denied being asked by the alférez to call Moya outside the house. Two witnesses had mentioned that Lara sent a soldier of his regiment to bring Moya outside, but neither knew his name. Roxas claimed he didn't see any soldiers or officers of his regiment at the baile. He didn't see any quarrel or commotion at the dance, but he did later hear the rumor that Alférez Lara had murdered Moya.

Ulibarrí completed the questioning in one day. Considering his job finished, he sent the case to Governor Manuel Armijo in Santa Fe, to be forwarded to the proper authorities. Armijo passed the case on to Comandante General Mariano Martínez because it involved military personnel. Martínez sent it to Colonel Pedro Muñoz of the Second Regimental Cavalry, but Muñoz was returning south to Mexico and was unable to handle the case. Martínez decided to forward the proceedings to Colonel don Juan Andrés Archuleta in Taos, prefect of the first district, with instructions to summon new witnesses and continue with the investigation.[23] Apparently, Martínez had second thoughts about the expediency of carrying the case out in Río Arriba, and he sent it back to Bado, where the crime had occurred. Don Damasio Salazar, captain of the auxiliary militia in Bado, was put in charge of the continuing investigation into the death of Antonio Moya.

Both Captain Damasio Salazar and Justice Santiago Ulibarrí had taken part in the defense of New Mexico in 1841. While the threat of a Texas invasion was at its peak, Manuel Armijo ordered the two of them to take scouting parties and guard the eastern frontier. Salazar captured a small party of Texans, including the journalist, George Kendall, who later wrote an account of the ill-fated adventure, defaming the character of his captor. The Texans were imprisoned in San Miguel del Bado until the rest of their party was captured, at which time they were rounded up and marched off to prison in Mexico City, some two thousand miles away. Salazar was in charge of escorting the prisoners as far as El Paso. A few weeks later, Captain don Juan Andrés Archuleta, in charge of the Taos militia, captured the remaining Texans and they too were sent off on the arduous trek to the capital.[24]

Now, two years after the infamous Texas Invasion, Captain Damasio Salazar was authorized to investigate the murder of Antonio Moya. He complied with the comandante general's orders and began to summon new witnesses to appear. The orders specified that he question Ramón López, in whose house the dance took place; Julio García, who informed the authorities of the crime; and the unnamed woman who danced with the suspect on the night in question. Alférez Lara, who was in custody and well guarded under an order of bien preso, was kept well informed of the proceedings of the case.

On 30 December, Salazar summoned the witnesses to appear before him. Ramón López, a 36-year-old farmer from Bado, was questioned about the events on that late October evening.[25] López told Salazar that on the evening in question he was at his home, where a baile was in progress. His friend don Gerónimo Baca had paid the juez of Bado for the license to host the dance.[26] López was not present during much of the dance and consequently did not witness any of the events under investigation, although he did hear from Gerónimo Baca and Manuel Sena that Alférez Lara had killed Antonio Moya during the baile. López was taken to view the dead man. Upon examining the wound he concluded that it had been inflicted by a sword.

López's son in law, Julio García, was sworn in next. Julio saw Moya die and heard his final words condemning Lara, but he had not been a witness to the crime. After Moya fell to the floor, Julio left the dance and ran to tell the judge. No new clues to the case were revealed by further questioning of the witness, and he signed his testimony Julio Garcilla.

Manuel Sena, the first witness questioned by Justice Ulibarrí, was brought in to see if he had anything to add to his previous testimony. Sena reported that his son Francisco had told him that he actually saw Lara stab Antonio Moya with his sword and then leave the dance with a soldier of his regiment.

Francisco Sena, Manuel's nineteen-year-old son, was immediately brought before Captain Salazar and sworn in. Francisco confirmed the story. He was in the doorway of the López home that night when the baile was in progress. He saw Alférez Lara leave the house and call to a soldier of the dragoons to follow him. It was dark outside, but Francisco could hear the two men talking. He heard the alférez say to the soldier, "You have seen how he has embarrassed me, this *paisano* Moya." The soldier admitted that he could not see how the alférez could bear this shame. Lara was apparently smoldering from the recent insult that he alluded to in his testimony. Francisco heard the officer order the soldier to bring Antonio Moya outside, and he heard the soldier call to Moya that his alférez wanted to see him. Moya went outside. From his position in the doorway, Francisco heard Alférez Lara say, "You have embarrassed me." With this simple explanation, Lara drew his sword and ran it through Moya's chest. Lara and the soldier departed in haste, as Moya staggered inside. Before he fell to the floor, he managed to cry out to the startled bystanders, "Seize Lara. He has killed me."

Francisco Sena swore that this was the truth. He knew nothing more. He did not recall seeing anyone else nearby who could have witnessed the murder. They were alone outside. Sena did not know of any argument between the two men. He had seen them sitting together earlier. He had not seen the alférez dancing with anyone. His statement was read to him, and he verified it, signing with a cross.

Salazar attempted to re-examine one more witness before he concluded his investigation. Finding Miguel Gerónimo Baca ill, he went to his home with two testigos de asistencia, but Baca had no more to add to his previous testimony. On the last day of 1843, Salazar returned the case to the comandante general, explaining that he had completed taking the testimonies with the exception of the unidentified woman with whom Lara had been dancing.

Comandante Martínez did not believe that Salazar had met his objectives in the case, and he ordered the captain to call the witness Felix Montoya back for further questioning. Montoya was not in Bado; it took some time to locate him. In the meantime, the prisoner, García de Lara, had written from the Santa Fe jail to the "excelentísimo comandante," asking that he be allowed to go home to regain his health. It seems that prison life did not agree with him, and he was suffering from severe pains in his chest. Lara further suggested that he could offer the necessary bond if he were allowed to go home. Mariano Martínez refused the offer but notified the prisoner that he would send the *practicante*, Francisco Ferrales, to heal him in the jail.

By the end of January, the witness Felix Montoya had been found and returned to San Miguel del Bado for further questioning. According to his previous testimony, Montoya was an eyewitness to the stabbing death of the victim. His second declaration added little more to the understanding of the case. He did say that he observed the whole incident from the doorway. If this was true, it seems that he should have been aware of the other eyewitness, Francisco Sena, who also claimed he was standing in the doorway. Montoya was asked who else was present, and he mentioned that there was another person whom he did not know. Perhaps it was Sena. Montoya did not know of any argument between Moya and the alférez, rather he witnessed their earlier friendship and saw the peso exchange hands. Like all the previous witnesses, he did not know the *compañera* who danced with Alférez García de Lara.

Once again, Salazar returned the case to the comandante, advising him that he had completed the extension of the testimonies as requested. Mariano Martínez took a second statement from Pedro Roxas, the soldier of the Second Regiment. Again, Roxas denied everything. He was not the soldier who was with the lieutenant at the dance. He did not see any other soldiers at the dance. No one gave him permission to attend the dance; he went of his own accord. He did not see Alférez Lara dance with anyone. He witnessed neither friendship nor animosity between the victim and suspect. Roxas claimed that he was advised of the incident back in the barracks by the sergeant of the guard, who informed the soldiers that Alférez Lara was in custody for the murder of Antonio Moya.

The testimonies were finally completed, and Comandante Martínez ordered Captain Salazar to summon the witnesses to ratify their statements.

The evidence in the testimonies was conflicting, and it was obvious that someone was not telling the truth. Comandante Martínez decided to enact careos, face-to-face confrontations between the opposing parties. This technique was used when there were conflicting testimonies, the suspect did not confess, and guilt could not clearly be established. It was hoped that someone might admit that he had "erred" in his previous testimony, and that some agreement might be reached as to what actually had occurred. Careos were not uncommon in the Spanish judicial system, although some jurists objected to them on the grounds that a witness might be intimidated by the presence of a more educated witness of a higher social standing.[27] Manuel García de Lara, in the Santa Fe jail, was advised that he would take part in this confrontation with his accusers, who were being summoned by Captain Salazar in Bado.

The witnesses had scattered to various locations. Salazar found it necessary to send letters to the justices of those places, asking them to locate these people and see that they return to San Miguel and report back to him. The Senas, both father and son, were contacted in Antón Chico, a few miles down the Pecos River from San Miguel. They promptly journeyed back to San Miguel and reported to Captain Salazar. Salazar sent them on to the capital, carrying with them the papers of the case, to be handed over to the comandante. The case file included an explanation that a letter had been sent to Real del Oro to find Felix Montoya, and that he should appear within the next few days.

Upon arriving in Santa Fe, Manuel and Francisco Sena reported to Mariano Martínez and ratified their earlier statements. Francisco was summoned to the jail for a confrontation with the prisoner. In his testimony, he claimed that he witnessed Alférez Lara strike down the victim with his sword, a charge that Lara vehemently denied. They both swore under oath to tell the truth. Their testimonies were read aloud; the contradictions were obvious. Sena asked the prisoner how he could deny that he murdered Moya when Sena witnessed the whole incident. Sena saw Lara send the dragoon to fetch Moya outside, where Lara stabbed him in the chest with his sword. Lara responded calmly; he had no disagreement with the deceased, he did not know anything about this soldier that Sena referred to, and Sena was lying. Each party remained firm, and the careo ended without coming to any agreement.

The soldier, Pedro Roxas, was called to appear before Mariano Martínez to ratify his earlier statements and to participate in a careo with Francisco Sena. They confronted each other, making various charges, and each remained adamant that he was telling the truth. Roxas insisted that he had talked to neither Lara nor Moya at the baile. Sena argued that he saw him from the doorway and heard him call Moya outside at Lara's request. Neither gave in, and this careo came to a halt.

Meanwhile, Juan Aragón, juez de paz of Real del Oro, had located the other eyewitness, Felix Montoya, and sent him off to the comandante in Santa Fe with apologies for the delay. Felix was ratified and brought "face to face," first with the prisoner, then with Roxas the suspected accomplice in the murder. In both careos, the participants affirmed their testimonies. Montoya admitted that he could not be sure Roxas was the same soldier he had seen with Lara, because it was night and his face was barely visible. Still, Montoya had seen with his own eyes that to which he had testified, and he heard what passed between Lara and the soldier. Roxas denied that he had spoken to the alférez at any time during the dance. The careos ended with no resolution.

Alférez Don Manuel Lara was brought from the jail to give his "confession." He was read his testimony, and he ratified it, changing nothing. Mariano Martínez charged him with the murder of Antonio Moya and read him the statements of the witnesses. Alférez Lara denied that he had committed the crime. Martínez asked the accused how he could deny that he had murdered Moya, when the victim himself had accused him just before he died. Proclaiming his innocence, the alférez responded that Moya's testimony, if it could be called that, should not be given much credence since he had drunk so much aguardiente and was hardly in his right mind.

Questioned about his acquaintance with the deceased and his obvious conversation with him prior to the incident, Lara argued that this was insignificant, hardly reason to charge him with Moya's murder. Lara was reminded that both Montoya and Sena had testified that he ordered a soldier to summon Moya outside, and when Moya obliged, Lara struck him with his sword. Again, Lara denied that he had killed Moya. He said that the witnesses had lied; they falsified the holy oath they had sworn, not understanding the seriousness of the consequences. Lara defamed the witness Francisco Sena, saying that he was a mere youth who claimed to be nineteen but appeared to be barely sixteen. That concluded the alférez's "confession."

Comandante Martínez notified Alférez García de Lara to name a defensor to promote his rights in the criminal case against him. Lara appointed Capitán Graduado Antonio Sena as his defender. Antonio Sena accepted the appointment and swore to perform this office loyally, on behalf of his client. The case, all forty-three folios, was handed over to the defense on 29 February 1844. Unfortunately we don't know what the defense had to say or what the final judgement was, since the documents end rather abruptly at this point.

Although we will never know how the case was adjudicated and what punishment the young officer received, if any, we can surmise that Lara did indeed murder Moya. What was his motive? He had to avenge the humiliation that Moya had inflicted upon him. The two men, suspect and victim, had not known each other before that evening, so whatever transpired between them at the dance was what sparked the violence that led to Moya's murder. Alférez Lara was a proud young Mexican military officer, and

Moya was a civilian and servant of one of New Mexico's wealthiest families. As the evening wore on, Moya's actions indicate that he may have been imbibing too much of the local aguardiente and offended the alférez. Moya gave Lara money for the dance and bragged about his employer's enormous wealth. Lara refused any additional money, and apparently he smoldered under this insult; a paisano servant had given him, an officer in the Mexican National Army, money to entertain the local Badeños.[28]

The word "paisano," meaning countryman or peasant, can also be used to refer to someone who is not in the military, a civilian. Conflict was not uncommon between the Mexican National soldiers and the local civilian populace. In January 1838, Governor Armijo issued a proclamation asking the citizens to do everything possible to avoid confrontations with the soldiers, not to raise prices in their stores, not to accept soldiers gear or horses as pledges, and not to attend gambling or drinking establishments with soldiers. Moya should have heeded this advice![29]

Whatever else passed between the two, the final insult occurred when Moya, in full view of other guests at the dance, walked into the room and plopped himself down in the same chair in which Lara was already seated. "Mil desvergüenzas!" What effrontery! A shameless act! The alférez was mortified! This show of vulgar familiarity was an insult that could not go unavenged.

The officer's swift and violent action, in what he must have perceived as the defense of his honor, was completely understandable to his fellow soldier, Pedro Roxas. Francisco Sena, an eyewitness, claimed that the soldier who abetted Lara in committing the crime admitted to Lara that he could not see how the alférez could bear the shame and the humiliation that Moya had inflicted on him. Pedro Roxas lied to enforce this code of honor for his alférez.

To the end, neither the alférez nor his soldier/accomplice ever admitted any part in the murder. Alférez García de Lara of the Second Regimental Cavalry was not about to be punished for killing a paisano who had made a fool of him in front of a crowd of people. The officer saw no wrong doing in his actions; he was simply defending his honor.

The Trial of José María Sebada for the Murder of Pablo Salazar

TOMÉ, 4 MARCH 1844

JUEZ ACTUANTE (JUDGE): don José Pino
PROMOTOR (PROSECUTOR): Juan Andrés Contreras
DEFENSOR (DEFENDER): José Ortiz
TESTIGOS (WITNESSES): Juan Antonio Baca; José Teodocio Varela; José Gabriel Sabedra; José Ignacio Salazar; Francisco Rubín
PERITOS (EXPERTS): Rafael Montaño; José María Lucero; don Luis Aguilar
CURA (PRIEST): Rafael Ortiz
ALCAIDE (WARDEN): Pedro Perea
FAMILIA DE DIFUNTO: Primo, José Ignacio Salazar; hermano, Rafael Salazar; hermano and juez de paz, don José Salazar; doña Dolores Salazar
OTROS: Miguel de Olona; Juan Montaño
TESTIGOS DE ASISTENCIA: Bartolomé Romero; Juan Lavadí; Antonio Barela; Andrés Zamora; Manuel Sisneros

TEN

Trouble in Tomé[1]

It was March in New Mexico, a time when the men of the community gathered under the guidance of a *mayordomo* (boss) to clean and prepare the *acequias* (irrigation ditches) for the coming year. Weeds and roots and the accumulated debris of winter were carefully cleared from the ditches to accept the flow of water that would soon flood the thirsty fields of the local farmers whose property adjoined the ditch.[2]

Most of the population was engaged in some form of agricultural or pastoral pursuit.[3] Subsistence farming was the rule; crops were grown for local consumption, or to use as barter since there was a general scarcity of cash on the frontier. New Mexicans grew corn, wheat, beans, chilies, onions, cotton, varieties of fruit trees, and a local tobacco called *punche*.[4] In this semi-arid land, farming depended on irrigation; maintenance of the irrigation system was a critical community enterprise. The control and distribution of water was vital, and conflicts over water rights were common, sometimes leading to bloodshed.[5] The death of Pablo Salazar of Tomé was the result of such a quarrel.

Tomé, one of several settlements in the lower Río Grande Valley, sprawled along the east side of the river in the shadow of a long volcanic hill known as the Cerro de Tomé. Tomé was a close neighbor to the villages of Valencia and Las Peraltas, settlements which may have been included in the census of 1827 that listed Tomé as having over two thousand inhabitants.[6] Some of the wealthiest families of New Mexico lived in this area of the Río Abajo, where they ran large herds of sheep in plain view of the Manzano Mountains, which stretched across the eastern horizon.

Pablo Salazar was laid to rest in Nuestra Señora de la Concepción, the parish church of Tomé, which had been constructed in the middle of the previous century when the grant was first made.[7] On 5 March 1844, the mortal remains of don Pablo were buried in the floor of the old church, against the wall, near the pulpit. The parochial priest, Rafael Ortiz, twin brother of Father Fernando Ortiz of Alburquerque, officiated at the funeral mass that morning.[8] It is likely that the Salazar family made a special "offering" to Padre Ortiz for the privilege of a burial within the church. Interment within the church, a practice frowned on by church hierarchy, was available only for those prominent and wealthy families who could afford the additional expense.[9]

Pablo Salazar was from such a family. The Salazar brothers had established themselves in the sheep raising business and had growing mercantile interests in the trade between the U.S. and Mexico. Although, not as wealthy or prominent as the Chávez, Otero, Perea, Ortiz or Armijo families, the Salazars had taken advantage of the business opportunities made available by the opening of the Santa Fe Trail. In 1832, Pablo trailed two sizable flocks of sheep southward; he sent three thousand head to either Chihuahua or Durango and eighteen hundred head all the way to Puebla, fifteen hundred miles away. In 1844, his brother, José Salazar, sent U.S. goods valued at $892 south down the Chihuahua Trail to trade in Mexican cities.[10]

Like other wealthy families, the Salazars were active in politics and the military. Both brothers signed the Plan de Tomé, a manifesto that disavowed the rebel government created by the Rebellion of 1837 and named Manuel Armijo as commander of the "liberating army," in charge of evicting the rebel "Governor" José Gonzales from the capital. Likewise, both Salazar brothers served at various times as captain of the militia. Pablo held the title of commander of the squadron when he was elected as a vocal for the first Departmental Assembly (member of the legislature) in 1843, and upon his death in 1844 he was captain of the militia of Río Arriba.[11] Pablo Salazar was a successful man, but all his business acumen and political connections could not compensate for one obvious and fatal flaw: don Pablo had an uncontrollable temper.

As was the custom, on the night preceding the funeral mass, a *velorio* (wake) was held in honor of the deceased. At a typical wake, friends, neighbors, and family members bearing lighted candles (*velas*) gathered at the home of the dead person to keep watch over the body. Women, their heads covered in black shawls, wept openly, and mourners would have spent the evening singing funeral hymns, offering prayers, and repeating the rosary for the departed.[12] These all-night vigils offered many opportunities for stories and gossip, and at Salazar's wake, the details of his death were freely discussed before witnesses had a chance to give their testimonies.

The story circulated that don Pablo, a man well known for his volatile temper, had provoked a quarrel with José María Sebada, a soap maker from Quila outside Culiacán, who was currently a vecino of Tomé. Sebada had made the mistake of questioning the distribution of water from the local acequia and thus had incurred the wrath of Pablo Salazar. Sebada controlled his anger while Salazar hurled verbal insults at him, but when don Pablo physically attacked him with slaps and blows, Sebada pulled a dagger from beneath his sarape and stabbed his assailant in the stomach. The entire incident occurred behind Dolores Salazar's house, in full view of several witnesses, including at least three members of the victim's family. Doña Dolores's relationship to the victim was not brought out in the records, and she was never asked to testify.

Don José Salazar was the current juez de paz of Tomé and had witnessed the struggle that ended his brother's life. Although he was an eyewitness to the crime, he refused to testify or act as judge because of his close kinship with the victim. Invoking las generales de la ley, don José disqualified himself and turned over the investigation of the murder to don José Pino. Pino had previously held the same office and was considered well qualified to handle the legal proceedings.

Pino was notified of the incident immediately after it occurred and was ordered to come at once to the scene of the crime. Following common legal practice, he brought with him two testigos de asistencia. Pino named don Luis Aguilar of Chihuahua as perito to make an examination of the wounds. Don Pablo died before he was able to give testimony, and Aguilar signed a statement that his death was the result of a single dagger wound, one inch wide and three inches deep, in the left side of the stomach. The murder weapon was given to the acting judge, José Pino, to hold as evidence, and a likeness of the blade was attached to the proceedings.

The accused was immediately apprehended without resistance and taken away to the Tomé jail. Three days after the witnesses had testified and Sebada had given his confession, the justice reduced him to formal prisión in the custody of Warden Pedro Perea, who saw that he was secured in shackles.

On 7 March, Justice Pino took the testimonies of five witnesses; only two of them had actually been present when the incident occurred. They were all farmers or workers from Tomé, who had been friends and neighbors of the deceased since childhood. The fourth witness, José Ignacio Salazar, was a first cousin of the victim, and he depicted their relationship as "*muy queridos*" (very close). Questioning revealed that each witness knew that Pablo was buried in the church of Tomé and that he had died as a result of a puñalada (stab wound) inflicted by José María Sebada. The first three witnesses learned about the tragedy from someone who had been present that morning outside the house of doña Dolores Salazar when the fight broke out.

Sixty-year-old Juan Antonio Baca was the first witness. He had learned of the tragic affair from Justice José Salazar, don Francisco Rubín, and don Miguel de Olona. Baca was sworn in, and in his testimony he repeated the story he had heard second-hand from his neighbors. The incident occurred behind doña Dolores's home, where Pablo Salazar and the soap maker José María Sebada quarreled. Salazar berated Sebada for complaining to the justice about his irrigation rights to water taken from the acequia del cerro. Salazar reminded Sebada that the priest was in charge of distributing the irrigation water for the benefit of the majority of the people. Sebada, not about to be dissuaded by the judge's brother, retorted that he was not getting water where it was needed and he wanted something done about it. Salazar flew into a rage and called Sebada a crazy old man, instigating the *riña* (quarrel) that led to Sebada's death.

A second witness, 28-year-old José Teodocio Varela, was called to testify. Varela did not witness the murder; he heard the story from the dead man's cousin the night of the wake. José Ignacio Salazar was present when his cousin Pablo was stabbed. Varela's statement was brief; he was only repeating what José Ignacio had told him. On the day in question, Judge Salazar called to Sebada, and they spoke together. A quarrel broke out between the judge's brother, Pablo, and José María Sebada. Pablo, began striking Sebada. The riña ended when Sebada suddenly pulled out his dagger and stabbed don Pablo.

José Gabriel Sabedra, was brought in for questioning, but he knew even less than the previous witness. He had heard of Pablo's death from don José Salazar and Juan Montaño, but they had not elaborated on the circumstances of the tragedy.

José Ignacio Salazar, the victim's forty-year-old first cousin and eyewitness to the crime, was sworn in. He was asked about motive. It was obvious to José Ignacio that his cousin had provoked the attack. The Salazars — don José, don Pablo, and don Ignacio — were gathered with their neighbors behind the house of doña Dolores. Upon seeing José María Sebada, don José called to him, and as he approached, the judge began to scold him. Standing nearby, don Pablo overheard the conversation and began heaping verbal abuse on Sebada. Calling him a crazy old fool who didn't know anything except how to make soap, don Pablo further insulted Sebada's intelligence by suggesting that he could not understand the workings of acequias. To all the insults Sebada replied, "Good Sir, I am as you say." Don Pablo then assailed Sebada, striking him with his hands. Sebada backed away, ducking the blows, and finally, drawing a dagger from under his sarape, he stabbed his attacker. José Ignacio and others ran to stop the fight when they saw the knife, but it was too late; don Pablo fell wounded. He was carried to his house, and Sebada was taken into custody by the victim's brother, Justice don José Salazar.

The last witness was 32-year-old Francisco Rubín, who was present behind Dolores Salazar's home that morning and witnessed the whole incident. He recalled a similar story. The judge called José María Sebada to censure him for his conduct regarding the acequia, and Pablo took it upon himself to harangue Sebada. He told him he was crazy, that the padre had tried to benefit him; Sebada, trying to keep calm, admitted that he knew he was crazy. It seemed that don José was purposely trying to provoke Sebada, for then he retorted that Sebada didn't know anything, except how to make soap. The taunting continued, and don Pablo began slapping Sebada with his hands. Sebada backed away, and adjusting his sarape on his arm, he addressed his aggressor with the warning, "Mire don Pablo" (look out). Pablo turned his back as if to leave, and it was with a look of disbelief that he saw Sebada pull out his knife. Indignant, Pablo turned around, and, hurling another insult, he seized his opponent by the hair. Sebada then plunged the dagger into don Pablo's abdomen. Don José, Francisco Rubín, and Rafael Salazar (another brother) ran forward and wrenched the weapon from Sebada. Don Pablo, mortally wounded, was still throwing punches; in his final breath he cried out, "They got me. I'm going. He's killed me, that man!"

These testimonies concluded, Juez Actuante don José Pino went the same day to the Tomé jail to take the statement of the accused. José María Sebada was not a native New Mexican. He had come from Quila, a pueblo just south of Culiacán in the Pacific coast state of Sinaloa, which until 1830 had been part of Sonora. He did not indicate how long he had been living in New Mexico, but in 1840 José María Sebada, listed as a widower from Tomé, had asked permission to marry Sarafina Varela.[13] Sarafina was probably still his wife when he came to trial for the murder of Pablo Salazar four years later. Sebada, in his forty-sixth year, listed his occupation as farmer and soap maker.

After Sebada was sworn in, Pino asked him if he knew why he had been imprisoned and to relate under oath what had happened. Sebada answered that he had killed the captain of the militia of Arriba, don Pablo Salazar. The incident occurred when Justice don José called to him and reproached him for a demand he had put before the magistrate regarding an irrigation dispute. Sebada attempted to justify his claim, but don Pablo, brother of the juez, took it upon himself to argue the issue with Sebada. Don Pablo called him crazy and foolish, no more than an ignorant old man, and Sebada responded calmly that he knew it. This further antagonized don Pablo, who struck out at Sebada with his bare hands and began slapping him. The rest was confusion. Don Pablo was hitting him and others were trying to restrain don Pablo, but the blows continued, and Sebada pulled out his knife. He did not recall exactly what occurred. Pablo continued hitting him, others were pushing him from behind, and in the fray he stabbed don Pablo. Sebada was thrown to the ground and knocked senseless. The next thing he remembered was being taken to jail.

Asked what else he had to say about the matter, Sebada added that he felt it was necessary for the presiding judge to make note of the effects of the beating that the deceased had given him. Justice Pino agreed that Sebada should be examined by two peritos to determine if the attack by Salazar had left any visible marks on his person. For this purpose, Pino named José María Lucero and Rafael Montaño. The following day they examined Sebada for bruises, cuts, and any indications that he had been assaulted. In separate testimonies they noted that he had a bruise on his nose on the right side, a bruised right eye, and discoloration of the skin of his right arm. They swore under oath that this was true and made the sign of the cross next to their names.

Before the defendant completed his testimony, he named four persons who had witnessed the fight between don Pablo and himself. Sebada asked that they be called in for questioning. The first was Juez de Paz don José Salazar, who once again refused to testify. The second, José Ignacio Salazar, the victim's cousin, had already testified. The last two individuals who Sebada named as witnesses were Miguel de Olona and Juan Montaño; both had been mentioned by previous witnesses.[14] There is no record that either Olona or Montaño ever testified.

The five witnesses who had testified were ratified. Their statements were read to them, and they swore that they were true, and that they had nothing more to say. These formalities completed, Pino ordered the suspect to appear before him to take his confession and make formal charges against him. Sebada was read his previous statement, which he verified as true. Pino questioned Sebada about the murder weapon. Was it the same knife that they showed him? Yes, he confessed it was the same. He was asked whose knife it was, why he carried it, and if he knew that it was a prohibited weapon. He replied that it was his knife and that he never carried it with him except on that day, when he had taken it with him to cut soap for José Salazar. A likeness of this seven-inch knife blade that had killed don Pablo was sketched on one of the pages in the proceedings.

Sebada was then charged with the homicide of don Pablo Salazar. The defendant answered that he understood the charge from his earlier testimony. The murder resulted from don Pablo's interference in Sebada's affairs and his terrible disposition, which was well known. Sebada was called by the juez, don José Salazar, to clear up a matter that did not concern don Pablo. Sebada had no dispute with don Pablo and he had no motive nor desire to harm him. Pino asked Sebada why, knowing Pablo Salazar's fearless temper, he had not avoided a confrontation. The accused man replied that they had never had any bad feelings between them, and he had no reason to suspect that any disagreement would occur. This ended José Sebada's confession and he was returned to jail.

The case was delayed when José Pino became ill and was unable to find anyone to replace him as the acting judge. However, by 19 July, Pino had regained his health and appointed Juan Andrés Contreras as the promotor fiscal to prosecute the case in favor of public interest. Contreras, a resident of Tomé, reviewed the case and prepared the prosecution, which he returned to Pino on 8 August. It was evident to the prosecutor that José María Sebada had perpetrated the murder of Pablo Salazar, a deed which he committed voluntarily and with premeditation. The evidence presented in the sumaria, both by witnesses and the suspect himself, was in agreement. It seemed obvious that Sebada's motive was pure vengeance against his aggressor. Don Pablo had turned his back to leave, when suddenly Sebada drew his knife with the intention of taking don Pablo's life. Contreras quoted this from Francisco Rubín's testimony. Such an act was deserving of the penalty that the law prescribed for such serious crimes. The prosecutor did not mention what this penalty might be, but he clearly felt that punishment was necessary to set an example for other wrongdoers.

In the local jail, José Sebada was notified that he should name a defender. If he did not know anyone capable of this task, the judge would appoint someone for him. Sebada requested that citizen José Ortiz of Santa Fe be appointed to defend him. Pino notified Ortiz of this appointment, and advised that if he accepted, he should come to Tomé to represent the defendant. The decree was dispatched to Santa Fe on 10 August. One month later, Pino noted that he was attaching Ortiz's reply to the proceedings and notifying the prisoner of such. The letter from Ortiz is not in the file and Pino's note is the final entry.

Once again, many questions are left unanswered. Did Ortiz accept the appointment? If so, what was his line of defense? Considering the case, it appears that a defensor might plead that Sebada had acted in self-defense. Pablo Salazar's death was the result of his own hot temper; through verbal and physical harassment, Salazar had provoked the attack. Both eyewitnesses testified to this effect. A defender might have asked that these two eyewitnesses, Miguel de Olona and Juan Montaño, be brought forward to testify as the defendant had requested. Their testimonies would have been more relevant than those of the first three witnesses, who were not present when the incident occurred but heard about it from one or more of the eyewitnesses.

Other than Salazar's well-known nasty disposition, was there any reason for his antagonism toward José Sebada? Pablo Salazar's obvious contempt for Sebada may have been due partially to their different social standing and background. Salazar was a native New Mexican from a relatively wealthy family, active in sheep raising, trade, and local politics; he was also a captain in the militia. Sebada, on the other hand, was not a native New Mexican; he was a poor farmer and soap maker born in a small pueblo in Sinaloa.

Sebada's request to the magistrate regarding his access to water from the acequia del cerro seems to have been the spark that ignited Pablo Salazar's wrath. It is unclear whether Sebada's complaint to Judge José Salazar over the acequia was aimed at another party or at the Salazar family itself. In his testimony, the defendant claimed that he had had no quarrel with Salazar prior to that day, and that don Pablo was interfering in something that did not concern him. Whether Sebada's complaint was with the Salazars or another party, it is clear that the violence was initiated as a result of a dispute over water rights.

ELEVEN

Murder within the Community

All communities, regardless of size or affinity, are prone to conflicts that could trigger violence. This violence is often directed towards women, but seldom perpetrated by them. Conflicts that lead to murder usually involve men, especially young men.[1] Over half of the cases of assault reported in the judicial records of this period occurred between Mexican males. In the three preceding cases, violence occurred between two unrelated males, and in each case it was the result of spontaneous uncontrollable anger, triggered by humiliation or injured pride. Inter-community violence can be sparked by various factors: competition for the favors of a woman, control of natural resources (water or land, for example), defense of honor (reaction to insult), or class prejudice. Then, as now, alcohol often acted as a catalyst that sparked the violent behavior.

From two of the cases discussed in this section, it is obvious that the baile or fandango could be a source of conflict as well as entertainment. Although the consumption of liquor was only mentioned in the Moya case, it seems likely that someone was imbibing the potent local whiskey that dulled the mind and intensified emotions at the Valdez fandango. One account by the American traveler, James Josiah Webb, found it remarkable that the New Mexican reveries were seldom broken by quarrels, unless by some brash young American; however, several complaints were brought before New Mexican justices regarding assaults and brawls at bailes, and both extranjeros and local New Mexican males were accused of being the assailants.[2]

Within the community, disputes occasionally arose over the control and distribution of water. The story of the murder of Pablo Salazar began with a conflict over access to irrigation water. The acequia system in New Mexico was an important social institution that called for co-operation between villagers. The principles of community irrigation system were based more on custom than on written law, and both land and water disputes were settled accordingly by alcaldes. Many cases of disputes over acequias can be found in the archives, testifying to the importance of water distribution in the arid communities of New Mexico that depended on crop irrigation for their livelihood.[3]

Although little understood today, the code of honor and the importance of maintaining honor were crucial to nineteenth-century Hispanic society. Honor was maintained by keeping a good public image. Those who allowed insults and humiliation to go unavenged risked losing their honor.[4]

The men charged with murder in the previous three trials reacted suddenly and violently to defend their honor after being insulted or humiliated. Juan Valdez, attempting to stop what he believed was an attack against his brother, rushed into a brawl that had broken out at his home, and began to pummel Andrés Márquez in the back. Surprised and angered by the attack, Márquez turned and struck Valdez full force in the stomach with his bare fist. No one was more stunned than Márquez, when his lifelong friend staggered and toppled over dead. Márquez claimed he had no motive for killing Valdez, that it was an accident, yet his swift assault on Valdez was not only to protect his physical self from Márquez's blows, but also to defend his injured pride and preserve his honor.

The defense of honor was most evident in the case of Antonio Moya's murder. Moya, servant of a wealthy New Mexican family, so humiliated the proud young Mexican military officer, Alférez García de Lara, that Lara found it necessary to redeem his honor by dispatching Moya with a thrust of his sword. The Alférez never confessed to the murder, but if we can believe one witness, his final words to the victim just before he killed him were "You have embarrassed me." Lara apparently felt that murder was justifiable to defend his honor and avenge his injured pride. In his testimony, the suspect used the words "mil desvergüenzas" to express his outrage at his victim's drunken impertinence. The soldier who brought Moya outside on the alférez's orders appeared to concur with his superior officer.

Don Pablo Salazar, a wealthy sheep rancher known for his explosive temper, provoked the violence that led to his death when he publicly humiliated the soap maker José María Sebada. Witnesses agreed that don Pablo had goaded Sebada into a fight with verbal and then physical abuse. Salazar had taunted Sebada, calling him a crazy old fool, slapping his face, and finally pulling his hair, before Sebada pulled a knife from under his sarape and plunged it into his antagonist's belly.

The defensor, if there was one, would surely have argued that this was a clear case of self-defense. Sebada was only defending himself from the slaps and blows of the cantankerous and haughty Salazar—Sebada had bruises to prove it—but was it self-defense to stab an unarmed man who was merely name calling, face slapping, and hair pulling? A more compelling motive for the stabbing death of Pablo Salazar is the defense of honor. Trying to ward off the conflict and defer to a man of higher social standing, Sebada had taken the verbal taunts, even admitting that he was what don Pablo had said, "an ignorant old man who knew nothing except how to make soap." Only after Sebada could take the insults and humiliation no longer, did he turn violent, stabbing the insufferable don Pablo in front of his family and friends.

In questions of honor, class and race played an important role.[5] Class conflict and prejudice were apparent in two of the trials. Both the Moya/Lara case and the Salazar/Sebada case show evidence of class hierarchy and prejudice. Alférez Lara referred to Moya as a "paisano." This term has various connotations, but most likely the young officer used it in a derogatory manner. Lara belonged to a battalion of troops that was not native to New Mexico and looked with disdain on the poor civilian populace. Pablo Salazar, a wealthy sheep rancher from Tomé, treated the soap maker from Sinaloa with contempt. His actions indicate a prejudice in native New Mexicans of the gente fina against poor immigrants from another district. Even in the small relatively cohesive communities of Mexican New Mexico, class distinctions did exist, and prejudice was not uncommon between classes.

When foreigners from North America began arriving in New Mexico, new class conflicts developed between the local populace and the newcomers. Eventually, the Mexican population became the conquered, and the new conquerors wrote freely of their prejudice and misconceptions about the land and people of New Mexico.

MANUEL ARMIJO

Armijo, shown here in full military regalia, was governor of New Mexico throughout much of the Mexican period. He served three separate terms: 1827–1829, 1837–1844, and 1845–1846.

(Photograph courtesy Museum of New Mexico, Santa Fe, negative no. 50809.)

DONACIANO VIGIL

A well educated and respected New Mexican, Vigil served as secretary to Governor Manuel Armijo at various times during his lengthy governorship. Vigil's signature appears on several of the documents in the Andrew Daily murder case. From 1847–1848 he served as territorial governor of New Mexico.

(Photograph courtesy Museum of New Mexico, Santa Fe, negative no. 11405.)

CHARLES BENT

A prosperous American trader living in Taos, Bent wrote letters to the American consul, Manuel Alvarez, protesting the slowness of Mexican justice when Americans were murder victims. Bent served as first territorial governor of New Mexico under the United States and was killed in the 1847 Revolt against American occupation.

(Photograph courtesy Museum of New Mexico, Santa Fe, negative no. 7004.)

JAMES WILEY MAGOFFIN

A prominent foreigner and wealthy merchant in both the Santa Fe and Chihuahua Trade, James Magoffin was the brother-in-law of Susan Shelby Magoffin, whose diary is one of the best accounts of life in New Mexico during the close of the Mexican era. It is believed that James Magoffin convinced Manuel Armijo to surrender New Mexico to U.S. forces in 1846. Magoffin was called to testify at the murder trial of John Patten, a fellow traveler over the Chihuahua Trail in 1844.

(Photograph courtesy Museum of New Mexico, Santa Fe, negative no. 10310.)

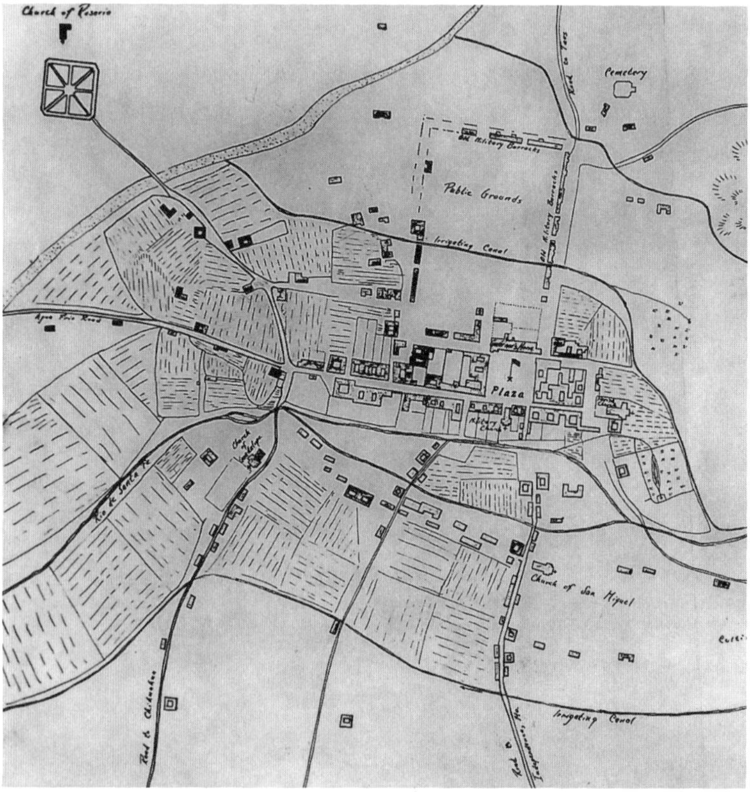

SANTA FE IN 1846–1847

Lieutenant J. F. Gilmore, U.S. Army Corps of Engineers, drew this map shortly after the American occupation. This is a close representation of Mexican era Santa Fe.

(Photograph courtesy Museum of New Mexico, Santa Fe, negative no. 101912.)

Left, PALACE OF THE GOVERNORS

The north end of the Santa Fe Plaza, shown here in this 1868 photograph, had probably changed little since the Mexican period. This building, commonly referred to as the Palace of the Governors, not only served as residence and office for the governor but also provided rooms for various military and civilian government agencies, including the guardhouse and jail.

(Photograph courtesy Museum of New Mexico, Santa Fe, negative no. 45819.)

SANTA FE

East De Vargas Street in Santa Fe photographed in 1884 may look much as it did during the Mexican period.
(Photograph courtesy Museum of New Mexico, Santa Fe, negative no. 6034.)

SANTA FE

A view of San Francisco Street in 1865 looking east toward the *parroquia* or parish church, where St. Francis Cathedral now stands.

(Photograph courtesy Museum of New Mexico, Santa Fe, negative no. 11330.)

MORA

An 1858 sketch of the road to Mora showing the east divide of the Sangre de Cristo Range in the background. This would have been the road James Bonney took in search of the alleged murderers of foreigner Joseph Pulsiphur in 1840.

(Photograph courtesy of the Museum of New Mexico, Santa Fe, negative no. 14761.)

DON FERNANDO DE TAOS

A sketch of the Spanish settlement of Don Fernando de Taos (present-day Taos) made shortly after the Mexican era came to an end. John Patten was apprehended just five miles from here, in Ranchos de Taos.

(W.W.H. Davis, El Gringo, *1857.)*

GAMBLING IN SANTA FE

John Patten came to town to gamble in such an establishment after the alleged murder and robbery of his partner Clemente in 1844.

(Albert Richardson, Beyond the Mississippi, *Newark, 1867.)*

Part Three

Extranjeros

✠ ✠ ✠

The Trial of Salvador Barela y Borrego and Diego Martín for the Murder of the Foreigner Andrew Daily

DOLORES DEL ORO, 28 FEBRUARY 1838

✠

ALCALDE, SANTA FE, JUEZ ACTUANTE, 1839: Luis Robidú
ALCALDE, 1840: Felipe Sena
ALCALDE, 1841: Francisco Ortiz y Delgado
ALCALDE, 1841: Albino Chacón
ALCALDE, 1842: Diego Beita
ALCALDE, 1843: Santiago Armijo
JUEZ DE PAZ, DOLORES: don José Francisco Ortiz
JUEZ DE PAZ, 1840: Juan Benavídez
JUEZ DE PAZ, SAN ILDEFONSO: Teodoro Gonzales
JUEZ DE PAZ, SAN JUAN: Diego Antonio Lucero
PREFECTO: Juan Andrés Archuleta
PROMOTOR (PROSECUTOR): Domingo Fernández
DEFENSOR (DEFENDER), FOR DIEGO MARTÍN: Francisco Ortiz y Delgado
DEFENSORES, FOR SALVADOR BARELA: José Dolores Madrid; Manuel Doroteo Pino (declined)
LICENCIADOS, CHIHUAHUA: Vitoriano Guerra; José Yrigoyen; Juan Nepomuceno de Urquidi; Ignacio Ochoa
TESTIGOS (WITNESSES): José Antonio Sánchez; Luis Lovato; Francisco Martínez; Francisco Esteban Martín (El Quemado); Tomás de Aquino Manchego
DOCTOR: don Henrique Masure
GOBERNADOR (GOVERNOR): Manuel Armijo
CONSUL (U.S. CONSUL): Manuel Alvarez
SECRETARIOS: Donaciano Vigil; Jorge Ramírez; Guadalupe Miranda; Vicente Vergara
SECRETARIO DEL TRIBUNAL, CHIHUAHUA: Lorenzo Tagle

OTROS: Future New Mexico governor, Charles Bent; reported the homicide, Santiago Godelese; brought in prisoners, Jesús María Sánchez; store owner in Dolores, Juan Langham

CHARACTER WITNESS: Juan Esquibel

TESTIGOS DE ASISTENCIA, 1838: Manuel Delgado; Joaquín Lomohano

TESTIGOS DE ASISTENCIA, 1839: Vicente Troncoso; José Ortiz

TESTIGOS DE ASISTENCIA, 1840: Pablo Domínguez; Ignacio Silva; José Serafín Ramírez; Luis Benavídez

TESTIGOS DE ASISTENCIA, 1841: José Ramírez; Juan García

TESTIGOS DE ASISTENCIA, SAN JUAN: Nicolás Lucero; Pablo Trujillo

TWELVE

Death in a Mining Camp[1]

1838

On 28 February 1838, in the mining town of Dolores del Oro, a murder took place that outraged the foreign community living in New Mexico. Between seven and eight that evening, two young Mexican miners entered the store of a foreign merchant, Juan Langham, and attacked the lone cashier, Andrew Daily, brutally bludgeoning him to death with rocks. By flickering candlelight, the two looted the store, taking money, gold, and various dry goods. After blowing out the candle, they fled into the night, not bothering to shut the door behind them.

Dolores del Oro was situated some twenty-seven miles south of Santa Fe on the west side of a lone mountain, originally named Sierra de San Lázaro by the Spanish but now known as the Ortiz Mountains.[2] The countryside is dry and rocky, cut by arroyos and covered with small scrub cedar and piñon trees. When word spread that gold had been discovered there in the 1820s, peones, farmers, and hired hands from all over the territory dropped their farm tools and rushed to stake claims to mine the dusty hillsides. The mining settlement that sprang up along the Arroyo Viejo was officially known as El Real de Dolores del Oro, but it was more commonly called El Placer after the placer gold deposits that triggered the boom.[3]

By 1832 several lode deposits of gold had been discovered in the canyons west of Dolores del Oro. The following year, two lucky prospectors struck a rich vein of gold on the side of the mountain. They decided to sell out, rather than mining it themselves. Lieutenant don José Francisco Ortiz, commander of the local militia garrison, and his partner Ignacio Cano bought out the prospectors' interest in the vein for one hundred pesos. In December 1833, the Santa Rosalia Mine and surrounding acreage was officially granted to Ortiz and Cano. A third partner, Damasio López (a Spaniard), helped to develop the mine but was soon crowded out of the business, and when Cano died in 1836, Ortiz became the sole owner of the mine. The mine, the mountains, and the land grant were henceforth known by the name Ortiz.[4]

José Francisco Ortiz, sometimes referred to simply as Francisco Ortiz, was a member of the New Mexico elite. The Ortiz family from Santa Fe had earned its wealth and prominence raising sheep and trading them down the Chihuahua Trail.[5] Francisco was a merchant, operating a store at the placers and one on the Santa Fe plaza as well.[6] Certainly he was the most prestigious figure in Dolores del Oro, where he occupied a fine adobe home and served as the juez de paz, the local judicial authority who would investigate the murder of the foreign merchant Andrew Daily.

Much less is known about the victim than the man who investigated his death. His name is spelled variously as (Andrés) Dele and Dayle in Spanish documents, and as (Andrew) Daily, Daley, or Doyle in English ones. Whatever the actual spelling of his name, we do know, through Max Moorhead, editor of Josiah Gregg's *Commerce of the Prairies*, that Andrew W. Daley had been a Santa Fe trader since at least 1834.[7]

Early in the morning following Daily's murder, a foreigner whose name appeared to be Santiago (James) Godelese, discovered Daily's body and hastened to report the murder to Justice Ortiz. Ortiz wasted no time. He immediately appointed two people, Manuel Delgado II and Joaquín Lomohano, as testigos de asistencia. Manuel Delgado II was the son of the prominent Santa Fe merchant of the same name and was also active in the sheep trade. The other testigo de asistencia, Joaquín Lomohano, had witnessed the original conveyance of the mine to Ortiz in 1833.[8] Both would serve as witnesses in the case throughout 1838, although the case dragged on for years after.

Next, Ortiz summoned Dr. Henrique Masure to accompany him to the scene of the crime. The few doctors on the Mexican frontier were usually foreigners who had made their way across the Santa Fe Trail after Mexican Independence.[9] Masure was no exception. Henrique and his brother Philippe Auguste, also a doctor, had both emigrated from Belgium to America and later to northern Mexico. Philippe Auguste Masure was mentioned in Susan Magoffin's well-known diary as the doctor who attended her while she was traveling to New Mexico in 1846 with her merchant husband.[10]

The foreigner, Godelese, lead the investigating party, which included Justice Ortiz, Dr. Masure, and the two testigos de asistencia. Finding their way through the sprawling mining town of ramshackle, wooden and jacal huts, they came to a place called *Paraje de las Norias*, near present-day Deer Spring.[11] Here the victim's body still lay, either inside of the store or outside (the records are not clear on this point). It was apparent that Daily had been beaten to death with two bloodied rocks that were found beneath his body. Dr. Masure counted twelve head wounds and an insignificant scratch on a finger of the left hand. The results of the doctor's examination were recorded by Ortiz and witnessed by his two assistants. Masure failed to sign the statement himself.

Ortiz attempted to determine exactly what had been stolen from the store. He noted in the records that linen and velveteen had been taken from the cupboards, and that gold and money were also missing. The justice did not mention who aided him in taking this inventory, if anyone. Perhaps it was the store owner Juan Langham, but his name is not mentioned, and it is probable that he was in Santa Fe at the time preparing for a trip back to the States that spring. Langham, a long-time Santa Fe merchant, died himself the following month "when he was seized with a fit of apoplexy" at Ocaté Creek. According to Josiah Gregg, Langham was traveling in the same merchant caravan with a party of twenty-three Americans, carrying between them some $150,000 in specie and bullion.[12]

Much of the gold bullion taken from the New Mexico mines found its way to the United States. Americans, who were forbidden from working as miners, accumulated the precious metal by setting up retail stores in the mining towns, where they devalued the price of gold and sold provisions at high prices to the miners. Merchants made a handsome profit, but the average miner, working with a spade and crude wooden bowl, seldom panned enough of the precious metal to afford a decent living. Under these conditions, it was no wonder that tempers flared and conflicts arose between Mexican miners and foreign shop keepers.[13]

The initial stage of the investigation completed, Ortiz named eight men to arm themselves and pursue suspects in the direction of Galisteo, although no one had yet been named as a possible suspect. The small community of Galisteo was on the road to Santa Fe, where it was believed the culprits were heading.

From Manuel Armijo's office in Santa Fe, a letter arrived directing Ortiz to keep the governor up to date on the Daily case and to apprehend the culprits as soon as possible, so that they could be punished for their crimes. Member of a wealthy Río Abajo family, the governor was active in the Santa Fe trade, sheep ranching, and anything else that would turn a profit. He had few friends among the foreigners residing in New Mexico. The portly governor was distrusted as an autocratic and arbitrary ruler by many foreign merchants, and he was certainly aware of the need to address this issue promptly.[14]

The following day, 4 March, Ortiz began taking statements from individuals who might have information about the murder. The suspects and witnesses in this case were all young indigent farmers from the Río Arriba, who had come to the placers with high expectations.

José Antonio Sánchez was the first person brought in for questioning. Sánchez was a 26-year-old farmer from San Gerónimo de Taos, the northernmost Indian pueblo in New Mexico, located about three miles northeast of the Spanish settlement of Fernando de Taos. Sánchez may have been a Taos Indian, but after Mexican Independence official records no longer required that ethnic background be made known.[15]

Sánchez testified that at about eight o'clock on the night of the sixth of the current month, Luis Lovato came to his home in Dolores and told him that Francisco Martín (called El Quemado), Martín's wife, Salvador Barela y Borrego, Diego Martín, and Tomás de Aquino Manchego had left the mining town for Arriba.[16] Lovato told Sánchez that Salvador Barela y Borrego and Diego Martín had confided to him that they wanted to kill Andrés Dele. Lovato had not taken the matter seriously, but later, after Daily was murdered, Lovato noticed that these two had various items from the shop where the deceased worked, and he grew suspicious. Sánchez's testimony fingered the chief suspects and witnesses in the murder case. However, the date (6 March) when he claimed to have had the encounter with Lovato is questionable, since he was now giving his testimony on 4 March. Justice Ortiz never questioned this discrepancy.

Luis Lovato, a 28-year-old farmer from Ojo Caliente, was called to testify. He verified Sánchez's testimony and added that after the murder he noticed that Salvador Barela y Borrego and Diego Martín had money and gold that they were spending freely. Furthermore, El Quemado (Francisco Martín), with whom Lovato worked, offered him gifts and spoke of digging up buried treasure. Then, Diego Martín and Salvador Barela y Borrego asked Lovato if he would go with them to Río Arriba, where they would have linen to make clothes with. Wisely, Lovato declined their offer. This was all he knew about the affair; his testimony was concluded.

The third witness, Francisco Martínez—not to be confused with Francisco Martín (El Quemado)—was thirty, single, a native of San Juan, and he worked as a miner with all four of the suspects. Martínez observed the same suspicious behavior displayed by Barela, Martín, and Quemado that Lovato mentioned in his testimony. Francisco Martínez roomed with Aquino Manchego, but he said that he did not know where Manchego slept on the night of the murder since his roommate often did not return home at night. Asked if he knew where Diego Martín and Salvador Barela y Borrego went on the night of the murder, Martínez responded that they went home to the ruined jacal hut that they shared with El Quemado.

The justice of Del Oro temporarily suspended the inquiries and dispatched a notice to all alcaldes and justices announcing the case against Salvador Barela y Borrego, Diego Martín, Tomás de Aquino Manchego, and Francisco Martín (alias El Quemado) for the murder and robbery of the foreigner Andrés "Dele." Ortiz asked that these culprits be captured and returned to his jurisdiction for the direct administration of justice.

On 8 March, in San Ildefonso, Juez de Paz Teodoro Gonzales heard that the same individuals had passed through the pueblo around nine that morning; they were carrying linen and calico. Gonzales asked to hire Jesús María Sánchez to find them.[17] The following day all four suspects were apprehended about fifteen miles north of the pueblo, in San Juan de los Caballeros, home of both Barela and El Quemado.[18] They were handed over to Sánchez, who was to escort them back to the Dolores jail. Once in custody, Salvador Barela y Borrego and Diego Martín confessed that they alone were responsible for the murder and robbery of Andrew Daily; the others had learned of the deed only after it was accomplished.

Juan Andrés Archuleta, prefect of the northern district and commander of the Río Arriba militia, compiled a list of the money and effects stolen during the robbery and handed over by the prisoners.[19] Jesús Sánchez delivered the list, along with the prisoners, to Judge Ortiz in Dolores del Oro. It included an insignificant number of pesos, several lengths of cotton and velveteen cloth, and a Navajo saddle blanket. Some of the money had been spent or given away, and Diego Martín had already managed to turn some of the cotton into stockings.

Textiles were scarce in New Mexico, especially for the poorer classes. New Mexicans had been weaving woolen and some cotton textiles since colonial times. Sarapes, blankets, *jergas*, and *colchas* were used for bedding, floor coverings, wall hangings, and clothing. These coarse domestic textiles and animal hides were almost the sole source of clothing, except for the very wealthy who could afford imported materials. However, new textiles began to come over the Santa Fe Trail into New Mexico; calicos, linens, velveteen, and finer cottons became available for the first time. Still, only the well to do could afford the prices that the merchants charged.[20]

On 12 March, the prisoners were back in Dolores, and Ortiz began taking their testimonies. Twenty-year-old Diego Martín and Salvador Barela twenty-five, were both single farmers from Río Arriba; Martín from

Ojo Caliente and Barela from San Juan. They gave separate but similar statements. Martín and Barela had planned to kill and rob the foreigner for at least two weeks prior to the event. Some time between seven and eight in the evening of 28 February, they came upon Daily, alone in the store in the Barrio de las Norias. They entered the store and attacked him : beating him over the head with rocks. Following the murder, Diego and Salvador looted the store, taking fourteen pesos in money, three pesos and six reales in gold, a roll of cotton, ten varas of velveteen, a scrap of striped cotton, and two varas of ribbon. Later Diego remembered a Navajo saddle blanket that he had also pilfered from the store. The two blew out the candle and quietly left the store, leaving the door slightly ajar.

Both Diego Martín and Salvador Barela confessed to the brutal premeditated murder and admitted that their only motive was robbery; they had no quarrel with Daily. They denied Luis Lovato's story, insisting that they had told no one of their plans to murder and rob the foreigner. Even after the deed was accomplished they told no one until the story was forced out of them, first by Quemado and then by Manchego, who were subsequently given some of the stolen items.

Next, Ortiz questioned El Quemado and Manchego, who were accused of being accomplices for accepting stolen goods and neglecting to report the crime. Francisco Martín was a 27-year- old farmer from San Juan whose curious nickname, El Quemado (the burnt one), may indicate that he had actually been burnt or more figuratively that he was generally an angry or resentful individual. When Quemado was questioned about what he knew of the foreigner's death, he denied any knowledge of the crime prior to when he encountered Salvador Barela y Borrego in the Galisteo arroyo, in possession of cloth and money that Quemado knew did not belong to him. After some prodding by Quemado, Salvador Barela confessed that he had murdered Daily and robbed the store. Quemado then pressured Barela into giving him half of the loot. Barela handed over five pesos and three varas of cotton, and they continued on their way.

Asked why he did not report the crime, Quemado claimed that he was traveling with his wife at night when he heard about the murder. The next day his wife was ill, and they passed the day in San Ildefonso. Quemado claimed that he was not aware that there was an alcalde in that pueblo. Ortiz asked him if he knew that traveling through villages in the night was illegal, and if he knew he had committed a crime when he received stolen goods. Yes, he knew, but he was tired and his wife was ill.[21]

Tomás de Aquino Manchego, a 28-year-old farmer from Ojo Caliente, was brought from the Dolores jail to testify. His story was similar to El

Quemado's. He met Martín and Barela traveling in El Río de la Cañada. Like Quemado, Manchego became suspicious when he saw the goods and money that they were carrying with them. After repeated questioning, Barela spilled the story of the murder. Diego Martín gave Manchego two pesos of the stolen money. This and the fact that he had neglected to report the crime made Manchego an accomplice. Manchego claimed that he had learned of the crime on the ninth, which according to the records was the day the four suspects were captured in San Juan.

Having completed the preliminary investigations, Ortiz forwarded the case to the governor's office on 16 March. One week later, Vicente Vergara, secretary to the governor, notified José Ortiz that they had forwarded the case to a licenciado in Chihuahua for legal advice. Vergara noted that the case was important, and the criminals should be properly punished for such a terrible crime.

Two weeks later, on 6 April, Salvador Barela and Diego Martín escaped from the Real de Dolores jail. The notice of the jail break, on the reverse side of folio eighteen, indicates that Justice Ortiz asked to be given permission to pursue and apprehend the criminals. However, if there was any attempt to capture the culprits, it was never officially recorded.

The year dragged to a close with no news from the Chihuahua lawyer. The criminals were still at large, and U.S. nationals living in New Mexico grew impatient with the slow pace of Mexican justice.

1839

Official indifference became obvious when over a year went by and no attempt had been made to capture the two confessed criminals and bring them to justice. However, if Mexican authorities seemed content with allowing Martín and Barela to go unpunished, the foreign community living in New Mexico was not. In early July 1839, a group of Americans made an official protest to the governor in Santa Fe, demanding that Daily's murderers be captured and punished.[22] The protest worked, and Salvador Barela and Diego Martín were surrendered to the authorities in San Juan.

Barela was from San Juan, probably not the pueblo but the Hispanic settlement in the vicinity of the pueblo. Barela, along with his partner in crime, had gone home. Why had two criminals wanted for murder not fled somewhere less obvious? Perhaps there weren't many places to hide in early-nineteenth-century New Mexico. Towns were small, and strangers would have been looked on with suspicion. Travel was restricted, especially for those too poor to own a horse. Few people ventured with impunity beyond established Mexican settlements, where wild tribes of nomadic indios bárbaros roamed, and constant hostilities and raiding made travel precarious. A dramatic example of the dangers of traveling into Indian territory occurred the same month and year that Barela and Martín were recaptured. In July 1839, twenty-five *comancheros/ciboleros* were murdered by the Kiowa or Comanche, forcing the subprefect of the northern district to suspend licenses to hunt buffalo or trade with these tribes.[23] Given these circumstances, there was really nowhere else to go, and the fugitives Barela and Martín went home to northern Río Arriba, where they felt secure among family and friends.

Official records in the criminal case do not mention who actually took Barela and Martín into custody; they state somewhat vaguely that the two were apprehended by order of the first prefecture, by virtue of a *reclamo* (protest) made by the foreigners. A letter written by U.S. Consul Manuel Alvarez is somewhat more specific. He wrote, "American citizens, who, shocked to see the confessed murderers of their countryman at perfect liberty, met together, took these individuals and presented them to his excellency [the governor] demanding immediate justice to be executed upon them."[24]

Case records do not indicate that Americans had any part in capturing the prisoners, escorting them to Santa Fe, or presenting them to the governor. On 8 July, Prefect Juan Andrés Archuleta sent notice to Justice Ortiz in Dolores, advising him that Barela and Martín had been captured and were being returned to his jurisdiction in order to complete the case against them. Barela and Martín were to be escorted to the Santa Fe jail the following day, by Justice Diego Antonio Lucero of San Juan, under tight security. Lucero's notice to the justices of the surrounding jurisdictions through which he would pass stressed the importance of speed and strict security. Was this because he feared the intervention of angry foreigners? Perhaps Mexican officials were already aware of the American's penchant for lynching.

Once Barela and Martín were incarcerated in the Santa Fe jail, a mob of unruly foreigners led by James Kirker and William Dryden forced a *memorial* on the governor, demanding prompt punishment of Daily's murderers. This incident began to turn ugly when Armijo threatened to call out the militia against the foreigners. Before any blood was shed, however, Armijo backed down and promised that justice would be served.[25]

Correspondence issuing from the governor's office that very day indicated that Armijo took the matter seriously, and his initial response was to carry the case to completion as soon as possible. Donaciano Vigil, acting as assistant secretary to Governor Armijo, wrote to Ortiz in Real del Oro, ordering him to present himself in Santa Fe the next day with all the papers in the Daily case. Vigil made it clear that absolutely no excuse would be tolerated. The case was to be concluded within eight days by the alcalde primero of the capital, with Ortiz present. The urgency of the order was due to what Vigil called a riot, that very morning, of U.S. citizens living in Santa Fe, who were demanding that justice be served in the case of their countryman Andrew Daily. Vigil added that the governor felt that the Americans' demand was reasonable.

Donaciano Vigil was a very prominent and well-educated New Mexican. Born in Santa Fe in 1802, he grew to adulthood during the last years of Spanish colonial rule. Young Donaciano was schooled at home by his father, Juan Cristóbal. It was an education that served him well; he went on to have a distinguished career in both the military and public service during the Mexican Era. Vigil was secretary to Manuel Armijo in the early 1840s and was well known to Americans as a merchant in the Santa Fe trade.[26]

The next entry in the Daily case was written on the same date, 9 July 1839, and it appears to be a very rough draft of a letter to the U.S. consul, from the governor of New Mexico. It was written in response to an anonymous letter from U.S. citizens, in which they asked for justice in the case of the murder of Andrew Daily, an end to the robberies, and punishment of the culprits of such deeds. In reply, the governor stated that Mexican laws must be observed for the sake of peace and tranquillity in both countries. Furthermore, foreign nationals living in Mexico must obey the laws of the Republic. He stated that the prisoners mentioned in the letter had arrived in the capital that day, and they would be judged and sentenced by Mexican laws, under Alcalde Primero don Luis Robidú. Robidú was a French-American who had settled in New Mexico in the early 1820s, where he prospered in the thriving fur trade, settled down with a local lady, and became active in Santa Fe politics.[27]

In the same letter, the U.S. consul was warned that he alone would be responsible to put an end to this uprising of U.S. nationals. The Spaniard Manuel Alvarez was serving as U.S. consul to Mexico during this period and would have been the recipient of the above letter from Governor Armijo. Alvarez was a merchant, active in the Santa Fe trade whose interests lay with the foreigners, and he often clashed with Armijo.[28]

The following day, José Francisco Ortiz arrived in Santa Fe and presented himself to the governor, who instructed him to continue with the proceedings. Donaciano Vigil, writing for the governor, reviewed the details of the case and instructed Ortiz on how the case was to be concluded.

He reminded Ortiz that the criminals, Barela and Martín, who so cruelly murdered Andrew Daily and then escaped from jail, had been captured and imprisoned in the Santa Fe jail. This had been accomplished, in spite of official indifference, by the efforts of the victim's countrymen. The public was outraged by this crime and by the way it had been handled so far. Governor Armijo ordered Ortiz to proceed with all haste to complete the case within eight days. He was to consult with a legal advisor by means of a special messenger and to take every precaution in securing the prisoners. Vigil warned that the jails were not secure for criminals of this type.

The preliminary hearings, or sumaria, had been completed the previous year, before the suspects escaped, and now the case was ready to progress to the plenario stage. Ortiz proceeded to the jail to inform the prisoners that in order to continue the case they must each name a defensor. Salvador Barela named Capitán don Manuel Doroteo Pino, wealthy sheep man of the Río Abajo and grandson of the famous Pedro Bautista Pino who acted as New Mexico's deputy to the Spanish Cortes in 1810.[29] Pino graciously declined the job of defending Barela, pleading that he was occupied making a peace treaty with the Navajos and could not possibly accomplish both. Ortiz accepted this as a valid excuse and named instead don José Dolores Madrid. Diego Martín asked for don Francisco Ortiz y Delgado to serve as his defensor. Madrid and Ortiz y Delgado both swore an oath to defend their respective clients to the best of their abilities and proceeded to the jail to make their acceptance known to the prisoners.

First, Barela was read his testimony and confession, and he verified it in the presence of his defender José Madrid. Madrid was then given twenty-four hours to study the case and prepare a written defense for his client. After Madrid returned his plea to Ortiz, it was attached to the case, and the same procedure was repeated by the other defendant Diego Martín and his defender Ortiz y Delgado. Perhaps it is not surprising that both defensores wrote almost the same plea for their respective clients. Each began by admitting that it would be useless to deny the truth of his client's guilt, since he had already confessed to the terrible murder of Andrew Daily. Therefore, the defensores begged that the justices show mercy and not impose the pena ordinaria, which the crime deserved.

The term "pena" ordinaria translates as the customary or usual punishment—a somewhat ambiguous term, since nowhere is it stated what was the usual punishment for premeditated murder. Certainly the pena ordinaria in this instance signified the death penalty since both defenders made emotional appeals, imploring the judges in the name of humanity and religion to commute the pena ordinaria to years in a presidio or perpetual banishment from New Mexico. These less severe punishments had both been used during Spanish colonial times.

Judge of the first instance, José Francisco Ortiz, following orders from the governor to complete the case within eight days, and since there was no asesor to consult in New Mexico, decided to pronounce sentence on the two criminals. On 14 July 1839, Ortiz condemned Barela and Martín to suffer the pena del último suplicio. There is no confusion of terms here; Ortiz ordered the death sentence. The criminals were to be executed by shooting, in front of the house where they had killed the foreigner.

Although Ortiz pronounced this sentencia difinitiva, his final judgement was hardly final, since he added that it was to be sent to a letrado for consultation and also to the Supreme Court of Justice before the sentence could be carried out. Ortiz must have felt pressured to make a decision of such magnitude, knowing full well that as the juez de paz he did not have the authority to carry out the death sentence without the approval of a higher legal authority.

With some relief, Ortiz sent the cumbersome stack of papers that constituted the Daily case, on to the governor's office, notifying Armijo of his "final judgement." In the Palace of the Governors, Secretary Donaciano Vigil received the case. He promptly notified Luis Robidú, alcalde primero of Santa Fe, of the sentence passed by Ortiz and ordered the alcalde to see that the case was consulted and the sentence confirmed by an *abogado* in Chihuahua. Rather than waiting for the regular mail service to carry the case to Chihuahua, Vigil ordered that the important file be sent by way of an *extraordinario violento* (special messenger).

There were 690 tortuous miles separating the New Mexican capital from the city of Chihuahua. Annual caravans traversed the Camino Real, generally departing Santa Fe in November and arriving in Chihuahua some forty days later. Regular mail service between the two points was scheduled to operate twice a month on the first and fifteenth. Dispatch riders setting out from Santa Fe and Chihuahua would exchange mail bags at a half-way point about thirty-five miles north of El Paso at a place called Rancho del Bracito. These relay riders carried the mail much faster than the cumbersome caravans, making the complete trip in twenty to thirty days. As the Mexican Era progressed, the mail service became more and more uncertain and irregular, due to increased Indian depredations, and it was often necessary to send important dispatches by special messengers.[30]

As his final duty in the case, Justice Ortiz went to the jail with his two assistants and the two defensores to inform the prisoners of the sentence he had passed on them. They acknowledged the sentence by making the sign of the cross next to their names, since neither knew how to write. If they made any comment about the harshness of their sentence, Ortiz did not record it, and the two were once again left to themselves in the filthy flea-ridden Santa Fe jail.[31] Alcalde Robidú was advised that he was now in charge of the security of the prisoners and could use the military as custodians.

The secretary of state delivered the case to Alcalde Robidú for its "prompt completion." Guadalupe Miranda, ex-schoolteacher, and one-time private secretary to Manuel Armijo, was secretary of state of the department from 1839 to 1841. In 1841 he became part-owner of the Beaubien-Miranda Land Grant. Later known as the Maxwell Grant, this huge (1,714,765-acre) tract was one of many given away during Armijo's governorship.[32] Miranda noted that the Daily case lacked a judge authorized for criminal cases according to the law of 23 May 1837, and according to the Supreme Court ruling of 11 November 1837 the alcalde was to handle such cases in the absence of a judge of the first instance. There is some confusion of terms here. Ortiz was called the judge of the first instance, presumably since he had handled the preliminary investigations in the case. He was a juez de paz, not a juez letrado; in other words, he was a local justice, but not a judge with actual legal training. Since there were no jueces letrados in New Mexico, alcaldes were allowed to handle criminal cases, and since Ortiz was not an alcalde, perhaps he could not legally be considered a judge of the first instance.

Alcalde Luis Robidú received the case and notified Ortiz to order the witnesses to appear in his jurisdiction, to have their previous testimonies verified. Three of the witnesses were still in Dolores del Oro, and Luis Lovato, Francisco Martínez, and Tomás de Aquino Manchego came forward to affirm their testimonies, taken over a year and a half previously. Antonio Sánchez was not to be found, and Francisco Martín alias El Quemado was not even mentioned in the summons, perhaps a result of confusion over the names.

Alcalde Robidú appointed Domingo Fernández to prosecute the case. Fernández, a native of Santa Fe in his early fifties, was an educated politician, merchant, and avid land speculator.[33] The alcalde gave him three days in which to formulate an accusation.

Promotor Fernández, in his tiny crabbed penmanship, wrote that society had been offended by the terrible premeditated murder of Andrew Daily. He acknowledged that the case had so far been handled competently by don José Francisco Ortiz, and wrote that only a few necessary conditions were lacking to legitimize the proceedings. He called upon Alcalde Robidú to complete these details. Robidú, zealous in his new role, accomplished these procedures. He went to the jail, where he ratified the testimonies of the two confessed prisoners, and he validated the statements of those witnesses who were no longer available: Dr. Masure who was now in Sonora, the parish priest who had buried Daily, and El Quemado.

Annoyed by these seemingly endless details, Guadalupe Miranda notified Robidú that the governor was demanding that the case be concluded immediately, whether that meant punishment of the criminals or an acquittal. Robidú was commanded to send the case by the next mail to a licenciado, and he was warned that if there were any further delays he would be considered negligent.

The case was hastily sent on to the defenders, first to Madrid and then to Ortiz y Delgado, for their final comments. Each stated that his client was guilty of the murder since he had confessed to it, and the defense could only appeal to mercy and beg for a lesser penalty, as had already been done in earlier pleas. On 20 August 1839, the forty-eight folios that now comprised the homicide case of Andrew Daily were sent to Licenciado don José María Yrigoyen in Chihuahua.

With the exception that the criminals were in jail, this year ended much like the previous one. No news was heard from the licenciado, and U.S. nationals continued to be annoyed that the Mexican courts were unable or unwilling to commit to the sentence that Ortiz had passed. Certainly New Mexican officials were just as frustrated by their inability to conclude the affair, hampered by a legal system that did not provide the authority to make important decisions.

1840

In February of 1840, Governor Armijo received a letter from U.S. Consul Manuel Alvarez. Alvarez's letter tactfully attempted to nudge Armijo into action, by thanking him for doing everything possible to see that justice would be done and Daily's murderers punished.[34]

In 1840, don Felipe Sena became alcalde primero of Santa Fe. Along with this office, Sena inherited the Daily case and all the problems that entailed. Felipe Sena was familiar with the workings of government. Like so many of the other persons involved with this case, Sena had a distinguished career in Santa Fe politics, serving several times as alcalde and for years as a *vocal* (member) of the Departmental Assembly.[35]

Sena received notification from Secretary Miranda that Yrigoyen, the licenciado in Chihuahua, had written that he was unable to advise the court on sentencing in the Daily case. Miranda went on to say that it appeared the case against the culprits was proven, the deed confessed, and the proceedings seemed to conform to the law. He agreed that grave crimes of this nature needed to be punished as a deterrent to other potential criminals, and he deplored the fact that after such a long time the deserved punishment had not yet been applied. Unfortunately, the case still needed to be sent to the Supreme Court for approval or rejection, and the governor wanted this procedure to be taken care of as soon as possible to avoid further delays and expenses, and to allay the fears and anger of the public. Further, Armijo was concerned about the possibility of a national claim by the government of the unfortunate victim.

After reviewing the case, Alcalde Sena decided that he could correct its serious defects by replacing some of the key proceedings. He immediately notified the prisoners that they were to give their confessions again. First Barela, then Martín was brought from the jail to appear before yet another magistrate. They listened to their earlier confessions, confirmed them, and Sena made formal charges against them for the murder of Andrew Daily.

Sena was insistent on discovering a greater motive. Why had they plotted to kill such a peaceful man for such meager rewards? They must have despised Daily to have murdered him so brutally. Perhaps they had hoped to take more in the robbery? It was no use; neither Barela nor Martín changed his confession. There was no greater motive. Diego Martín added that they had only stolen necessities. One obvious source of conflict between miners and merchants that could have lead to violence was the common practice of devaluing gold from the mint price of $20 to $16 per ounce. American traders who established stores in the placers made a ready profit in gold bullion through such unethical procedures.[36] Shop keepers charged high prices for foodstuffs, supplies, and other essentials. Did Barela and Martín resent the merchants who wound up with the lion's share of their small earnings? Was this resentment the motive Sena was searching for? If so, the two prisoners never admitted it.

Sena halted the confessions and once again went on to ratify the witnesses who were still in the department and to guarantee those who were absent. This time, Luis Lovato and El Quemado (now using his full name, Francisco Esteban Martín) were available to confirm their testimonies. Antonio Sánchez and Tomás Manchego were absent from New Mexico, but Donaciano Vigil and Juan Esquibel vouched for their characters as witnesses.

Once again the case was given over to the defense for final comments and approval. José Dolores Madrid, representing Salvador Barela, and Francisco Ortiz y Delgado, representing Diego Martín, again begged the court to have mercy on their clients and to commute their sentences to years in a presidio and banishment from the department. Ortiz y Delgado repeated his client's plea, asserting that his only motive had been necessity, and the defense hoped that the court would be humane, as was its nature when dealing with the destitute.

José Francisco Ortiz moved to Santa Fe in 1840.[37] Juan Benavídez, the new justice in the placers, took over Ortiz's role in the Daily case. He forwarded a notice certifying the burial of Andrew Daily to Alcalde Sena, which Ortiz had failed to record back in 1838. The notification did not include the date of interment, but it contained a description of the burial, recounting how the body had been washed and laid out in clean clothes and buried in a wooden box on a major street in Real. Ordinarily burials were within the campo santo adjacent to the church, or, in the case of important persons, the interment might take place within the church itself. Daily was a foreigner and presumably not Catholic, which may explain the unusual location of his burial. As a mining camp with a mostly transient population of miners, Dolores did not have a church or resident priest.

After attaching the death certificate to the case file, the alcalde considered the case to be complete to his satisfaction. He notified the prisoners and their defensores that a sentence would be passed the following day, 28 March 1840, at ten o'clock in the morning, in his office. At that time, Sena recapped the case against the two defendants and reconfirmed the death sentences that had been handed down by José Ortiz on 14 July of the previous year. However, this sentence would not be carried out without the approval of the Supreme Court of Justice of the Republic. Consequently, the case would be sent to the Supreme Court, which would then direct it to a second court for final judgement. The prisoners and their defendants were given the right to confer power on a procurador *de pobres* (legal counselor for the poor), who would represent them in that tribunal, and the case was forwarded to the Supreme Court in Mexico City.

While officials in Santa Fe awaited word from Mexico City, the foreign community grew impatient. Up north in Taos, Charles Bent, renowned Indian trader and partner in Bent's Fort, had become the spokesman for the large group of Americans who had settled in Río Arriba. Friend and business partner of Manuel Alvarez, Bent was a vociferous letter writer, keeping the consul informed of all the grievances that the foreigners had against New Mexican officials.[38]

On 1 December 1840, Bent wrote to Alvarez complaining that four

American citizens had been murdered in the last few years and no one had been punished. He advocated the death penalty for murderers and declared that it was the duty of the authorities to see that it was carried out.[39] Although Bent did not mention the names of these four victims, Alvarez was well aware of who they were, and two weeks later, in a letter to Powhatan Ellis, the U.S. minister to Mexico, he wrote, "Of my own knowledge this is the fourth murder committed upon American citizens in this Department, the first Mr. Gordon, the 2nd was Kennedy, the 3rd was Daily, the 4th was we presume Joseph Pulsiphur."[40]

In addition to these four Americans who had allegedly been murdered by Mexicans, there was at least one case where both victim and murderer were non-Mexicans. Bent had written a year earlier to Alvarez asking that a William Langford be tried for the murder of Sermon Nash.[41] Only two of these homicides — Daily and Pulsiphur — were recorded in judicial records found in the Mexican Archives; presumably the others were never brought to trial.

Murders, robberies, and other crimes against foreigners that went unpunished angered Americans and further aggravated hostile feelings between Mexicans and the foreign community. Racial tension increased in New Mexico with the possibility of an impending invasion by the neighboring Republic of Texas, and the following year would see increased animosities as the rumors of invasion became a realty.

1841

In January 1841, the Supreme Court of Mexico wrote to the governor of New Mexico, advising him to return the Daily case to the judge of the first instance, in the place where the crime had been committed. That justice was to reopen the case and pass judgement with the aid and advice of an asesor. So far the case had been plagued by incompetence, but the court hoped that the governor would be zealous in his duties and see that this case would be handled efficiently in the future. It should be sent immediately to a letrado and then returned to the Supreme Court.

Guadalupe Miranda sent the proceedings and the orders from the Supreme Court to the alcalde primero of Santa Fe and advised the U.S. consul of the decision.[42] In 1841, the new alcalde primero was don Francisco Ortiz y Delgado, defender of the prisoner Diego Martín. Since it was not possible to act as both judge and counsel for the defense in the same case, Ortiz y Delgado was disqualified as judge, and the case was passed to Alcalde

Segundo Albino Chacón.[43] Complying with the order of the Supreme Court, in March, Chacón sent the case off to a legal adviser in the department of Chihuahua.

In July, the prisoners petitioned to be released on bail. They both promised to find two well-known and respected people who would act as bondsmen. These fiadores would be held responsible for the culprits' immediate appearance before the judge, whenever summoned; otherwise, they would be subject to the same penalty as the criminals. Chacón broached this subject with the governor, who informed him that he could not accede to this request without the consent of the U.S. consul. Chacón wrote to Alvarez for advice on the suitability of such a move.[44]

Alvarez answered promptly. The case was being consulted by a letrado, and it was hoped that it would be returned in the next mail. He reminded Chacón that it was his duty to handle the case and see to the punishment of the criminals; in criminal cases of this type, laws outline procedures, and they should not be altered by the opinions of functionaries.[45]

Clearly Alvarez was worried that the murderers would be set free. The following year, he wrote in his memorial to U.S. Secretary of State Daniel Webster that Chacón's letter was "proof sufficient, that he [the governor] does not intend to have the murderers of Americans punished."[46]

Governor Armijo had other problems on his mind that summer. Since the previous year rumors of an impending invasion from Texas had occupied his thoughts. To complicate matters, both the presidios and militias were undermanned and ill equipped, and the central government had not responded with any enthusiasm to his letters requesting reinforcements and supplies. Furthermore, the loyalty of the many foreigners living in Santa Fe and Taos was suspect, and it appeared that some Anglos had conspired with the Texans.[47]

William Dryden, one of the Americans who had led the mob that demanded the punishment of Daily's murderers, was sent by Texas President Mirabeau Lamar to New Mexico in 1840 to ascertain popular sentiment towards Texans. Two naturalized citizens and long-time residents of Taos were implicated in the Texan conspiracy along with Dryden. They were John Rowland and William Workman, who operated a mill and distillery at Ranchos de Taos and had married into local families. As anti-foreign sentiment grew, Rowland and Workman packed up their families and gathered a group of some twenty Anglos and a few New Mexicans and fled to California.[48]

Dryden assured Lamar that New Mexicans would welcome a Texan invasion. With a great deal of optimism generated by this bit of bad advice, an expedition of fifty merchants escorted by 270 soldiers and one howitzer left Austin in mid-June of 1841. The supposed purpose of the expedition was to establish commercial relations between the young Republic and New Mexico. However, the "merchant" caravan's ratio of soldiers to merchants belied the notion that their intent was purely commercial. The young Republic of Texas, whose independence had not yet been recognized by Mexico, was jealous of New Mexico's prosperous Santa Fe trade and harbored a belief that the Texas border with New Mexico was the Río Grande.[49]

New Mexicans made little distinction between Americans and Texans, both being considered extranjeros, and tensions between foreigners and New Mexicans escalated during the Texas Invasion of 1841. When Armijo left the capital on 16 September to fight the Texans, who were expected to arrive at any moment, an angry mob led by Armijo's nephew Tomás Martín burst into Consul Alvarez's office on the plaza and gave him a severe beating. Fortunately, Guadalupe Miranda put an end to the violence, and Alvarez sustained only minor facial lacerations.[50]

In Fernando de Taos that same fall, the murder of yet another U.S. citizen was indicative of the racial violence that existed. Frances Lacompte, a deaf mute, was clubbed to death by men sent by the local authorities to find out why he had not answered a summons.[51]

When the much-touted Texas expedition finally arrived on the eastern New Mexican frontier in September 1841, it turned out to be a rag-tag band of exhausted half-starved men who were quickly taken prisoner by Armijo's forces. The Texans were ill-prepared. They lost their way on the staked plains, were harried by hostile plains tribes, ran out of provisions, and were forced to split up their party under two commands. By early October, the last Texans had surrendered and begun a long forced march to prison in Mexico City some two thousand miles away.[52] Among their number was George Wilkens Kendall, editor of the *New Orleans Picayune*, who later wrote an excellent, if somewhat prejudiced, account of the affair, detailing the insults and injuries incurred by the Texans on the grueling march to the Mexican capital.[53]

1842

Nothing was heard from Chihuahua for over a year. The news that finally did reach New Mexico was disappointing for those who wished for a speedy end to the Daily affair. On 10 May 1842, Lorenzo Tagle, secretary of the

Superior Tribunal de Justicia de Chihuahua, wrote to the officials in New Mexico. In exquisite calligraphic script he announced that Licenciado don Ignacio Ochoa was unable to advise the case against Barela and Martín, and the case was being returned to the alcalde segundo in Santa Fe.

This correspondence was acknowledged three months later by the new alcalde segundo, Diego Beita. Beita promptly sent the case back to Chihuahua to yet another legal advisor, the wealthy Chihuahua merchant and lawyer, don Juan Nepomuceno Urquidi.[54] Urquidi received the case, now containing seventy-some folios, and was quick to reply that he was much too busy as a public servant and secretary of the department of Chihuahua to be able to advise this most important case. He begged the judge to excuse him from this duty, adding that there were many competent lawyers in Chihuahua who could handle the Daily case.

Urquidi's reply was dated 24 September 1842, but it was not received by Alcalde Santiago Armijo in Santa Fe until the following spring. Armijo decided that since it was his duty to save the case from further delays, he would send it the following day to Licenciado don Vitoriano Guerra who would advise on what procedures were to be followed.

1843

Don Vitoriano's response was dated 21 August 1843, some six months after the alcalde in Santa Fe had sent the case to him. He had been extremely busy, traveling in Jalisco on official government business, and since his return he had been overloaded with work from both civil and criminal courts. Once he had time to consult the case, the licenciado filled four folios, outlining the errors and discrepancies that he had found in the proceedings in the Daily case. Guerra was appalled that the judges in New Mexico had pronounced two death sentences without consulting a letrado, that they had multiplied the proceedings unnecessarily, and that everything had been handled incompetently. Nevertheless, he would tell them what should have been done.

Don Vitoriano started at the beginning. There should have been an auto cabeza de proceso written in general terms and based on Godelese's discovery of the body. The investigation of the crime did not include enough detail. Exactly where was the body found—in the house or outside? Was it lying face up or down? How deep and wide were the wounds? Which wounds had actually been responsible for the victim's death? Dr. Masure should have filed a complete statement. The rocks that were the murder weapons should have been collected and labeled as evidence. Was it a forced entry into the store? What exactly was missing from the store? There should have been orders for the burial procedure, according to the religious beliefs of the deceased. The reproofs went on and on. The licenciado felt that these errors must be corrected if possible in order to ascertain the truth about the crime.

Furthermore, there were some discrepancies in the dates referred to by witnesses. In his testimony, Antonio Sánchez mentioned an occurrence on the sixth of the current month; how was this possible when he was being questioned on the fourth? Both Sánchez and Lovato knew the murder was premeditated and they did not inform the authorities. For this offense, they should have been detained in jail. All six men involved in the crime should have been given warrants for their arrest: Diego Martín and Salvador Barela as the principal perpetrators, and the other four as accessories. At this point, each witness should have taken an oath and been ratified.

According to Guerra almost every step of the legal process had been bungled. He went on to detail the proceedings of a criminal case, many of which the authorities in New Mexico had accomplished and others they had not. The licenciado explained how to take the prisoners' confessions and how to make charges against them based on testimonies and depositions. He emphasized the importance of questioning each suspect about his motive for committing the crime. He discussed the naming of the promotor fiscal and the defensor, and the procedure for ratifying and guaranteeing witnesses who were no longer available in person. He explained that after the judge created the act of publicación de probanzas which made the evidence in the case known, the proceedings were to be sent to the prosecution and the defense for them to sum up their arguments. At this point the case was ready to send to a letrado who would be able to advise on the sentence that should be pronounced.

Licenciado Guerra concluded by saying that "This is my opinion. You will do what you think is correct."[55] He gave no opinion on sentencing; apparently the magistrates in New Mexico were to correct the errors that he had pointed out and submit the case once again to a licenciado.

The licenciado's long letter dictating procedures to correct the errors in the Daily case was an exercise in judicial futility. On 25 August 1842, one year before don Vitoriano wrote his lengthy dictum, U.S. Consul Alvarez advised U.S. Minister Waddy Thompson that "the murderers of the American citizens Andrew Daily and Joseph Pulsiphur are in absolute liberty."[56] A few months later, Alvarez wrote another letter to the minister making it clear who was responsible for the prisoners' release. Alvarez enclosed in his letter "a copy of an official letter from Governor Armijo to one of the alcaldes for the release of one of the murderers of Andrew Daily, the last of the murderers they had in prison."[57]

So ended the case of the extranjero Andrew Daily, a case whose history had dragged on for five and a half years. The conclusion of the case could hardly have been satisfactory to the foreign community who saw it as a travesty of justice, yet New Mexican officials were handicapped when it came to dispensing justice in homicide cases.

The Case against Juan Cristóbal Armijo, Juan Angel Apodaca, and Asunción Montoya for the Murder of the Foreigner Joseph Pulsiphur

LA JUNTA, SEPTEMBER 1840

✠

ALCALDE, SANTA FE, 1841: Justo P. Pino
ALCALDE, 1841: Francisco Ortiz y Delgado
ALCALDE, 1842: Antonio M. Ortiz
ALCALDE, 1844: Tomás Ortiz
JUEZ DE POLICIA, MORA: Antonio Trujillo
JUEZ DE PAZ, MORA: Miguel Mascarenas
JUEZ DE PAZ, LAS VEGAS: Manuel Durán
TESTIGOS (WITNESSES): Ignacio Lucero; José Guadalupe Ortega; Manuel Benavídez
GOBERNADOR (GOVERNOR): Manuel Armijo
CONSUL (U.S. CONSUL): Manuel Alvarez
SECRETARIO: Guadalupe Miranda
OTROS: Santiago Bone (James Bonney); Encarnación García; Mr. Slover; Joaquín Montoya
RECLAMANTES (CLAIMANTS): María Juliana Armijo; Luis Canuto Leiba y Villas Dando; Francisco Trujillo; Juan de Dios Trujillo; Martín Armijo
OTROS (SIGNED THE PETITION FOR CLAIMANTS): Manuel Benavídez; Manuel Gonzales; José Salazar; Ignacio Lucero; Matias Mansana; Juan de Dios Aguilar; José Guadalupe Ortega; Antonio Vigil
TESTIGOS DE ASISTENCIA: Francisco Baca y Ortiz; José Francisco Sandoval; Teodoro Quintana; Guitano Tapia; Domingo Fernández; Crestino Tapia; Antonio José Rivera; José Guadalupe Ortega; Juan Lorenzo Mire; José Francisco Sena; José García; José de Jesús Ortiz; Juan Luis Trujillo; José Candido Ortiz; Tomás Rivera

✠

THIRTEEN

The Missing Peddler[1]

✢

In mid-September 1840, while the murderers of Andrew Daily were still locked up in the Santa Fe jail awaiting word of their fate from the Supreme Court, and the Texans were yet in the planning stages of their infamous invasion, another incident occurred that further aggravated racial tension in New Mexico. An itinerant Mormon trader with a wagonload of merchandise drawn by two horses approached the eastern settlements of the department of New Mexico. He arrived at a place known as La Junta, at the confluence of the Mora River and Sapello Creek, two small wandering streams that flow eastward into the Canadian River. The stranger camped there for the night among the cottonwoods, willows, and tall grass, some twenty miles from the nearest settlement of Las Vegas. He was never seen again.

His name was Joseph Pulsiphur, a fact not immediately known. He was traveling alone, or possibly with a Mexican companion, when he left the Arkansas River and began his journey south into New Mexico. Several months after his disappearance, Charles Bent wrote to Consul Alvarez of the matter, expressing conviction that the foreigner had been the victim of foul play: "I have not as yet bean able to asertain, the name of the Mexican that left the Arkansas in company of the Mormon that was murdered near the De Mora."[2]

There were two major forks of the Santa Fe Trail: the Cimarrón Cutoff and the Mountain Branch. Both trails followed the Arkansas River west before turning south towards Santa Fe. The peddler most likely entered New Mexico on the Mountain Branch, which crossed the Arkansas River near Bent's Fort, a way station for travelers and a trading post established by the Bent brothers and Ceran St. Vrain in 1834. Pulsiphur probably stopped at Bent's Fort before traveling south across the formidable but beautiful Ratón Pass and into present-day New Mexico. The Mountain Branch then descended into the plains where it made a series of river crossings, including the Rayado and Ocaté, skirted mesas and buttes, and finally merged with the Cimarrón Branch at La Junta.[3]

In the late 1840s La Junta became a rendezvous for caravans going east on the Santa Fe Trail. A small community developed there around a store and ranch established by Samuel Watrous in the years following the U.S. takeover. In 1879, when the railroad came through La Junta, putting an end to the Santa Fe Trail, the name was changed to Watrous.[4] When Joseph Pulsiphur pulled up his horses and brought his small wagon to a halt at the Mora and Sapello Rivers, La Junta was just an uninhabited crossroads on the Santa Fe Trail. A few years later the land at the confluence of the Mora and Sapello was granted to a group of petitioners headed by Santa Fe merchant John Scolly, and in 1844 when the American trader James Josiah Webb came across the trail he found two Americans settled on the Scolly Grant.[5]

One of the settlers was James Bonney, a Kentuckian and naturalized Mexican citizen, who lived about a mile and half from the crossing of the two rivers. Webb described his dwelling as a single room dug out of the ground and roofed with poles covered over by earth and grass. Bonney had settled on the Scolly Grant with his common-law wife, María Juana Mascarenas, and three or four children, the eldest of whom was a teenage son.[6] In 1840, James Bonney would lead the investigation into the disappearance and possible murder of the foreign peddler, Joseph Pulsiphur. At this time Bonney and his family had not yet moved to La Junta, but they had been living for many years in the Las Vegas/Mora area.[7]

Mora, nestled in the eastern foothills of the Sangre de Cristo Range, was actually composed of two tiny villages settled in the upper valley of the Mora River. San Antonio de lo de Mora, now called Cleveland, was at the upper end of the valley, and Santa Gertrudis de lo de Mora, now Mora-proper, was established at the lower end of the same valley. The Mora Grant was decreed by Governor Pérez in 1835, and the entire area was referred to as Lo de Mora or De lo Mora in early documents.[8]

Las Vegas, settled by residents of San Miguel del Bado in 1835, was the first village encountered by westbound travelers. Like Mora, Las Vegas was actually two small plazas located in the grassy meadows on either side of the Gallinas River.[9] Las Vegas would grow rapidly after American occupation, but in 1840 it was still a small village, described by Webb in 1844 as having a population of only three or four hundred.[10] Two years later when the caravan that carried Susan Magoffin stopped in the Vegas settlement, she found that she was the object of the greatest curiosity among the natives, who had never seen an Anglo woman before.[11]

In these small frontier communities, any activity out of the ordinary was immediately observed, eliciting curiosity, suspicion, and gossip among the settlers. In the fall of 1840, suspicion fell on Juan Cristóbal Armijo, who had been selling calico, tobacco, rifles, and gunpowder out of his house in Mora. Where had Armijo obtained this foreign merchandise?

In Santa Fe, U.S. Consul Manuel Alvarez heard rumors that an American had been killed in Lo de Mora, and in November he commissioned James Bonney to search for evidence and suspects in the case of the missing peddler.[12]

On 12 November, Bonney left Vegas for Mora to find the suspect Juan Cristóbal Armijo and bring him in for questioning. Mora was thirty miles to the north, up a winding wagon road, through low, rolling, pine-covered countryside. On that early-winter day, the impressive granite face of Cerro del Tecolote (later called Hermit's Peak), visible to the west, may have had a light dusting of snow. Traveling by mule or horseback, it would have taken Bonney the better part of the day to reach his destination.

Arriving in Mora, Bonney was informed by a Mr. Slover that he was going to purchase a rifle and some tobacco from said Armijo. Bonney accompanied Slover to the upper town of San Antonio with the intention of bringing Armijo in for questioning, but when they arrived, Bonney was informed that he had missed Armijo who was now on his way to Las Vegas. Bonney questioned Armijo's neighbors in Mora and confirmed that he had been selling some of the foreigner's goods.[13]

Bonney headed back to Las Vegas, hoping to catch up with him, but the slippery Armijo had eluded his captor once again. Informants in Vegas now advised Bonney that Armijo had "gone to the buffalo," perhaps alluding to the eastern plains, home of the great shaggy beasts.[14] Armijo obviously had friends who were keeping him informed of Bonney's movements and helping him to keep one step ahead of the law.

In Las Vegas, Bonney offered a reward to anyone who might have knowledge of the stolen goods. He learned that a certain Juan Angel Apodaca of the same village had recently been engaged in peddling various articles to his neighbors. Bonney went to Manuel Durán, the juez de paz of Vegas, to report his suspicions, and together they proceeded to Apodaca's home. A search of the premises turned up some calico cloth, a horse, and a pocket book belonging to the foreigner.[15]

The pocket book provided the first clue to the identity of the missing foreign peddler. Bonney wrote to Alvarez, "We found a small pocket book containing a few receipts and a note of thirty dollars in favor of Joseph Pulsiphur which appears to be the name of the person missing."[16] This letter, dated 17 November 1840, indicates that Joseph Pulsiphur was still a "missing person," and according to case records, his body never was found. Apodaca admitted to Justice Durán and James Bonney that two other people were involved in this business: Juan Cristóbal Armijo and Asunción Montoya, a servant of Joaquín Montoya of Peña Blanca. However, Apodaca denied any knowledge of the merchant Joseph Pulsiphur, claiming instead that the goods had been taken from a wagon that the three men had discovered abandoned in a gulch near the river crossing.[17]

Bonney explained all this in his letter to the consul, in which he also advised Alvarez that he was on his way back to Mora to search Armijo's house for stolen goods. He added that he would also attempt to locate the peddler's wagon. Consul Alvarez would be kept informed of Bonney's discoveries.[18]

The investigation moved slowly, and, with the Andrew Daily homicide in mind, the foreign community living in New Mexico became agitated over what was considered the poor administration of justice. From Taos, Charles Bent wrote to Manuel Alvarez, "We are all equally interested in having theas murderers punished this is the fourth merder that had bean comitted on American citizens within the last fue years, and as yet neather of the murderers have been punished."[19]

Within two weeks Alvarez complained to Powhatan Ellis, the U.S. minister to Mexico, that "for want of an equal administration of justice Santa Fe was near becoming the theater of the most bloody rencountre. The case of Pulsiphur has created much interest and has awakened all the sympathies of the many victims that have suffered innocently." He went on to say that although Governor Armijo had promised that he would see that justice was administered, the consul had observed that "between his saying and doings there is a very wide difference."[20]

On 13 January the following year, James Bonney asked permission to search for Joseph Pulsiphur's killer. He asked for help from Encarnación García, who gathered eight armed men, and together they headed into the Gallinas Mountains, where Bonney was certain the killer was hiding. Although his name was not mentioned, the "killer" that Bonney went in search of was most likely Juan Cristóbal Armijo. At some point, they were notified that the murderer had been found in Vegas and was to be handed over to the authorities the following day. As a result, the juez de paz of Lo de Mora, Miguel Mascarenas, probably one of Bonney's in-laws, did not give consent for the manhunt and the search was called off.

The justice of Las Vegas wrote to the governor that he had allowed one of the culprits out on bond because he was ill. This letter of 18 January has disappeared, but the governor's secretary, Guadalupe Miranda, referred to it in a letter to Alvarez.[21] Perhaps Armijo had been captured and allowed to escape by feigning illness! Nothing in the records indicates that either Armijo or Montoya was ever apprehended, and no further mention is made of this incident.

Miranda was annoyed. This action of the authorities was contrary to the spirit of the law. Through the apathy of the jueces de paz of Lo de Mora and Las Vegas the criminals had not been taken into custody. From this point forward the alcalde primero of Santa Fe was put in charge of proceedings and James Bonney was authorized to find evidence and suspects.[22]

By mid-January, James Bonney had found the foreigner's wagon and brought the remaining merchandise to Las Vegas, where he handed it over to the juez de paz, Manuel Durán. Durán forwarded the effects and an inventory to Justo Pastor Pino, the current alcalde primero of Santa Fe. Justo Pino was the brother of Manuel Doroteo Pino, who in 1839 had declined the offer to defend the criminal Salvador Barela. Pino was now in charge of the Pulsiphur case. The goods — including clothing, various types of cloth, dyes, tobacco, blankets, foodstuffs, paper, traps, a chair, and a horse — were given to Consul Alvarez, perhaps with the idea that he would sell them and send the proceeds to the relatives of the deceased, as Charles Bent had suggested in one of his many letters.[23] However, Alvarez apparently held the goods until August and returned them to the alcalde of Santa Fe, at that time Francisco Ortiz y Delgado, who was defending Diego Martín, the other prisoner in the Daily case.

Bonney, who had been given the authority to collect evidence, had confiscated all the stolen goods he could find among the citizenry of Lo de Mora and the articles that had been bartered and found in Armijo's home. The inventory, signed by Justice Mascarenas, included such articles as a jacket, mattresses, soap, salt, a locally grown tobacco called punche, onions, a broken lance, and candles. These items were all inventoried on one small sheet. Another page recorded several *fanegas* (one fanega was equal to about one and a half bushels) of wheat, corn, and beans; hides of buffalo and wolf; and a putrefied bear skin. Bonney assumed that these items found in Armijo's house had been taken in trade for the goods of the dead man. He continued to keep some of these articles, including sacks of corn and other grains, locked up in the Armijo home.

Certain citizens of Mora were angry. They filed a formal protest with the governor stating that in October of the previous year they had traded their recently harvested grain to Juan Cristóbal Armijo in exchange for certain commodities that he had received from a foreigner. Armijo had led them to believe that he had traded two mules for the merchandise that he was selling, "Pero hoy Senor que Dios a' clarado la verdad" (but today Sir, God has cleared up the truth). They now knew that the merchandise they had purchased in good faith was stolen from a murdered man. They claimed that James Bonney had taken all the goods and had locked up all their seed in Armijo's house. They asked the governor, in the name of the "most holy laws of the Mexican nation," to see that justice was done. It was only fair that their grains and money be restored to them. One of the claimants was María Juliana Armijo, daughter of the suspect Juan Cristóbal Armijo. María declared that there were sixteen fanegas of wheat and three and a quarter fanegas of beans stored in her father's house that she had harvested, and Bonney refused to give them to her. Another claimant, the *maestro* Luis Canuto Leiba, had traded six sacks of corn and seven fanegas of wheat to Armijo for a horse, and now James Bonney had taken his horse. Francisco Trujillo had paid Armijo four pesos for eight varas of *indiana* (calico) and now he was out both his pesos and the cloth. Eight more citizens of Mora came forward to sign a petition certifying that the grain that Bonney had locked up in Armijo's house was planted and harvested by Martín Armijo, his brother-in-law Juan de Dios Trujillo, and his father Juan Cristóbal Armijo.

Miguel Mascarenas called three of those who signed the petition to testify as to what more they knew about the seed locked in Armijo's home. Ignacio Lucero, a sixty-year-old farmer who had helped clean the grain, swore that the grain locked in Armijo's home was from the work of his (Armijo's) family, not obtained by trading stolen goods. Manuel Benavídez, the ditch boss, knew that the harvest in question belonged to the brother, and he knew they had planted wheat, corn, and beans. José Guadalupe Ortega testified that the seed locked in Armijo's house belonged to the claimants; in particular, he knew that Juliana had gathered six fanegas of grain and stored them in her father's home. He added that the articles that had been removed from the house belonged to Armijo's children.

On 3 February 1841, in Santa Fe, Alcalde Francisco Ortiz y Delgado ordered a case to be formed against Juan Angel Apodaca, as an accomplice in the death of Joseph Pulsiphur. Apodaca was spending time in the Santa Fe jail, where he may have been in contact with Diego Martín and Salvador Barela, who were awaiting final judgement in the case against them for the murder of Andrew Daily. The 36-year-old farmer from Las Vegas was brought from the jail and questioned about what had occurred on 19 September the previous year that had led to his imprisonment. Apodaca related the following story to the alcalde.

On that autumn day, he, Asunción Montoya, and Juan Cristóbal Armijo were following some horses herded by gentiles. Gentiles was a generic name given to members of various non-Christianized tribes, including Ute, Navajo, Apache, Comanche, Kiowa, and Pawnee. Also known as indios bárbaros (wild uncivilized Indians), these people were nomads who roamed freely over the sparsely populated territory, raiding isolated Mexican settlements. Gentiles had not adopted Spanish ways and were considered fair game for raids and slaving parties by Hispanics. Throughout the Mexican Era indios bárbaros and Mexican citizens on the frontiers distrusted and feared each other as enemies, yet they often traded with each other out of necessity. The Comanches, Pawnees, Kiowas, and Jicarilla Apaches all threatened the eastern settlements of New Mexico, and it was most likely a small band of one of these indios bárbaros that the three men had encountered.[24] Tired of following the gentiles, Apodaca and his two companions decided to stop for the night in the Gallina Arroyo and rest their own tired mounts. Armijo went on ahead to the junction of the Mora and Sapello Rivers. The following morning, Apodaca and Montoya continued on. Crossing the Sapello River, they heard Armijo shouting to them. Armijo had discovered a wagon and two horses.

The wagon was loaded with goods. Apodaca went into a detailed account of the contents: calico, cotton, muslin, a chair, a carbine, a barrel of gunpowder, forty barrels of lead, a sack of ammunition, three axes, a saw, a drill, four traps, thirty-six bunches of tobacco, four boxes of soap, five jars of tin leaf plate, twenty-one knives, nine skeins of purple thread, nine volumes of good-quality blue thread, a bucket, a jar of tin leaf, a handful of awls, a roll of white paper, a pair of pants and two vests, a piece of black kerchief, a sack of wheat flour, and twelve small white blankets.

Following this lengthy inventory, Apodaca mentioned that the three men had discovered the driver of the cart in the Gallina Arroyo and they had questioned him about the gentiles. Oddly, they never asked him about the wagonload of goods that he was transporting. Apparently, Apodaca, Montoya, and Armijo had encountered the cart driver before they split up for the night and before Armijo discovered the cart. Apodaca's testimony is confusing. Was the cart driver the Mexican companion of the peddler that Bent mentioned in his letter to Alvarez, or was he Joseph Pulsiphur? In an earlier testimony, Apodaca denied any knowledge of the peddler.

Next, Apodaca recalled that after he and Montoya had caught up with Armijo they questioned him about the foreigner whose wagon he had found. Armijo told them that he had spent the night camped with the extranjero, who promised to pay him if he would conduct him to Taos, but the foreigner suddenly fled to his own land. Apodaca and Montoya asked Armijo why the peddler had run away. Had he left in the night? Armijo was not very specific. His companions were suspicious and asked pointedly if Armijo had killed the foreigner. Armijo denied this vehemently, and together they searched the area looking for the missing peddler. When it was affirmed that he was nowhere around, Apodaca and Montoya suggested that they inform the authorities. Armijo dissuaded them, saying that the foreigner had left for his homeland and they should divide up his merchandise among themselves.

After dividing up the goods, the three went together as far as Las Vegas, where they split up. Apodaca went on to his home in that town; Armijo went north to Mora; Montoya traveled south another ten miles to the small village of Tecolote located on a creek of the same name. Asked why he had not informed the juez de paz in Las Vegas about the peddler and the wagonload of goods, Apodaca confessed that he had been afraid. Later, James Bonney reported him to Justice don Manuel Durán. As a result, the two of them searched his home, where they found some calico and a horse that he had taken from the wagon, and they arrested him. The alcalde suspended the investigations at this point, hoping that the other two suspects would soon be apprehended and their testimonies would help to clear up the matter.

In late February, Alcalde Ortiz y Delgado received the petition from the citizens of Mora, attached to a letter from Justice Mascarenas. After reviewing the protest, the alcalde ruled in favor of the claimants and ordered Mascarenas to open up Armijo's house and return their goods.

On 1 March 1841, Alcalde Ortiz y Delgado, the judge of the first instance, decided it was time to take Apodaca's confession and make charges against him, even though the other culprits had yet to be brought in. Further questioning added little new information to Apodaca's statement. Although this was called a confession, the suspect did not confess. He denied that he had any part in the death of the foreigner, and if Armijo had killed him, he knew nothing about it. He declared his earlier testimony to be the truth. Apodaca was charged with being an accomplice in the death because he had not informed the authorities when he first arrived in Vegas. Why had he waited until he was denounced to the justice before turning over the stolen goods? Apodaca reiterated his earlier answer—that he had been afraid of the consequences of informing the authorities and Armijo had warned him not to tell the justice.

Once again the proceedings were suspended, awaiting the capture of Montoya and Armijo. Tipped off that Montoya had returned to his home in Peña Blanca, about thirty miles west of Santa Fe, Manuel Alvarez passed the information on to the authorities in the capital. The Santa Fe alcalde forwarded the warrant for Montoya's arrest to the justices in either San Miguel or Las Vegas, many miles away on the eastern frontier.[25] As a result, the order was never acted on and Montoya remained free.

On 18 May, Ortiz y Delgado received news from Mascarenas that two sons of the fugitive Juan Cristóbal Armijo had been captured in the Mora vicinity with a load of corn and one of wheat, armed with a carbine and a bag full of ammunition. They were imprisoned and questioned as to the whereabouts of their father. They confessed that he had gone with his wife to hide in Pecos. Did Armijo and his wife take refuge in the ruins of the Pecos Pueblo, or in Cañon de Pecos the Hispanic settlement situated a few miles to the north on the Pecos River? The once-thriving pueblo of Pecos, decimated by Comanche raids and small pox, and weakened by the encroachment of Mexican settlers, was completely abandoned by 1838, and the ruins of its church and dwellings became a much-noted landmark on the Santa Fe Trail.[26] Pecos was in the jurisdiction of San Miguel del Bado, and the news of Armijo's whereabouts was forwarded to the juez de paz of that village. There is no evidence that it was ever acted upon.

There was some suspicion that Juan Cristóbal Armijo was related to the governor, which could have explained his apparent immunity to the law. In fact, Manuel Armijo did have a nephew by the same name; however, it is unlikely that they were the same person. The governor's nephew, by his brother Juan, was married to Juana María Chávez in Alburquerque in 1830, but the suspect had two grown sons and a daughter in 1841. Further, the Armijos were among the most prominent and wealthy New Mexican families, and in 1848 a United States judge described Juan Cristóbal Armijo as a prominent citizen of Bernalillo.[27] The murder suspect appears to have been a man of poor means, living in a remote mountain village, who found it necessary to sell stolen goods to his neighbors to augment his income. Obviously, there was more than one Juan Cristóbal Armijo.

By mid-July, Apodaca had been in the Santa Fe jail for almost nine months. As a result of the par de grillos, the irons that restrained him, he had become quite ill. He petitioned the governor to allow the alcalde to remove these restraints until his health was regained. The governor obliged, after the alcalde filed a report stating that the fetters had indeed endangered the prisoner's health, and the offending restraints were removed.

The proceedings in the case slowly ground to a standstill. In August and again in December, Alvarez wrote to Waddy Thompson, U.S. minister in Mexico that "the murderers of the American citizens Andrew Daily and Joseph Pulsiphur are in absolute liberty."[28] Then, on 14 February 1842, the new alcalde of Santa Fe, Antonio M. Ortiz, suspended the proceedings in the case.

There is no mention of when Apodaca was released from jail or when the search for Armijo and Montoya was called off. Joseph Pulsiphur's body was never recovered, and his death remains a mystery. One final notice appeared in the Santa Fe records four years after Pulsiphur's disappearance. On 6 July 1844, Tomás Ortiz presided over a public auction of the moth-eaten goods of el extranjero murdered near Las Vegas.[29]

The Trial of John Patten for the Murder of his Partner don Clemente

ON THE ROAD TO SANTA FE, 25 APRIL 1844

✠

ALCALDE: Francisco Ortiz y Delgado

ALCALDE: Tomás Ortiz

JUEZ DE PAZ, DEL BADO: Gregorio Vigil

TESTIGOS (WITNESSES), SANTA FE: James Gidding (don Santiago Guidinas); William Smith (Guillermo Esmite); Andrew L. Constant (Andrés Constante)

TESTIGOS, DEL BADO: James (Santiago) Magoffin; Ralph Bennet Fulton; John Snelling; William McDermot (?); Gabriel Valdez

ALCAIDE (WARDEN): Pedro Sandoval

GOBERNADOR (GOVERNOR): Mariano Martínez de Lejanza

SECRETARIO: José Felix Zubia

OTROS: don Mariano Chávez; Felipe Sena

TESTIGOS DE ASISTENCIA, SANTA FE: Domingo Fernández; Manuel Baca y Delgado; José Sánchez

TESTIGOS DE ASISTENCIA, DEL BADO: Francisco Narvaiz; Santiago Trujillo; Alarid

✠

FOURTEEN

Two Frenchmen[1]

During the Mexican Period, the capital of Santa Fe was a small dusty village of one-story adobe homes and jacal huts interspersed with orchards and fields of wheat and corn, all strung along a clear meandering river at the western edge of the Sangre de Cristo Mountains. The villa of Santa Fe was comprised of several individual *barrios*, each with its own parish church or other familiar landmark. The heart of Santa Fe was the town square, or plaza, a simple collection of unimposing one- story adobe buildings grouped around a barren, sun-baked square of earth. Not until a few years preceding the American takeover did one of the governors, don Mariano Martínez de Lejanza, have the foresight to plant cottonwood trees to shade the capital's plaza.[2]

The *parroquia* (parish church) of San Francisco once faced the east end of the plaza, but by the Mexican Era part of the plaza had been filled in with residences and government offices until the church was no longer directly off the plaza. The northern side of the square was occupied by the casas reales (Palace of the Governors), a long rectangular structure containing various civil offices, a customs house, warehouses, the governor's quarters, offices of the Departmental Assembly, and the national jail. The Palace of the Governors also housed the quartermaster, the commissariat, and the guardhouse for the crumbling Santa Fe presidio that lay immediately to its north. Across from the Palace of the Governors, on the south side of the plaza, stood the military chapel of La Castrense, already in ruins before the American occupation. Other buildings around the plaza included private residences and shops, and rooms rented to American merchants upon their arrival in town.

The Santa Fe plaza was a lively, noisy place at the terminal of both the Santa Fe and Chihuahua Trails. Here, caravans unloaded their merchandise, and teamsters unhooked their horses and mules. The center of town became a camping place and stock corral, where camp fires burned, and pigs and chickens roamed freely. Food vendors hawked fresh fruits and vegetables, baked goods, and meats under the shade of the *portales* (porches) of the buildings that faced the square. Church bells pealed from the various chapels and parochial churches, and the lively music of bailes and fandangos resounded from numerous dance salas. Entertainment included gambling at ever-present cock fights and card games like the popular *monte*.[3]

According to a census conducted in 1827, Santa Fe's population was somewhat over five thousand. Most of the adult males were occupied as farmers, laborers, and craftsmen. The same census listed twelve people who were considered merchants.[4] The number of merchants increased throughout the Mexican Period as the Santa Fe trade prospered and more caravans arrived in town with merchandise to sell or trade.

One of the merchants who had a store on the Santa Fe plaza was don Francisco Ortiz y Delgado, who had served as the defensor for Diego Martín in the Daily homicide case. In 1844, Ortiz y Delgado was alcalde segundo of Santa Fe and regidor segundo (councilman) on the Santa Fe ayuntamiento (municipal council), which met in one of the adobe buildings on the east side of the plaza.

Around five or six o'clock one afternoon in late April 1844, a group of North Americans was gathered on the plaza chatting at don Francisco's store, when one of them—William Smith—revealed to the alcalde and proprietor of the store that he feared a murder had been committed. The conversation came to a halt when Smith disclosed his suspicions. A Frenchman, Juan Bautista Paton (Patten) oddly nicknamed el Tejano (the Texan), had arrived in Santa Fe alone, leading his master's mule and gambling with gold coins (*onzas de oro*).[5] Smith felt certain that el Tejano had murdered his boss, another Frenchman whose name Smith did not know, and stolen his mule, his gold coins, and possibly other belongings as well. Patten had since left Santa Fe and was heading in the direction of Taos.

During the early years of the Mexican Era, numerous Frenchmen and French-Americans had come into the Taos area as trappers and fur traders, and like the Anglos a number of them decided to settle in New Mexico. Their presence is evidenced by the numerous French surnames found in church and civil records and travelers' journals of the time. Some were natives of France and others were born in Canada or the United States, but like their Anglo counterparts in New Mexico they were all classed as extranjeros. Also like the Anglos, many of them learned Spanish and married into the local population. Some acquired land, established businesses, and became active in politics.[6]

After listening to Smith's tale about the two Frenchmen, the shop owner and alcalde, don Francisco, directed Smith to report the suspected crime to the governor's office. The governorship was at this time in the process of changing hands. Due to ill health, Governor Armijo resigned the military command to Mariano Martínez de Lejanza in December 1843, and appointed don Mariano Chávez to take over civil authority the following January. When Chávez departed the capital in early April to see to personal matters in the Río Abajo, Felipe Sena took over the role of civil governor. Meanwhile, Mariano Martínez was appointed governor by the Mexican president, but he did not receive the official news until 29 April 1844, four days after the Patten case was first brought to the attention of the governor's office.[7]

On 25 April, from the office of the governor, an order went out to the justices of Pojoaque, Cañada, Río Arriba, and Taos to search for and apprehend the man called el Tejano on suspicion of murder and robbery. The order was signed by Governor Martínez's secretary, José Felix Zubia, who added that the suspect should be handled with respect, and necessary precautions should be taken in returning him safely to the alcalde of Santa Fe.[8] The notice warned that the foreigners who had brought about these charges would be held responsible in case their suspicions proved false.[9] After signing the auto cabeza de proceso, Ortiz y Delgado called two of the foreigners, William Smith and James Gidding, to appear as witnesses. William Smith, whose name appears as Guillermo Esmite in the records, was the first to be sworn in and questioned. Smith was a 36-year-old widower from Kentucky, who was residing in Santa Fe and working as a clerk in John Scolly's store at that time. Scolly, Smith, and Gidding were among the grantees of the La Junta (sometimes called Scolly) Land Grant, where Joseph Pulsiphur had met his end a few years earlier, before the land was granted by Governor Armijo.[10]

Smith testified that he had been with a group of Americans when a Frenchman approached him and asked if two of his countrymen had arrived in town. Smith told the Frenchman that he had seen only the one called el Tejano, who had shown up with a horse, a mule, some money, and gold coins. The other Frenchman responded that when el Tejano left the wagons, he had nothing more than one carbine and a skinny horse. The other Americans were listening, and it was agreed that the governor should be informed of this.

James (Santiago) Gidding was sworn in and asked to testify about what he knew of this incident. The 32-year-old Kentuckian was also a merchant, living in Santa Fe and married to a local woman, Petra Gutiérrez.[11] Gidding's story verified Smith's testimony. He reported that a Frenchman had come to town inquiring about two other Frenchmen, and Gidding had acted as interpreter. The Frenchman, who remains anonymous in the records, asked the same questions of Gidding he had asked of Smith, and his answers indicated that el Tejano had come to town alone, with his companion's possessions. It seemed certain that el Tejano had killed his companion and robbed him somewhere on the road. This incident was reported to the governor, but apparently nothing came of it, until Ortiz y Delgado ordered it reported a second time.

Just a few days after the order went out to arrest the suspect, John Patten was taken prisoner in Ranchos de Taos by Andrés Constante, another foreigner, who was living in Santa Fe with his Mexican wife of four years, Ramona Sandoval.[12] Andrew L. Constant, was twenty-four years old, a native of St. Louis, Missouri, and a tailor by trade. Constant stated that he had come upon Patten in Ranchos de Taos, a small settlement in the Taos Valley about five miles south of Don Fernando de Taos (Taos-proper). They had traveled some twenty varas (about eighteen yards) chatting with each other, before Constant told el Tejano that he had come by order of the most excellent governor to take him into custody for murder. Constant produced the arrest warrant, and in a panic Patten tried to wrestle the carbine from Constant's partner, but it was no use. Patten swore that he had not committed the crime and refused to hand over his pistol. After realizing it was impossible to escape, he surrendered to the two men, and they returned to Los Ranchos, where the local justice gave Constant eight men to aid in escorting the suspect back to Santa Fe, seventy to eighty miles to the south over a rugged road.

The road to Santa Fe wound its way up out of the Taos Valley through pine- and cedar-covered mountains to where sweeping vistas of the snow-capped mountain peaks and deep canyons of the surrounding country would have met the travelers' gaze. Constant and his party may have stopped at Embudo, a small settlement twenty-some miles from Taos where Embudo Creek flows into the Río del Norte (Rio Grande), and a French-Canadian trapper, Jean Baptist Chalifoux, operated a trading post.[13] From Embudo the road to Santa Fe followed the course of the Río del Norte. Winding along the east side of the river, it passed through the San Juan Pueblo, the villa of La Cañada, and the San Ildefonso Pueblo before it left the river valley and turned east to Pojoaque, then south to Tesuque Pueblo, and another eight miles on to the capital.[14]

It probably took two days to escort the prisoner from Taos to Santa Fe, where he was promptly incarcerated in the run-down jail on the north side of the plaza. On 1 May, Patten testified before Alcalde Francisco Ortiz y Delgado. Asked if he knew why he had been imprisoned and by whose orders, Patten replied that he did not know. He knew only that he had been captured in the Ranchos de Taos by Andrés Constant, acting on the orders of some judge, but he did not know why.

The alcalde entered the defendant's name in the records as "Juan Bautista Paton," but the signature, written boldly at the end of the testimony, is John Patten. Neither spelling appears to be French, but the 33-year-old carpenter, a current resident of Santa Fe, claimed to be a native of France.[15]

As he gave his testimony, the following story unfolded. Patten and his companion, the Frenchman don Clemente, whose full name he did not know, had been traveling from Chihuahua in the same caravan as don Santiago Magoffin, a well-known, prosperous, North American merchant. Patten did not mention what business he and Clemente were engaged in or why they were coming from Chihuahua. He did say that the two parted company with the other travelers south of Alburquerque at the house of don Mariano Chávez, a wealthy respected merchant and sheep man of the prominent New Mexico Chávez clan. One of wealthiest men in New Mexico, don Mariano would send $26,474 worth of American goods south to Chihuahua that same year of 1844. Perhaps one of his agents was in the caravan returning to New Mexico that spring in company with the Frenchmen. Chávez's extensive estate spread for miles along both sides of the Río Grande, encompassing fields, pastures, groves of cottonwoods, and one of the grandest adobe homes on the remote New Mexican frontier.[16]

Patten and Clemente left don Mariano's *hacienda* and traveled on alone. Although he did not mention it, they probably spent the night at Chávez's and continued their journey the following day. The Chihuahua Trail was not a uniform route; rather, it was a series of roads and pathways that led in the same general direction, each taken at the discretion of the wayfarers who traversed it. The main route wound north along the east bank of the Río Grande Valley until it reached the pueblo of Santo Domingo, where it turned eastward away from the river in the direction of Santa Fe. An alternative route followed the river for a few more miles north to Peña Blanca before leaving the Río Grande and turning eastward.[17] Travelers then faced the formidable La Bajada Hill, a tortuous ascent up a steep basalt escarpment that separated the Río Arriba from the Río Abajo. There were foot trails that wound up over La Bajada, and it was possible to work one's way along through the canyon of the Santa Fe Creek, but an easier route was to travel eastward in the sandy bottom of the Galisteo River until one skirted this rugged terrain and could turn northward toward the capital over less troublesome ground.[18]

According to Patten, he and his companion "left the river" about three in the afternoon, probably near the Santo Domingo Pueblo where the Galisteo Creek empties into the Río Grande. Here the road traversed the top of a long sandstone ridge before abruptly descending into the wide sandy bottomlands of Galisteo Arroyo.[19] Later that afternoon, at an undetermined location, the Frenchmen decided to make camp for the night. Strong spring winds, common to New Mexico, were blowing dirt and dust around the two weary travelers as they argued about whether to set up camp on high or low ground. The exact location of their camp is not known; however, it was indicated that the incident occurred on the wagon road between the pueblos of Cochití, Santo Domingo, and San Felipe, and the mining camp of Real del Oro. Were they close to La Bajada Mesa and fearful of tackling the steep ascent in the gusting winds, or were they somewhere in the Galisteo Arroyo? Wherever they made camp that night, they had decided to settle on the low ground and save the ascent until morning.

In the early morning, as the moon began its descent, casting a pale eerie light over the vast expanse of mesas and plains, Patten suddenly awoke in the stillness. Where were the animals? His horse and the mule were no where to be seen. He woke Clemente, but the other Frenchman seemed unconcerned. Patten got up, and, leaving his weapon on the camp bed, he went in search of the animals. He had been gone about thirty minutes when he heard a shot and someone cry out. He hastened back to camp, where he found his companion dead and the carbine lying beside the fire, not on the bed where he had left it.

At this point in his story, Patten was interrupted with a barrage of questions from the alcalde. What road did he take after he saw that his companion was dead? To which justice did he report this? Did he leave Clemente? Did he observe his wounds? What did he do with the dead man's possessions? Had the dead man carried any money, silver, or gold? John Patten replied that he had been frightened by the event and did not stay long enough to examine Clemente's wounds. He left his dead companion and all his belongings and fled down the road to Santa Fe; he did not stop until he got there. No, he did not inform the authorities about the incident. The mule that the Americans claimed was Clemente's was in fact his own; he had purchased it for thirty pesos in the Rinconada Canyon. Patten did not know if his companion had silver or gold, but he doubted it because he had lent Clemente money on various occasions. Once the questioning was over and the testimony had been read back for his verification, Patten signed his name next to the alcaldes's signature, and it was witnessed by the two attending testigos de asistencia.

The alcalde declared an auto de bien preso, and Patten was given over to the custody of Pedro Sandoval, the alcaide of the public jail of Santa Fe. Sandoval, typical of many New Mexicans of the time, could not read or write, but he signed the judicial act with a cross to show that he understood his responsibility to guard the prisoner.

José Zubia, secretary of the governor, penned a note to Ortiz y Delgado explaining that he was forwarding testimonies taken by Gregorio Vigil, the juez de paz of San Miguel del Bado, from merchants who had traveled with the Frenchmen from Chihuahua. These testimonies had been solicited by a superior order from the governor on 28 April. On 30 April, Vigil ordered Santiago Magoffin and Benjamin Fulton to appear before him to testify regarding their knowledge of John Patten.

James Wiley Magoffin (called don Santiago Magoffin in the documents) was a prominent extranjero, generally respected by both North Americans and Mexicans. He became established in the Chihuahua and Santa Fe trade in the mid-1820s and operated stores in Saltillo and Chihuahua. In addition to being a wealthy merchant, Magoffin acted at various times as U.S. commercial agent and diplomat to Mexico. He was well connected in Mexican circles through his marriage, in 1830, to doña María Gertrudis Valdez y Beremende. Doña María was from a prominent Chihuahua family and a cousin to New Mexico's Governor Armijo. Magoffin's brother Samuel, also a merchant, was married to Susan Shelby Magoffin, whose diary about her travels over the Santa Fe Trail in 1846–47 stands as one of the best sources on New Mexico at that time.[20]

James Magoffin stated that he did not know John Patten, except that they had traveled together from Chihuahua as far as the home of don Mariano Chávez at La Peralta.[21] Here Patten and his companion, Clemente, split from the main group and went on alone. They were not heard from again, until Patten arrived in Santa Fe with Clemente's mule, where he was seen gambling with gold coins. Questioned about the firearms that the Frenchmen carried, Magoffin revealed that Patten had a good-quality rifle and that Clemente went about unarmed. This exchange ended his testimony, which was taken under oath and read to him twice before he signed and ratified it.

The second witness to testify before the juez de paz in Del Bado was called Benjamin Fulton, but he signed his statement Ralph Bennet Fulton. Like Magoffin before him, Fulton admitted that he did not know much about Patten, other than that they had traveled from Chihuahua in the same caravan. He knew that Patten had a companion called Clemente and they seemed to be good friends. At don Mariano Chávez's home the group parted company. Fulton went on towards the gold fields of El Placer on 21 April around three in the afternoon, leaving the two Frenchmen still in the company of the other merchants at don Mariano's.[22]

When questioned about possessions and weapons, Fulton verified that Clemente carried no weapon, while Patten had both a rifle and a pistol. Clemente rode a mule with a dark, reddish brown saddle and had in his possession eleven gold coins that he showed to Fulton. The witness did not know how much silver the Frenchman had, but he carried on his hips a little bundle wrapped in leather chamois — for what purpose Fulton had no idea. Patten, except for his palomino horse, his weapons, and a single peso, owned no more than the clothes on his back. The Frenchmen left the company on 22 April, the day after Fulton himself had departed. He learned from his companions, John Snelling, William J. McDermot, and Gabriel Valdez, that Patten had arrived in Santa Fe on 25 April.[23] These same three were also sworn in. They verified and signed Fulton's statement. Fulton, McDermot, and Snelling were all citizens of the United States. Gabriel Valdez was James Magoffin's brother-in-law. Although he listed himself as a native of Monclova in Coahuila, he came from a prominent Chihuahua family and was a merchant active in the Santa Fe trade.[24]

The case ended abruptly with one final note, dated 28 July 1844 and signed by Tomás Ortiz in Santa Fe. There is no title given for Ortiz; he was probably the new alcalde, replacing Ortiz y Delgado. He was the same Tomás Ortiz who only three weeks before had auctioned off the remains of Joseph Pulsiphur's merchandise. Ortiz wrote that he was closing the murder case against Juan Paton since the investigations had found nothing of merit and nothing had been proven about the death of the Frenchman Clemente.

This case had a great deal in common with the Pulsiphur case. In both instances there was no corpus delicti and there were no substantial witnesses, only circumstantial evidence. If the crimes did occur, the motive in both cases was probably robbery. In neither case does it appear that the authorities attempted to find the victim's body, or if they did, the search was not documented. It is curious that the authorities investigating the murder of the Frenchman made no attempt to locate his companion who had come to town looking for Clemente and Patten. This third unnamed Frenchman had raised the suspicions against el Tejano leading to his arrest, and he should have been a prime witness in the case. Patten's negligence in not reporting Clemente's death to the authorities is certainly suspicious, and it seems likely that he did indeed kill his partner and steal his gold coins, his mule, and his other belongings. Then, after enjoying a little gambling in the capital, he fled north to avoid the authorities.

The Trial of the Foreigner Julian Collins for the Murder of José Armenta

CAÑON DE PECOS, 4 SEPTEMBER 1845

✠

ALCALDE, SANTA FE: José Francisco Baca y Terrús
JUEZ DE PAZ, DEL BADO: don Tomás Sena
TESTIGOS (WITNESSES): Felipe Salas; Manuel Archuleta; Pablo Armenta
OTRO: don Jesús María Ortiz
TESTIGOS DE ASISTENCIA: Simón Delgado; Miguel Antonio Lovato

✠

FIFTEEN

An Acquittal[1]

One final homicide case involving an extranjero is extant in the New Mexican archives of the Mexican Era. On the evening of 1 September 1845, José Armenta was shot and killed in Cañon de Pecos, and his neighbor, 24-year-old Julian Colenes (Collins), was tried for the murder.

Cañon de Pecos, also called Cañon del San Antonio del Río Pecos, is the present-day village of Pecos, situated just a few miles north of the Pecos Pueblo. The Cañon de Pecos Grant was made to a group of settlers headed by Juan de Dios Peña in 1815, ostensibly to serve as a defensive outpost against incursions of the indios bárbaros. The grant seriously encroached on Pueblo lands, as did the Los Trigos Grant, settled the year before to the southeast of the Pueblo. The early nineteenth century saw an increase in the Hispanic population of the Pecos Valley, as that of the Pueblo Indians declined rapidly. In 1838 the Pecos Pueblo was abandoned altogether.[2] Cañon de Pecos was in the jurisdiction of San Miguel del Bado, about twenty miles down the Río Pecos. Don Tomás Sena, juez de paz of Del Bado, made the preliminary investigations in the homicide case against Collins.

Unfortunately, these documents have not survived, and it is uncertain what the events were that led to Armenta's death. Only seven entries remain in the file of this homicide case. All of them, with the exception of the final one, were dated 4 September 1845, and all were signed by the alcalde primero of Santa Fe, José Francisco Baca y Terrús, and his two testigos de asistencia, Simón Delgado and Miguel Antonio Lovato.

Jesús María Ortiz, resident of Cañon de Pecos, and probably a member of one of its original families, was given the responsibility of escorting the suspect and witnesses to Alcalde Baca in Santa Fe.[3] It was a journey of about twenty-five miles that wound through green, piñon- and juniper-clad hills, around the northern edge of Glorieta Mesa, over the pass of the same name, through Apache Canyon, and northwards to the capital. It was about two in the afternoon when the dusty travelers arrived in the Santa Fe plaza.

Ortiz turned Collins over to the alcalde, along with the three witnesses, an official letter from the justice in Del Bado, and the preliminary investigations in the case. Unexplained by the few surviving records is the collection of weapons that Ortiz also handed over to the alcalde to be held until the conclusion of the case. These weapons included a knife, a hand axe, and a rifle. The latter was probably the murder weapon. Alcalde Baca acknowledged the receipt of these items and persons, and immediately ordered that Collins be served with an arrest warrant. The warden of the Santa Fe jail issued the warrant and promised to keep the prisoner under his custody.

Next, Baca asked the three witnesses, who had already testified in Del Bado, to appear before him to have their statements ratified. From these ratificaciónes, we know that the three witnesses were all from Cañon de Pecos, all Catholic, and probably all farmers, although the final witness, Pablo Armenta, did not mention what work he did. The first two witnesses, eighteen-year-old Felipe Salas, and Manuel Archuleta who did not know his age ("de edad quien sabe"), had nothing to add to their testimonies. Pablo Armenta was probably related to the deceased José Armenta, although this was not brought out in his testimony and he was not disqualified as a witness.[4] Pablo verified his previous testimony and was asked if he knew whether or not the foreigner and the deceased had any ill feelings towards one another. He answered with certainty that the two were the best of friends and neighbors; Collins had even promised to work for José Armenta without pay.

The defendant, Julian Collins, was then given the opportunity to ratify his statement and make any additional comments. He had nothing more to add, and, like the witnesses, he was unable to sign his name. In the ratificación it was noted that his earlier statement, given in Del Bado, was recorded in folio one of the proceedings. This notation indicates that he had given testimony before the witnesses. The usual procedure in the sumaria was the reverse: witnesses testified first and the defendant was heard from only after the testimonies had stacked up against him.[5]

There were other uncommon features in this case. It appears that the juez de paz of Del Bado did not issue a court order for the investigation of a crime, which should have been the first legal act of the proceedings. Instead, the alcalde in Santa Fe wrote that his first entry would serve as the *cabeza de proceso*. In most criminal cases the suspect was referred to as "el reo," which indicated the status of guilty, culprit, criminal, or simply the defendant. Collins was never called "el reo," but was always referred to as "el extranjero" (the foreigner). Furthermore, the alcalde in Santa Fe never ordered the prisoner to be restrained in irons. Perhaps from the beginning this case was considered an accidental shooting rather than a homicide.

For whatever reasons, the odds were in favor of el extranjero, the only foreigner to be tried for murder of a vecino during the Mexican Era.[6] In a final undated entry, Alcalde Baca ordered that Julian Collins be acquitted of the homicide of his friend José Armenta.

SIXTEEN

Conflict with Foreigners

For over two centuries Mexico's far northern frontier was protected from the incursions of foreigners. Spanish colonial policy forbade trade with foreigners in frontier provinces, fearing the encroachment of other nations on her soil. The few extranjeros who found their way to New Mexico prior to Independence did so at risk of being jailed for their efforts.[1] The policies of the young Mexican Republic opened the floodgates, and extranjeros began arriving on the Mexican frontier in large numbers.[2]

Anglo-Americans were the most numerous of the foreigners to arrive across the newly opened Santa Fe Trail. Two well-known names among them were the renowned trapper, buffalo hunter, and scout, Christopher (Kit) Carson, and Charles Bent, fur trader, entrepreneur, and for a short time governor of New Mexico. Many Frenchmen and French-Americans made their way into New Mexico during the early years. Some of the more prominent included Ceran St. Vrain, the Robidoux brothers, Carlos Beaubien, and Gervais Nolan. They were all involved in trapping and the fur trade in the Taos area.[3] Other nationalities were present, but only in small numbers. Very few Spaniards remained in New Mexico after their expulsion in 1827, but some, like Manuel Alvarez who became the U.S. consul, found their way back to New Mexico. Anglos and French were the best represented groups on the frontier. New Mexican's generally referred to them all as extranjeros.

These aggressive and eager foreigners proved to be a mixed blessing. They opened shops on the Santa Fe plaza that they supplied by annual merchant caravans back to the States. They returned bringing coveted articles of trade: cloth, textiles, iron tools, ammunition, even books and paper. They brought new ideas, new crafts, and "Yankee ingenuity." These foreigners eagerly exploited the boundless opportunities they found in New Mexico. Up north in Taos, extranjeros became involved in the lucrative fur trade, trapping beaver until that animal was all but extinct.[4] Some opened distilleries, where they manufactured the famous local whiskey called Taos Lightning.[5] From forts they built along the wilderness frontier, they traded whiskey and guns to the nomadic "indios bárbaros" in exchange for captives and buffalo hides, thus upsetting the delicate relationship between New Mexican settlements and these bellicose tribes. From Taos, the native priest Padre José Martínez complained about these norteamericanos in an *exposición* to the Mexican president, Santa Anna, printed in 1843.[6]

In order to carry on their prosperous trade and mercantile, interests it was expedient to learn Spanish and become naturalized citizens. Many took this a step further: marrying local señoritas and professing the Catholic faith, they were able to gain entrance into New Mexican society. A number of these enterprising extranjeros began to accumulate large amounts of land given to them in the form of grants. The largest land grants in New Mexico were made during the Mexican Era by Governor Armijo; several of them involved foreigners who had become naturalized citizens in partnership with native New Mexicans.[7] Some well-educated and respected foreigners even acquired positions in local government.[8] It soon became apparent that the United States coveted Mexico's far north to fulfill its own "manifest destiny." Extranjeros, those North American traders and merchants, paved the way for the United States' occupation that would soon put an end to the Mexican Era.[9]

Although many norteamericanos grew to love both the land and the people of New Mexico, they shared a strong cultural bias and spoke critically of New Mexicans and their lifestyles. They wrote articles, diaries, and books about New Mexico that stirred the interest of their countrymen while espousing their obvious racial prejudice against Mexicans.[10] George Frederick Ruxton, an English adventurer who wrote about his travels in northern Mexico, described Mexicans as "liars by nature," "treacherous and faithless to their friends, cowardly and cringing to their enemies; cruel and lazy." Ruxton visited New Mexico in 1847, and his unfavorable comments on Mexican nature were colored by the recent massacre of Governor Bent and others during the 1847 Rebellion in Taos.[11] Another example of flagrant racism was Rufus B. Sage's *Scenes in the Rocky Mountains*, first published in 1846. Sage, a newspaper man and trapper from Connecticut, came to Taos for a brief visit in 1842 and wrote, "There are no people on the continent of America whether civilized or uncivilized, with one or two exceptions, more miserable in condition or despicable in morals than the mongrel race inhabiting New Mexico."[12]

With this type of attitude prevalent in foreigners arriving in New Mexico at this time, it is easy to see why animosity grew between them and the local inhabitants. With good reason, Anglos were often considered arrogant and racist, and although they brought much-coveted material goods, their presence was deeply resented. Violent confrontations between them and the local populace were not unusual.

Merchant caravans left New Mexico laden with thousands of dollars in gold bullion from the placer mines. This whetted the appetites of other North Americans, and did not go unnoticed by New Mexicans, who saw the meager resources of their poor country being whisked away by norteamericanos.[13] Extranjeros made money in the mining camps by establishing shops from which they sold supplies to miners. Merchants often devalued the gold that they received in payment and charged high prices for their merchandise, not unusual practices in boom towns but definitely a cause of conflict between Mexican miners and foreign merchants.[14] Resentment caused by this treatment may have been a factor in the brutal murder of the foreign merchant Andrew Daily.

When Diego Martín and Salvador Barela were arrested for the murder of Andrew Daily, they had in their possession goods stolen from the store where Daily was cashier. Both Martín and Barela confessed to the crime, explaining that their only motive was robbery; they claimed they had no quarrel with Daily. The two men were poor farmers from Río Arriba who had come to the gold mines south of Santa Fe where they dreamed of striking it rich. They traded at the stores in the mining camp where they lived, and most of their hard-earned gold dust went to pay for essentials. Diego Martín told authorities that he and Barela had stolen only necessities, and an inventory of the stolen goods indicated that this was true. Before he was captured, Diego Martín had already made himself a pair of cotton stockings from the stolen cloth.

However, if the only motive was robbery, one wonders if it was really necessary to bludgeon the storekeeper to death. Was there a deeper motive? In 1840 when Alcalde Sena took over the investigation, he tried in vain to find the "real" motive for the violent crime. He suggested that the suspects must have hated Daily to have murdered him so brutally. There is no evidence to indicate that Daily had been deliberately cheating miners and he may well have been an honest man. Although Martín and Barela denied that they had any other motive than robbery, one witness testified that the two had told him before the murder that they wanted to kill Daily.

The two suspects denied that they had told anyone of their plans, but they did admit that the murder and robbery were premeditated.

If, in the cases presented here, honor was the motive that instigated the murder of fellow Mexicans, robbery was often the motive in the murder of foreigners. Robbery was the apparent motive in the Daily, Pulsiphur, and Clemente murders. In each case the suspects were in possession of what were presumed to be stolen goods. John Patten came to Santa Fe with gold coins and a mule that witnesses testified belonged to his partner Clemente. When they were caught selling goods that did not belong to them, Juan Angel Apodaca and Juan Cristóbal Armijo became suspects in the case involving the missing (and presumed murdered) Mormon peddler, Joseph Pulsiphur.

Unlike the Daily case, the Clemente and Pulsiphur investigations were both dropped for lack of any conclusive evidence. In both cases, the incident occurred in an isolated place, and the victim's body was never recovered. The suspects never confessed to the crime, and in the case of Pulsiphur the major suspect was never even apprehended.

Conflicts between foreigners and New Mexicans were inevitable, and there were many incidences of violent assaults against extranjeros. The news of murders and acts of violence against foreigners spread rapidly among the foreign community. Foreigners living in New Mexico were quite vociferous when they felt they were not being treated fairly by Mexican authorities. From Taos, Charles Bent wrote numerous letters to his friend and business associate, Manuel Alvarez, the Spaniard acting as U.S. consul in Santa Fe. Bent complained about the mistreatment of foreigners living in New Mexico. He was especially critical of Mexican justice. Consul Alvarez attempted to correct these injustices and corresponded frequently with Governor Armijo's office and with officials in the United States. In 1842 Alvarez sent a memorial to Secretary of State Daniel Webster, outlining all the grievances of the Americans who had been living in New Mexico since 1837.[15]

The Daily and Pulsiphur cases, occurring within a couple years of each other and prior to the Texan Invasion, caused the biggest stir among foreigners because they both involved a foreign victim and alleged Mexican suspects. Foreigners were frustrated and outraged at what they considered to be the ineptitude of local authorities in handling these two cases that involved their countrymen. Gregg complained about how the Daily case was handled and compared it unfavorably to the swift justice of the American courts in the trial concerning the merchant José Antonio Chávez, who was robbed and murdered in 1843 by Missourians on the United States end of the Santa Fe Trail.[16] Americans were confident that they knew how justice should be handled. Their views on swift justice and capital punishment were soon to be proven by the aftermath of the 1847 Revolt and the Territorial Period, in general.

Not all violent attacks against foreigners were brought to trial. Charles Bent complained to Consul Alvarez in December 1840 that four Americans had been murdered and not one of the culprits punished.[17] Two of these were Daily and Pulsiphur. According to Alvarez, the names of the other two Americans who had been murdered in New Mexico were Gordon and Kennedy.[18] Alvarez wrote in his 1842 memorial to Secretary of State Daniel Webster that a U.S. citizen, Frances Lacompte, had been clubbed to death by Mexican officials in Taos.[19] There is no record of any investigation into the deaths of these three Americans who were allegedly murdered by Mexicans.

Other violent attacks against extranjeros included one Amado Piérotin, a French doctor and merchant residing in Santa Fe, who was savagely beaten and robbed by a group of four or five dragoons from the Veracruz Squadron in 1842. Piérotin was lucky and he survived the attack, but he was never the same afterwards. In 1844, when James Josiah Webb arrived in Santa Fe, among the foreigners he found living there was the French doctor, who was in very poor condition due to a beating he had received, which had broken his jaw to the point where it never healed and he had to tie it shut with a piece of cloth. Like the Daily case, this unfortunate affair dragged on for years with no satisfactory conclusion. This was partially due to the military fueros and overlapping legal jurisdictions.[20]

During the Texas Invasion resentment ran high against foreigners, and Consul Alvarez was severely beaten by Manuel Armijo's nephew who broke into his office with a mob of rowdies. Fortunately for Alvarez, the governor's secretary Guadalupe Miranda stopped the attackers, but not before Alvarez's face had been lacerated by a knife. The Spaniard, Alvarez, a foreigner himself, was one of the strongest voices for the extranjeros. He also had close connections with the Santa Fe trade and its prominent merchants, especially Charles Bent.[21]

Extranjeros were also brought to trial for assaulting New Mexicans. In September 1839, Juez Louis Robidoux presided over a case where a young American, Robert Beal, shot a Mexican soldier, José María Guerrero, at a baile in Santa Fe. Guerrero sustained a painful gunshot wound, but did not die and was able to testify at the trial. He felt that Beal had shot him while attempting to defend himself from other Mexicans who were throwing stones at him. Beal had surrendered his pistol as requested when he entered the house where the dance was in progress, but asked for its return when he found himself overwhelmed by Mexicans hitting him with sticks and stones. The brawl started when another American made improper advances to one of the ladies at the dance and then insulted her partner. The Mexican males went outside and armed themselves with sticks and stones and began to attack the Americans inside the house. Understanding that Guerrero was out of physical danger and that Beal had acted in self-defense, Robidoux, himself a foreigner, concluded the sumaria and forwarded the case to Governor Armijo for further instructions.[22]

In 1843, another American, known only as Maese, found himself in jail for starting a riña at a baile in Santa Fe. When the alcalde who was present at the baile attempted to stop the fight, the American brandished his sword and seized the magistrate's cane of justice (*vara de justicia*) from his hands. Maese refused to give up his weapon but was eventually disarmed and packed off to the local cárcel. The American's lack of respect for local authority was duly noted by witnesses.[23]

The only homicide case that was tried against a foreigner for the murder of a Mexican citizen was the trial of Julian Collins, who was accused of shooting his neighbor José Armenta in Cañon de Pecos. Unfortunately, the preliminary investigations were lost, and very little is known about the case. From the few scraps of evidence that remain on record, it appears that the Anglo, Collins, and his Mexican neighbors were good friends. Julian Collins was acquitted by the Santa Fe alcalde on the testimony of witnesses, one of whom was a relative of the deceased. If the statements of the witnesses had survived, they might have given testimony to friendship rather than conflict between Mexican vecinos and Anglos in at least one small New Mexican village.[24]

Obviously not all New Mexicans and foreigners despised each other. There was more advantage to be gained from mutual cooperation than conflict, and both sides profited in some way from the new business opportunities and social alliances that developed during the Mexican Era. Still, there were many New Mexicans who did not profit by the influx of North Americans and saw them as a threat to their way of life. New Mexico already suffered from an unequal distribution of wealth, and class distinctions widened during the Mexican Era, as the ricos became more wealthy through new trade opportunities, and increasing numbers of extranjeros began to compete for limited available resources.

The Mexican Era that had begun with such optimism and good feeling began to witness a mounting tension as more and more foreigners took up residence, acquiring wealth, land, and even political prominence. This social climate resulted in the 1847 Revolt, a brief but bloody affair that broke out in Taos just months after the U.S. occupation began. The victims of the Taos Revolt were foreigners and their New Mexican sympathizers. Among them was Charles Bent, the once vociferous proponent of foreigners' rights in New Mexico. Bent was appointed governor by Kearny after the occupation began, a position which may have increased the ill will towards him from local families, who saw not only their land being snatched up by greedy foreigners but their political power as well.[25]

With the United States' conquest of New Mexico, North Americans had their chance to show the Mexicans what their brand of justice was all about. Treason trials were conducted following the 1847 Revolt, and at least seven New Mexicans were hastily convicted and executed. Unlike the years under Mexican rule, New Mexico witnessed as many as sixty-two (a conservative estimate) legal executions under the U.S. Territorial government.[26] Further, this era became known for vigilantes and mob lynchings, a testament to the fact that the legal system on the American frontier still did not operate fast enough to satisfy impatient North Americans, who it appeared valued swift punishments over fair trials.

Conclusion

As witnessed in the homicide cases that were tried during the Mexican Era, the investigations of violent crime and the trials of suspects were conducted along well-established lines, even though there were no lawyers, judges, or anyone with any legal training in New Mexico. Gabriel Haslip's study of crime and justice in eighteenth-century Mexico City describes judicial procedures for homicide cases that closely resemble those applied in New Mexico.[1] It appears that New Mexicans were well aware of the basics of Spanish judicial practices.

Legal professionals had no desire to live on poor remote frontiers, when they could practice their profession in a populated area where they would be well paid and could enjoy the advantages of city life. The Spanish had always been a litigious people who took full advantage of their legal system to settle grievances and redress wrongs, and records indicate that New Mexicans were making full use of the courts, without benefit of lawyers, counselors, or judges formally educated in law.

One lawyer did come to New Mexico during the Mexican Era. Antonio Barreiro was sent by the central government to advise territorial authorities on legal matters. He was appalled by what he found. New Mexicans filed lawsuits, litigated against neighbors in land and water disputes, and brought charges against persons who had caused them injury—all without the aid of a legal professional.[2]

In frontier areas such as New Mexico, a handful of educated persons served in a variety of offices and ran the affairs of state. Local government was not separated into tidy branches; executive, legislative, judicial, and often military functions were managed by the same official. Incidences of crime were reported to the alcalde or juez de paz in the jurisdiction where they were committed. This official would then investigate the crime, question witnesses, appoint a prosecutor, see that the suspect had a defender, arbitrate the case, and possibly hand down a sentence. The same magistrate was involved in every step of the judicial process, and as such he could hardly have acted as an impartial judge. As a safeguard to arbitrary judgement or abuse of power in more serious crimes, such as homicide, local justices were not granted the authority to hand down the final sentence, and the case was sent to legal advisors in Chihuahua.

Although frontier justice was plagued by a multitude of problems, on the positive side, alcaldes and jueces de paz were not completely ignorant of laws and legal protocol. They were informed of current legislation and had access to the major compilation of Spanish law, a copy of which was kept in the capital.[3] Local justices were knowledgeable about legal procedures that they were expected to follow. They were the prominent men of their communities, chosen for their abilities and literacy to act as judges and leaders. Frontier judicial procedure was based less on Spanish legal precepts than on Spanish values, community tradition, and a strong sense of right and wrong. This common-sense approach to justice may have shocked big-city lawyers like Licenciado Barreiro, but it appears to have worked on the frontier.

If it appears that homicides were never punished in New Mexico, it must be noted that this was not the fault of frontier justices, who did not have the authority to pass judgement in such serious crimes. Although most prosecutors asked for the death penalty, it was never pronounced except in one unusual case. The justice in the Daily case was pressured into handing down a judgement, but he was probably aware that it would not be carried out. The reasons most prosecutors gave for requesting the death sentence were to punish the criminal, to deter other criminals, and to satisfy public vengeance. Remorse could be a mitigating factor in the sentencing of criminals, and the prosecution often cited lack of remorse as a justification for the death penalty.

It was easy for the prosecutor to demand capital punishment. Not only was it expected of him, but also he knew that judgement rested with a higher authority and he was not responsible for the final outcome. As we have seen, a final judgement and sentencing was never handed down by New Mexican courts, and even the justices of higher courts in far off Chihuahua were reluctant to pass any sentence on homicide cases. Local justices must have been relieved that they did not have the authority to make final decisions on capital crimes. In the small communities of New Mexico, where everyone knew everyone else and much of the population was related in one way or another, a decision to condemn a fellow vecino to death and then carry out the execution would have put a terrible stress on the local magistrate.

Capital punishment was not rare only in New Mexico, but throughout Mexico under both Spanish colonial and Mexican administration, thus contradicting the "Black Legend" of supposed Spanish cruelty. Statistics collected by Taylor show that out of fifty-six cases of homicide in eighteenth-century Oaxaca, ten resulted in capital punishment, and in central Mexico only four out of 152 murders were punished by execution.[4] Only the most heinous criminals were punished by death: incorrigible highwaymen who robbed and murdered their victims, rapist-murderers, repeat murderers, and especially brutal murderers. Even so, capital punishment was not common. Corporal punishments, fines, and exile were among the sentences meted out to convicted murderers, but the most popular punishment in eighteenth-century Mexico was forced labor in obrajes and presidios. Towards the end of the colonial period, presidio terms were the most common type of punishment for convicted murderers, and at least half of those convicted were pardoned or released without punishment.[5]

In New Mexico, culprits did not go completely free; most of them spent some time in jail awaiting a final judgement that could take months or years, as the case was sent back and forth between contending parties and down to Chihuahua and back to be advised by an asesor. Even in central Mexico, where there was no shortage of judges and lawyers, prisoners often languished in jail awaiting their sentence. A similar plight shared by prisoners all over Mexico was the unhealthy condition of the jails. Not just on the New Mexican frontier were jails described as dark, filthy, vermin-infested places; this was the norm in Mexican jails throughout the country. In addition, prisoners in Mexican and New Mexican jails alike were expected to support themselves. Most were too poor, however, and extended imprisonment made it necessary for the state to support them.[6]

The few homicide cases that were tried in New Mexican alcalde courts between 1821 and 1846 and whose documents survive in the archives don't just reveal how the local judicial system functioned; they also provide a picture of society from the perspective of the less-fortunate majority. Most of the trials included testimonies and statements from "common people," uneducated vecinos, who otherwise would never have left any word of their existence. Admittedly, these are very brief and somewhat formal "encounters," due to the official nature of the questioning; still, court trials are more personal than many other sources of social history because they allow the "silent" folk to speak.

Testimonies of witnesses and "confessions" of suspects give us a small but important glimpse at how these people lived and thought, and how they viewed their world. In addition, the voices of men who acted as judges, prosecutors, and defenders are a record of the belief systems and prejudices of the elite educated portion of the population. Through these trials we get a better understanding of how New Mexicans viewed their world—their concept of society, justice, honor, the role of women, and the importance of family and religion in their lives—and how these world views influenced their behavior.

If we knew nothing about post-colonial, pre-territorial New Mexico except what we learned from these few homicide trials, we would still be able to piece together a basic knowledge of that society. It is apparent that New Mexico was still a predominantly agricultural-pastoral society, in a semi-arid land dependent on irrigation. This was a frontier society, remote from the amenities available in more urban, central locations. There was a lack of lawyers and doctors, and a shortage of priests. This was a stratified society. As evidenced in the case files, there was an "upper-crust" that lived well, having land, animals and servants, and a poorer class, who worked as independent farmers and artisans, or as servants and day laborers for the wealthy.

The state of public education can also be evaluated from the trial records. Obviously, illiteracy was common, especially among the poorer people, who signed their testimonies with crosses. Not all witnesses were poor and illiterate; others called to testify were able to sign their testimonies, and many did so with a flourish (*rúbrica*).[7] The men who served in judicial capacities were able to read and write, and had a basic knowledge of Spanish legal practices and access to some written judicial works as well. From this disparity in literacy, we might infer that public education on this frontier was sporadic and that the upper classes probably benefited from private schooling.

Poor and wealthy alike enjoyed the entertainment of bailes and fandangos, where dancing, drinking, and merriment were a welcome relief from the uncertainties and rigors of frontier life. That these festive occasions were often broken by fights and violence and were the scene of two of the murders should come as no surprise to anyone. Modern-day parties and large social gatherings are a common arena for confrontations that often lead to violence.

New Mexico suffered from the hardships and unpredictability of unsecured borders between her settlements and various nomadic tribes, a powerful expanding nation to the north, and a recently independent republic to the east. One juez de paz mentioned that conflicts with both Navajos and Tejanos had disrupted New Mexico in 1843. The justice, in Corrales, was using this as an excuse for his tardiness in forwarding a case file to the defensor in Santa Fe. Although his excuse had nothing to do with the actual trial, it contributes important information about conditions in New Mexico during this time period.

Without too much inference, we glean from the case records that this was a class-conscious society with certain prejudices and misconceptions about non-Hispanic neighbors, genízaros, and Pueblos. At least one case witnessed the contempt shown by some members of the wealthy class against fellow Mexicans of a lower economic and social background, and another hinted at possible animosities between local people and the Mexican military units stationed in New Mexico.

The arrival of more and more extranjeros who came as merchants and settled in New Mexico must have given rise to conflicting feelings among the local people. Eager for foreign goods yet suspicious and envious of the foreigners who brought them, the poorer classes of New Mexicans felt threatened by these norteamericanos. According to these case trials, robberies committed against foreigners often netted little more than simple material goods not readily available to the poorer people in New Mexico. The cases also indicate that there were some North Americans who settled peacefully among New Mexicans.

Even a cursory glance at the case files brings to mind the importance of the Catholic faith in the lives of Hispanic New Mexicans. When witnesses were sworn in, they were asked to state their name, age, marital status, occupation, place of residence, and religion. The religion of Hispanic witnesses was always "Católico," sometimes written "RCAR" (religión católico apostólico romano). In one case, the trial of Francisco Rael, the defendant was asked to prove that he was Catholic, and his religion was questioned when the priest could not find his baptismal records. In almost every case where a Catholic died, a priest was called to see that the victim was given a Christian burial. A shortage of clergy is evident in trial records. Small communities had no resident priest; often the priest had to be summoned from the parish church many miles away. Consequently, victims of violent attacks who did not die immediately often did not receive last rights.

The cases involving domestic violence indicate a patriarchal society in which women were controlled and coerced into proper behavior by the males in their family. One alcalde spoke of "correcting" a wife's behavior; a prosecutor advised that it would have been alright for the husband to use "force" to make his wife do his bidding. This was suggested as a way to deal with a wayward wife's disobedience — an alternative to the violence that had occurred. One prosecutor commented about "bonds of love that all husbands should possess for their wives," and one alcalde, when speaking of wife-murder, said it was "the worst crime that a man could commit."

The comments of these men, who had been called upon to serve in trials as judges, defenders, and prosecutors, reflect the views of a paternalistic, male-dominated society, a society that believed in the sanctity of marriage and the family, and the need for men to control women. This world view included the concept of honor, which played an important role in several of the murder cases. Men were expected to be aggressive in defense of their honor and the honor of their family.

Here we have a fundamental understanding of New Mexico Hispanic society based solely on a handful of murder trials. Murder trials tell us about crime and the administration of justice, but they also expose a great deal about the society in which they occur. Almost every aspect of Hispanic society in Mexican New Mexico was touched on in these few homicide cases.

Glossary of Spanish Terms

Abogado: Lawyer
Acequia: Irrigation ditch
Acusador: Complainant, accuser
Aguardiente: Locally made whiskey or brandy
Alcaide: Warden, jailer
Alcalde: Civil official with judicial, legislative and executive functions; mayor, magistrate, justice of the peace. Santa Fe had two alcaldes, primero (first) and segundo (second).
Alcalde constitucional: Replaced the alcalde mayor of colonial times
Alcaldes mayores: Magistrate who presided over alcaldías during colonial times
Alcaldía: Political division of New Mexico under the Spanish crown
Alférez: A field-grade military officer, ranking between a second lieutenant and a colonel
Alguacil: Constable, peace officer, sheriff
Asamblea: The legislature under the departmental plan (first called the Junta)
Asesor: A legal adviser
Asesoría: Office of legal adviser
Audiencia: Superior tribunal during Spanish colonial times
Auto cabeza de proceso: Court order for the investigation of a crime
Auto de bien preso: Act to insure that a prisoner was secured
Auto de prisión: Arrest warrant
Auto de prueba: Act or writ of evidence to ratify the witnesses
Ayuntamiento: Municipal council, city hall

Baile: Dance, ball, party
Bando: Edict, proclamation
Barrio: Small community or neighborhood adjacent to larger community

Bosque: Woods or wooded area along a river bank or other body of water, usually cottonwoods

Cabeceras: Head city established in each partido
Cabo: Corporal
Cabresto: Horsehair rope, rope (regional usage)
Cabestro: Halter
Campo santo: Cemetery
Cantor: Singer, religious song leader
Cárcel: Prison, jail
Careo: Comparison or confrontation between witnesses and/or defendant
Cargos: Charges, accusations
Casas reales: Palace of the Governors on the Santa Fe plaza where the government offices were located
Ciboleros: Buffalo hunters
Cirujano: Surgeon
Colcha: Bed covering, quilt
Comancheros: People who went out into the plains to trade with the Comanche
Comandante: Military commander
Comandante General: Commander general
Compadrazgo: Relationship between parents and godparents of a child
Compañera: Female companion
Confesión: Confession
Cordón de nervio: Sinew cord
Cortes: Spanish legislative body
Criado: Servant
Criador: Person engaged in the occupation of raising or breeding stock
Cura: Secular priest
Curador: Legal guardian for a minor, legal defender of Indians
Curandero: Folk healer
Chicharra: Insect, cicada, katydid

Declaración: Testimony
Dedo: Finger or toe; as a unit of measure, forty-eighth part of a Spanish vara
Defensor: Counsel for the defense
Desvergüenza: Shamelessness, impudence
Difunto: The deceased; used in these cases to refer to the murder victim
Diligencias matrimoniales: Marital investigations to determine if impediments to a marriage exist
Diputación: Territorial legislature

Embargo de bienes: Confiscation of suspect's goods to pay court costs
En fragante: In the very act

Escribano público: Notary public
Escrito: Bill, brief, writ, written plea
Exposición: Petition, address
Extraordinario violento: Special messenger or courier
Extranjero: Foreigner, stranger

Familia: Family
Fandango: Dance, shindig
Fanega: Grain measure equivalent to one and a half bushels
Fe de heridas: Examination of the wounds of the victim (also called reconocimiento de heridas)
Fiador: One who posts bond or bail for another
Folio: Sheet of paper folded in the middle, making two leaves or four pages of a document; folios in legal cases were numbered only on the front side of each leaf
Formal prisión: Lawful imprisonment
Fueros: Special privileges given to military and religious personnel that allowed them to be tried in their own tribunals

Generales de la ley: Disqualification of a potential witness due to some legally disabling personal circumstance (age, close friendship or kinship ties, "interest," etc.)
Genízaros: Detribalized Christian Indians living among Hispanics. These people or their forbearers were captives ransomed by the Spanish and brought up in Spanish households as servants. Once their ransom was paid, they were free to leave. Not being accepted as either Indian or Spanish, genízaros often were forced to settle frontier areas where they formed a defensive buffer between indios bárbaros and Hispanic settlements.
Gente de razón: Literally "people of reason;" settled people of Hispanic culture, regardless of ethnic background
Gente fina: Small group of elite families that controlled the wealth and dominated society
Gentiles: Non-Christian, nomadic Indians (Apaches, Comanches, Kiowas, Navajos, Pawnees, Utes, Wichitas, etc.) that roamed the fringe areas around Mexican settlements, trading with or making raids against the inhabitants.
Golpe: Blow, slap, hit, or stroke
Grillos/grilletes/par de grillos: Fetters, shackles, or irons to secure a prisoner
Guitarristas: Musicians who play the guitar

Hacienda: Estate, lands
Hermandad: Brotherhood
Hermano carnal: Full brother
Hispanos: Hispanics; people of Spanish descent, native to the American Southwest

Indiana: Calico
Indios bárbaros: Literally "wild Indians" (see Gentiles)

Jacal: Dwelling made of sticks and twigs, and patched with adobe clay (wattle and daub); also refers to this type of construction
Jefe político: Political chief, governor
Jerga: Course twilled wool used for rugs, carpets
Juez/jueces: Judge/judges, in New Mexico; usually did not have any formal legal training
Juez actuante: Acting judge
Juez de paz: Magistrate, justice of the peace, replaced the alcalde constitucional when New Mexico was a department (after 1836)
Juez de primera instancia: Judge of the first instance
Juez letrado: A judge trained in the law
Juicio criminal: Criminal trial, judgement
Juzgado: Jurisdiction of a court

Las posadas: Miracle play performed at Christmas
Letrado: Lawyer, counselor
Leyenda negra: "Black Legend" purporting Spanish cruelty, dating from time of conquest and spread by countries jealous of Spain's power
Licenciado: Licentiate
Luminarias: Festive lights, lit especially at Christmas time

Maestro: Teacher; master of a trade or profession
Mala vida: Bad life
Manta: Covering; woven cotton cloth used in making clothing
Mayordomo Boss, foreman, ditch boss, overseer, sponsor of the annual church fiesta
Memorial: Petition, memorial, memorandum
Monte: A popular card game where money was wagered
Mozo: Youth, lad, manservant

Noria: Machinery for drawing water from a well; in common usage, a well

Obraje: Workshops where wool was manufactured; sometimes used as a place where criminals were detained and forced to labor
Onza de oro: Doubloon; a gold coin worth about sixteen silver pesos or sixteen U.S. dollars.

Padre: Father, priest
Paisano: Countryman, peasant; civilian; also roadrunner (a native New Mexican bird)
Panaderos: Spanish dance
Papel común: Common paper, not stamped for official use
Papel sellado: Stamped paper used for official business

Paraje: Place, spot
Parroquia: Parish church
Partidario: Shepherd who contracted to herd the flocks of another in return for a portion of the animals
Partido: A political division of New Mexico from 1823 to 1836; also a system of stock raising where a shepherd contracted to take care of a flock of sheep in exchange for part (partido) of the flock
Patrón: Boss
Plaza: Square, place, village
Pena capital: Capital punishment, death penalty
Pena del último suplicio: Capital punishment, execution
Pena ordinaria: Customary penalty
Peninsulare: Spaniard, born in Spain but living in the Americas
Penitentes: Common name for members of the religious confraternity the Brotherhood of Our Father Jesus the Nazarene (la Cofradiá de Nuestro Padre Jesús Nazareno)
Peón: Unskilled laborers who often became indebted to the patrón
Perito: Expert, expert witness
Peso: Mexican unit of money roughly equal to one U.S. dollar during the Mexican Era
Plenario: Stage in judicial proceedings following the sumaria, and preceding the sentencia, when both parties in a case offer their respective positions
Pobladores: Settlers
Portales: Portico
Practicante: Practitioner; one who practices medicine under the guidance of a physician. Since there were no medical doctors in New Mexico at this time (with the possible exception of the surgeon for the Santa Fe Company or a foreign doctor) this term may have applied to a curandero.
Prefectura/subprefectura: Political divisions of the department of New Mexico after 1836 (partidos)
Presidio: Place where soldiers were garrisoned; sometimes used as a place to send prisoners
Procurador: Attorney, counselor
Procurador de pobres: Attorney appointed for someone who could not afford to pay legal fees
Procurador síndico: Attorney elected as part of the town council
Promotor fiscal: Prosecutor
Protector de Indios: During colonial times, an agent that acted as a legal representative for Indians in the Spanish courts
Punche: A locally grown New Mexican tobacco
Publicación de probanzas: Make public the evidence in a judicial case
Puñalada: A stab with a *puñal* (a dagger or poniard)

Rancho: Small farmstead
Ratificación: Ratification; a process by which the witnesses and prisoner verified their statements
Razón: Explanation to clarify legal proceedings
Real: Coin worth one-eighth of a peso; mining town
Reclamo: Claim, protest
Recopilación (Recopilación de leyes de los reynos de las Indias): Compilation of the laws of the kingdom of the Indies, promulgated in 1680
Regidor: A municipal councilman
Reo: Convict, criminal, defendant
Ricos: Wealthy people
Río Abajo: Downriver; the geographic area south of the La Bajada Mesa
Río Arriba: Upriver; the geographic area north of the La Bajada Mesa
Riña: Argument, quarrel, dispute
Rúbrica: Mark or flourish added to a signature, sometimes written without the signature

Sala: Main room in the home, a parlor; law court
Salteadores: Highwaymen
Santa visita: Visitation (inspection) by a church official
Sarape: Woven blanket worn as a shawl or cloak
Sello cuarto: Official paper that was folded into quarters (folios) and stamped on the front and back
Sentencia: Judgement of a case, sentencing
Sentencia difinitiva: Final judgement
Sin comunicación: Referring to a prisoner denied communication
Sin vergüenza: Shameless, immoral
Sirviente: Servant
Sumaria: Preliminary investigation of the crime by a magistrate
Superior tribunal de justicia: Superior court of justice

Tacha: Challenge; disqualification of witness
Teguas: Hard-soled hide Indian moccasins
Terna: List of candidates for governor sent by the diputación to the National Congress in Mexico City
Testigo: Witness
Testigo acusador: Witness accusing the defendant
Testigos de asistencia: Attending witnesses; ordinary citizens who witnessed legal proceedings, acting in the absence of escribanos (notaries)
Tierra sagrada: Holy ground, cemetery

Vado: Ford, river crossing
Valse: Waltz

Vara: Spanish unit of measure equivalent to a yard (approximately thirty-three inches)
Vara de justicia: Staff of justice, symbol of office
Vecino: Neighbor, citizen, resident; head of the household
Velas: Candles
Velorio: Wake or vigil held prior to a funeral
Vergüenza: Literally "shame;" for women, a code of modesty and purity; for men, a good reputation with fellow citizens
Villas: Cities that were founded by a charter
Violinista: Musicians who played the violin
Vocal: Member of the legislature

Notes

INTRODUCTION

1. Colonel Stephen Watts Kearny received his commission as Brigadier General while he was in Las Vegas, New Mexico, before he entered Santa Fe. John P. Wilson, "The American Occupation of Santa Fe," in *Santa Fe: History of an Ancient City*, ed. David Grant Noble (Santa Fe: School of American Research Press, 1989), 104.

2. For a brief history of the Sender Collection, see Richard Salazar, comp., introduction to *Calendar to the Microfilm Edition of the Sender Collection, 1697–1884* (Santa Fe: Archives Division of the New Mexico State Records Center and Archives, 1988).

3. David J. Weber, *The Mexican Frontier, 1821–1846: The American Southwest Under Mexico* (Albuquerque: University of New Mexico Press, 1982), 195. Census statistics for these years are sketchy and sometimes conflicting. For census information during the years 1820–21, see Lansing Bartlett Bloom, "New Mexico Under Mexican Administration, 1821–1846," *Old Santa Fe* 1 (July 1913): 28–30. A census for 1827 showing a total population of 43,433, excluding nomadic tribes, is quoted in H. Bailey Carroll and J. Villasana Haggard, eds., trans, *Three New Mexico Chronicles: The Exposición of Don Pedro Bautista Pino 1812; the Ojeada of Lic. Antonio Barreiro 1832; and the additions by Don José Agustín de Escudero, 1849* (Albuquerque: The Quivira Society, 1942), 88–89. Virginia Langham Olmsted, G. R. S., has collected censuses for three years in *New Mexico Spanish and Mexican Colonial Censuses, 1790, 1823, 1845* (Albuquerque: New Mexico Genealogical Society Inc., 1975). The 1790 one is the most complete, the 1823 census is mostly for the various barrios in Santa Fe, and the 1845 census is incomplete, giving figures mostly for the northern and eastern communities. Other censuses are scattered inconsistently throughout the archives.

4. Josiah Gregg, *Commerce of the Prairies*, ed. Max L. Moorhead (Norman: University of Oklahoma Press, 1954), 165.

5. David J. Weber, "The New Mexico Archives in 1827," *New Mexico Historical Review* 61 (January 1986): 54.

6. This was Governor William A. Pile, in 1869. Fortunately, a wood hauler from Cieneguita rescued these documents and returned them to the territorial librarian many years later. Daniel Tyler, *Sources for New Mexican History, 1821–1848* (Santa Fe: Museum of New Mexico Press, 1984), 12, 13.

7. Bent to Alvarez, 10 December 1839, Benjamin Read Collection (hereafter cited as BR), no. 39.

8. Thomas E. Chávez, *Conflict and Acculturation: Manuel Alvarez's 1842 Memorial* (Santa Fe: Museum of New Mexico Press, 1989), 57.

9. Ibid., 26–27.

10. John E. Sunder, ed., *Matt Field on the Santa Fe Trail* (Norman: University of Oklahoma Press, 1960), 229–30.

11. Journals and accounts kept by foreigners and merchants who visited New Mexico during the Mexican Period, or shortly after, are especially helpful sources. These works have become important, if somewhat biased, accounts of New Mexico during this time. Some of the best known works of this nature are as follows: Josiah Gregg, *Commerce*; Stella M. Drumm, ed., *Down the Santa Fe Trail and into Mexico: The Diary of Susan Shelby Magoffin, 1846–1847* (1962; reprint, Lincoln: University of Nebraska Press, Bison Books, 1982); James Josiah Webb, *Adventures in the Santa Fe Trade, 1844–1847*, ed. Ralph P. Bieber (1931; reprint, Philadelphia: Porcupine Press, 1974); Sunder, *Matt Field*; Albert Pike, *Prose Sketches and Poems, Written in the Western Country*, ed. David J. Weber (Albuquerque: Calvin Horn Publishers, Inc., 1967); W. W. H. Davis, *El Gringo, New Mexico and her People* (1857; reprint, Lincoln: University of Nebraska Press, Bison Books, 1982); Lewis H. Garrard, *Wah-To-Yah and the Taos Trail*, ed. Ralph P. Bieber (1838; reprint, Philadelphia: Porcupine Press, 1974).

12. Among the published accounts written by New Mexicans, Mexicans, or Spaniards about early-nineteenth-century New Mexico are three works translated and edited by H. Bailey Carroll and J. Villasana Haggard in *Three Chronicles.* Donaciano Vigil, a native New Mexican of the time, wrote about the problems of New Mexico at the end of the Mexican Era: David J. Weber ed., *Arms, Indians, and the Mismanagement of New Mexico: Donaciano Vigil, 1846* (El Paso: Texas Western Press, 1986). Another work written by a Spaniard complained of the problems foreigners living in New Mexico faced during the latter half of the Mexican Era: Thomas Chávez, *Conflict*; see also David J. Weber, ed., *Northern Mexico on the Eve of the United States Invasion: Rare Imprints Concerning California, Arizona, New Mexico, and Texas, 1821–1846* (New York: Arno Press, 1976). In this last selection, imprints 4–7 pertain to New Mexico, and they include writings by Manuel de Jesús Rada (1829) and writings by and about the Taos priest, Antonio José Martínez (1843).

13. According to sociologists, these are nearly universal categories of association in which homicides occur. William B. Taylor, *Drinking, Homicide, and Rebellion, in Colonial Mexican Villages* (Stanford: Stanford University Press, 1979), 85.

14. Charges against women for assault or homicide are quite rare. See ibid., 83–88, on aggressor/victim relationships. Although Taylor studied cases from central and southern Mexico, the conclusions he draws are relevant to any study of domestic violence.

15. Charles Ross Cutter, "Judicial Practice in Northern New Spain, 1700–1810" (Ph.D. diss., University of New Mexico, 1989), 140. Gutiérrez defines three categories of civic status: vecinos (landowners), residentes (residents), and naturales (natives) of a certain town or settlement. Ramón A. Gutiérrez, *When Jesus Came, the Corn Mothers Went Away: Marriage, Sexuality, and Power in New Mexico, 1500–1846* (Stanford: Stanford University Press, 1991), 104. All three terms were used in the cases; most considered themselves vecinos.

16. David J. Weber, ed., *Foreigners in their Native Land: Historical Roots of the Mexican Americans* (Albuquerque: University of New Mexico Press, 1987), 61.

17. See for example, George Frederick Ruxton in LeRoy R. Hafen, ed., *Ruxton of the Rockies: Autobiographical Writings by the author of "Adventures in Mexico and the Rocky Mountains" and "Life in the Far West"* (Norman: University of Oklahoma Press, 1950), 182; also Rufus Sage in Weber, *Foreigners*, 71–74.

CHAPTER ONE

1. For a general work on the Mexican Era on the northern frontier, see Weber, *Mexican Frontier*; Bloom, "Mexican Administration," and Marc Simmons, *New Mexico: An Interpretive History* (1977; reprint, Albuquerque: University of New Mexico Press, 1988), 107–31.

2. Captain William Becknell, the first foreigner successfully to traverse the Santa Fe Trail with a wagon and open up trade with New Mexicans, earned for himself the title "Father of the Santa Fe Trail." According to Max Moorhead (*Royal Road*, 60 nn. 12, 13, the journal of this historic trip was written up by his brother: Thomas Becknell, "The Journals of Capt. Thomas Becknell, from Boone's Lick to Santa Fe, and from Santa Cruz to Green River," *Missouri Historical Review* 4 (January 1910): 65–84; see also Larry M. Beachum, *William Becknell, Father of the Santa Fe Trade* (El Paso: Texas Western Press, 1982.)

3. David J. Weber, *The Taos Trappers: The Fur Trade in the Far Southwest, 1540–1846* (Norman: University of Oklahoma Press, 1970).

4. Rebecca McDowell Craver, *The Impact of Intimacy: Mexican-Anglo Intermarriage in New Mexico, 1821–1846*, Southwestern Studies Series, no. 66 (El Paso: Texas Western Press, 1982).

5. For information on land grants see Victor Westphall, *Mercedes Reales: Hispanic Land Grants of the Upper Río Grande Region*, New Mexico Land Grant Series, ed. John R. Van Ness, vol. 1 (Albuquerque: University of New Mexico Press, 1983).

6. Max L. Moorhead, *New Mexico's Royal Road: Trade and Travel on the Chihuahua Trail* (Norman: University of Oklahoma Press, 1958); John O. Baxter, *Las Car-*

neradas: Sheep Trade in New Mexico, 1700–1860 (Albuquerque: University of New Mexico Press, 1987).

7. Janet Lecompte, "Manuel Armijo's Family History," *New Mexico Historical Review* 48 (July 1973): 252–53.

8. Armijo's first term in office was from 1827 to 1829. In 1837 Armijo took over as governor, after he put down a rebellion in which the unfortunate governor Albino Pérez lost his life. Armijo remained in office until 1844, when he retired for health reasons; however, he resumed the governorship again eighteen months later in 1845, shortly after Jefe Político Mariano Martínez de Lejanza, an unpopular outsider, was removed from that office. Daniel Tyler, "Gringo Views of Governor Manuel Armijo," *New Mexico Historical Review* 45 (January 1970): 23, 28, 37.

9. This was more than half the amount of land granted by both Spanish and Mexican authorities in the entire history of the region. Westphall, *Mercedes Reales*, 52.

10. Peonage in New Mexico was closely tied to the partido system of raising sheep, especially on the large estates of the Río Abajo families. Partidarios, were shepherds who contracted to care for the herds of wealthy sheep ranchers, in exchange for a certain number of the sheep. Indian raids and inclement weather often resulted in losses that the partidario was unable to repay, leading to a form of peonage to the wealthy patrón. See Weber, *Mexican Frontier*, 212; Baxter, *Las Carneradas*, 28–29. José Agustín de Escudero's "Noticias" in Carroll and Haggard's *Three Chronicles*, 41–42, gives an idealized version of how the partido system worked.

11. Janet Lecompte, *Rebellion in Río Arriba, 1837* (Albuquerque: University of New Mexico Press, 1985).

12. Regarding the distinction between the Río Arriba and Río Abajo, see Lecompte, *Rebellion*, 3–7, and T. M. Pearce, ed., *New Mexico Place Names: A Geographical Dictionary* (Albuquerque: University of New Mexico Press, 1965), 133.

13. G. Emlen Hall and David J. Weber, "Mexican Liberals and the Pueblo Indians, 1821–1829," *New Mexico Historical Review* 59 (January 1984): 5. The Pueblos themselves were not a homogeneous entity; each tribe had its own governor, and they did not all share the same language. There were three major linguistic groups (Keres, Zuñi, and Tanoan) among the Pueblos, and the last was further divided into three separate languages (Tewa, Tiwa, and Towa). See Warren A. Beck and Ynez D. Haase, *Historical Atlas of New Mexico* (Norman: University of Oklahoma Press, 1985), 57.

14. For a detailed account of Indian hostilities against New Mexican settlements in the last years of the Mexican Period, see Ward Alan Minge, "Frontier Problems in New Mexico Preceding the Mexican War, 1840–1846" (Ph.D. diss., University of New Mexico, 1965), 283–97. For an account written by a native New Mexican of the time, Donaciano Vigil, in 1846, see Weber, *Arms*, 1–8. Father Martínez wrote an exposition to Santa Anna in 1843, complaining about Indian hostilities caused by North Americans depleting the animals that the natives depended on for their food

supply. Antonio José Martínez to Sr. General Antonio López de Santa Anna, 1843. Weber, *Rare Imprints*, imprint no. 5.

15. On the Taos trade fair, see Bloom, "Mexican Administration," *Old Santa Fe* 1 (July 1913): 39, and Weber, *Taos Trappers*, 10. On the Abiquiú trade fair with the Utes, see Frances Leon Swadesh, *Los Primeros Pobladores: Hispanic Americans of the Ute Frontier* (Notre Dame: University of Notre Dame Press, 1974), 47.

16. Magnaghi says that the best definition of genízaros was made by Fray Agustín Morfí in 1779: "This name is given to the children of the captives of different [Indian] nations who have married in the province." In eighteenth- and nineteenth-century New Mexico genízaros were considered as "children of the enemy." Russell M. Magnaghi, "The Genízaro Experience in Spanish New Mexico," in *Spain and the Plains: Myths and Realities of Spanish Exploration and Settlement on the Great Plains*, ed. Ralph H. Vigil, Francis W. Kaye, and John R. Wunder (Niwot: University of Colorado Press, 1994), 115–20.

17. According to Swadesh, some genízaros were Pueblos who had been expelled from the pueblo because they had become too Hispanic in their actions. Swadesh, *Primeros Pobladores*, xviii.

18. On the decline of the presidios and the poor defense of the northern Mexican frontier, see Weber, *Mexican Frontier*, 107–21, and Lecompte, *Rebellion*, 9–11; on military problems, Antonio Barreiro, "Ojeada," in Carroll and Haggard, *Three Chronicles*, 74–82.

19. On the decline of the church during the Mexican Period, see Weber, *Mexican Frontier*, 69–82, and Antonio Barreiro, "Ojeada," in Carroll and Haggard, *Three Chronicles*, 53–55.

20. Marta Weigle, *Brothers of Light, Brothers of Blood: The Penitentes of the Southwest* (Santa Fe: Ancient City Press, 1976).

21. Weber, *Mexican Frontier*, 234. Licenciado Antonio Barreiro lamented, in his "Ojeada Sobre Nuevo Mexico" in 1832, that the schools were in a deplorable condition, there was a scarcity of books, no newspapers, and no printing press. Carroll and Haggard, *Three Chronicles*, 95–96.

22. Weber, *Mexican Frontier*, 231, 360 n. 103. For a recent work on literacy and education in New Mexico during the Spanish colonial period, see Bernardo P. Gallegos, *Literacy, Education, and Society in New Mexico, 1693–1821* (Albuquerque: University of New Mexico Press, 1992).

23. After its arrival in New Mexico, the press was purchased by Ramón Abréu, and for a month it was used by Antonio Barreiro, who published New Mexico's first newspaper, *El Crepúsculo de la Libertad* (The Dawn of Liberty). A rather exalted title for a paper that was used primarily as a campaign devise for Barreiro's re-election to the National Congress.

Two other newspapers appeared in the 1840s, both edited by Donaciano Vigil: *La Verdad* was published from November 1842 to June 1845 and was succeeded by the short-lived, *El Payo*, which only lasted a few months. Annabelle Oczon, "Bilingual and Spanish-Language Newspapers in Territorial New Mexico," Calvin Horn Essay, *New Mexico Historical Review* 54 (January 1979): 45–46. Examples of early printing on this press are included in Henry R. Wagner, "New Mexico Spanish Press," *New Mexico Historical Review* 12 (January 1987): 1–40. Padre Martínez was the first native secular priest in New Mexico. A well-educated man himself, Martínez recognized the need to improve education in New Mexico. He opened a coeducational primary school in Taos in 1826, and in 1833 he was given permission to open a seminary. Ray John de Aragón, "Padre Antonio José Martínez: the Man and the Myth," in *Padre Martínez: New Perspectives From Taos* (Taos: Millicent Rogers Museum, 1988), 129–130.

24. Josiah Gregg, *Commerce*, 143. The census in 1827 lists only one doctor, a surgeon in Santa Fe. This was probably the doctor at the presidio. Weber, *Mexican Frontier*, 236.

25. Bloom, "Mexican Administration," *Santa Fe* 1 (1913): 28–31. This is a 21 percent average annual rate of increase, which was twice as much as Mexico as a whole experienced but much less than Texas or California. Weber, *Mexican Frontier*, 195.

26. Some villages that originated during the Mexican Period were Antón Chico (1822), Tecolote (1838), Las Vegas (1835), the two towns of Mora, San Antonio, and Santa Gertrudis (by 1835), and in the west, Cubero (1833). Many new settlements were founded as family groups splintered off from one town and moved into the next valley to find new pasture for their flocks. Often settlers were driven off by nomadic Indians. Richard L. Nostrand, "The Century of Hispano Expansion," *New Mexico Historical Review* 62 (October 1987): 361–86.

27. Weber, *Mexican Frontier*, 195.

28. On U.S. expansionism during this period, see Josefina Zoraida Vásquez and Lorenzo Meyer, *The United States and Mexico* (Chicago: University of Chicago Press, 1985), 25–50.

29. James Magoffin was the brother-in-law of Susan Shelby Magoffin, who was in a merchant caravan following behind Kearny and his Army of the West in 1846. James caught up with the caravan and the army at Bent's Fort in July. He went on ahead with a small party into Santa Fe, where he met with Governor Armijo. Drumm, *Magoffin*, xxiv–xxvi.

30. Simmons, *Interpretive History*, 125–27.

CHAPTER TWO

1. Barreiro, "Ojeada," in Carroll and Haggard, *Three Chronicles*, 60.

2. Speaking of the alcaldes mayores of pre-Independence New Mexico, Cutter suggests that they were entrusted with these positions because they were literate and respected men of good social standing who learned through experience. Cutter, "Judicial," 121, 123–25.

3. Tyler, *Sources*, 4.

4. Tyler, *Sources*, 4–6.

5. The four villas and the pueblos they administered were as follows: Santa Fe (Bado, Cochití, Jémez, and Alameda); Alburquerque (Isleta, Tomé, Belén, Laguna, and Socorro); Santa Cruz de la Cañada (San Juan, Abiquiú, and Taos); El Paso del Norte (San Lorenzo and Isleta del Paso). Bloom, "Mexican Administration," *Santa Fe* 1 (1913): 158.

6. In 1836, the department of New Mexico was divided as follows. First Prefectura: Partido 1 — Santa Fe, Bado, San Ildefonso; Partido 2 — Cañada, Taos, Abiquiú, Ojo Caliente, San Juan, Chama, Trampas. Second Prefectura: Partido 1 — Cochití, Jémez, Sandía, Alburquerque; Partido 2 — Isleta, Valencia, Tomé, Belén, Sabinal, Socorro, Laguna, Zuñi, and Acoma. Tyler, *Sources*, 10.

7. The 1844 division of New Mexico worked as follows. Río Arriba, or Northern District: headed by Santa Cruz de la Cañada — Chimayó, Truchas, Trampas, San Juan, Taos, Mora, Abiquiú, Rito Colorado, Ojo Caliente, Río de Chama, and Chamita; Central District: headed by Santa Fe — San Ildefonso, Sierra Blanca, Jémez, Algodones, Angostura, Santa Ana, Zia, San Felipe, Santo Domingo, Chile, Cochití, Bado, Tecolote, and Vegas; Río Abajo, or Southeastern District: headed by Alburquerque — Bernalillo, Corrales, Alameda, Ranchos Padillas, Valencia, Tomé, Laguna, Belén, Sabinal, and Socorro. Tyler, *Sources*, 10. Minge gives quite a different version of the 1844 restructuring of the department under Governor Mariano Martínez. Minge, "Problems," 212–13.

8. Marc Simmons, *Spanish Government in New Mexico* (Albuquerque: University of New Mexico Press, 1968), 212–13.

9. Tyler, *Sources*, 7, 8.

10. Lynn Perrigo, "New Mexico in the Mexican Period, as revealed in the Torres Documents," *New Mexico Historical Review* 29 (January 1954): 35; Tyler, *Sources*, 8–10,

11. Tyler, *Sources*, 4, 5, 10. Only four of New Mexico's governors during the Mexican Era were not from New Mexico. They were Colonel José Antonio Vizcarra (1822–23), Colonel Antonio Narbona (1825–27), Colonel Albino Pérez (1835–37), and General Mariano Martínez (1844–45). Bloom, "Mexican Administration," *Santa Fe* 2 (1915): 224.

12. Tyler, *Sources*, 4, 5.

13. Weber, *Mexican Frontier*, 37.

14. Simmons, *Spanish in New Mexico*, 177–78.

15. Weber, *Mexican Frontier*, 37–38; Tyler, *Sources*, 8.

16. Weber, *Rare Imprints*, imprint no. 4, Manuel de Jesús Rada.

17. Carroll and Haggard, *Three Chronicles*, xx.

18. Bloom, "Mexican Administration," *Santa Fe* 2 (1914): 12; Carroll and Haggard, *Three Chronicles*, xx–xxi, 60–61.

19. Barreiro, "Ojeada," in Carroll and Haggard, *Three Chronicles*, 45.

20. Weber, *Mexican Frontier*, 38.

21. Bloom, "Mexican Administration," *Santa Fe* 2 (1914): 136.

22. Minge, "Problems," 211–14.

23. Weber, *Mexican Frontier*, 234–35.

24. Even in high government offices it was possible to find persons who were illiterate; two of the seven deputies to the departmental junta in 1837 could neither read nor write. Bloom, "Mexican Administration," *Santa Fe* 2 (1914): 13, 14.

25. Josiah Gregg, *Commerce*, 143.

26. Gregg mentioned that *hombres buenos* (arbitrators) were often called upon to aid the acting judge in deciding a case. Josiah Gregg, *Commerce*, 164. (In the homicide cases reviewed in this work, the term "hombres buenos" never occurred.)

27. "firmo con testigos de asistencia actuando por receptoria por falta de escrivano [*sic*] publico que no lo hay." Juan José Lucero, Corrales, 22 December 1842, Mexican Archives of New Mexico (hereafter cited as MANM), roll 32, frame 134.

28. "La presente causa se sigue en papel común por no haber de oficio en la administración pr[ovinci]al de rentas según se le [h]a comunicado por aquella oficina en oficio de 3 del corriente y para que no padesca nulidad alguna por la falta indicada." Jesús María C. de Baca, juez de paz, Santo Domingo, 22 January 1846, MANM, roll 10, frame 496.

29. "Destinado solamente para las causas criminales." Due to the scarcity of stamped paper, out-of-date paper was often updated and used later. The case of Juan Valdez, adjudicated in 1826 was written on paper dated 1810–11 and contained the royal seal of Carlos IV. The paper had been updated several times with the seal of Fernando VII and dates as late as 1817. MANM, roll 5, frame 1016.

30. Josiah Gregg, *Commerce*, 164–65.

31. Weber, "Archives," 55–56.

32. Perrigo, "Torres Documents," 35.

33. Simmons, *Spanish in New Mexico*, 186.

34. Cutter suggests that alcaldes mayores of pre-Independence New Mexico were chosen for their abilities and leadership qualities. They were literate and respected men in their communities and not deserving of the contempt with which contemporary and modern writers have often viewed them. Cutter, "Judicial," 118–24.

35. This procedure is detailed in ibid., 156–229.

36. Ibid., 160–61, 208.

37. In the eight homicide cases where a body was found, five were either examined by peritos or the acting judge. One was examined by Mariano Larrañaga surgeon of the Santa Fe Company, one by a foreign doctor Henrique Masure, and another by a cirujano whose name appeared to be Autin Reina.

38. Licenciado Vitoriano Guerra, who consulted the Daily case, gave a fairly detailed rundown of how a homicide case should have been conducted. Guerra to juez de primera instancia, Santa Fe, 21 August 1843, MANM, roll 25, frames 205–12.

39. Gregg claimed "Generally speaking, however, the process of examination is gone through without a single oath being administered; and in the absence of witnesses, the alcalde often proceeds to sentence upon the single statements of the

contending parties." Josiah Gregg, *Commerce*, 164. This was definitely not true in homicide cases.

40. See the Gonzales case where an old mare is taken from the prisoner and sold at an auction to pay his expenses in jail. MANM, roll 32, frame 146. Bloom gives the charge at one peso per day. Bloom, "Mexican Administration," *Santa Fe* 1 (1913): 152.

41. Alcalde Baca, 7 June 1826, MANM, roll 5, frames 1044–45.

42. Sender Collection, roll 1, document 124.

43. If it is possible to draw any conclusions from so few homicide cases, it would appear that the defense was weakened in plenario proceedings in the Mexican Era. During colonial times, the first stage of the plenario was the naming of a defensor, followed by the ratification of the accused in the presence of this defensor. Cutter, "Judicial," 192–93. The Mexican homicide cases indicate that the suspect was called upon to make a formal confession before he was allowed to name a defensor. The Mexican cases also reveal that the juez de paz or alcalde normally appointed a promotor fiscal to prosecute the case against the suspect, but in colonial times apparently this was not the case.

44. Cutter, "Judicial," 191–92. The Moya and Salazar cases are examples of incomplete plenarios.

45. Ibid., 192. For examples see the Herrera, Armenta, Pulsiphur, Daily, and Moya cases.

46. Ibid., 199.

47. Mariano Martínez in the trial against Alférez Lara for the murder of Antonio Moya. MANM, roll 33, frames 958–72.

48. Cutter, "Judicial," 194–95.

49. "Por estar ynposibilitado, [*sic*] por las Generales de la Ley para conoser [*sic*] o dar fe de un asesinato que acaba de perpetrarse en la persona de mi hermano d. Pablo Salasar,." Letter from juez de paz of Tomé, don José Salazar, 4 March 1844. MANM, roll 36, frame 346.

50. This step in the plenario was not mentioned by Cutter. It appears that no prosecutor was appointed during colonial times and that the magistrate who had investigated the crime was the prosecutor as well.

51. Cutter mentions that some individuals hired procuradores to defend them. This apparently was the case with Francisco Rael, accused murderer of his servant boy Juan José Montoya. MANM, roll 33, frames 1020–22.

52. In at least one case, the alcalde was able to find a lawyer visiting in the department who could advise a case. Anastacio Sandoval advised the accused murderer Juan Antonio Chaves that he was turning the case over to Licenciado Jesús María Palacio in La Peralta, 5 August 1846. MANM, roll 41, frame 533.

53. Licenciado Vitoriano Guerra to juez de primera instancia in Santa Fe, 21 August 1843, MANM, roll 25, frames 205–12.

54. According to a law from *Novísima Recopilación* written on the back of a letter

from Juan B. Vigil y Alarid to Francisco Ortiz y Delgado, 19 November 1838, "Porque la cárcel no fue establecido para castigar, sino para custodiar a los presos mientras se substancian sus causas." MANM, roll 25, frame 260.

55. Order of Juez de Paz José Francisco Ortiz, Santa Fe, 14 July 1839, MANM, roll 25, frames 141–43. In colonial New Mexico any sentence calling for capital punishment was sent to a superior court such as the audiencia in Guadalajara for approval. Cutter, "Judicial," 217–18.

56. Gregg, *Commerce*, 166.

57. Taylor, *Drinking*, 98; Gabriel James Haslip, "Crime and the Administration of Justice in Colonial Mexico City, 1696–1810" (Ph.D. diss., Columbia University, 1980), 202–03; Cutter, "Judicial," 218.

58. Robert J. Tórrez, "Justice in Spanish Colonial and Territorial New Mexico: A Comparative Perspective," Lecture, 1989, 13–14, 18–21. For a discussion of the murder of the Frenchman and subsequent punishment of the accused, see Lansing B. Bloom, "The Death of Jacques D'Eglise," *New Mexico Historical Review* 2 (October 1927): 369–79. Also Cutter, mentioned that after examining hundreds of cases during the period 1700–1810 he only found a few examples of the death sentence that had actually been carried out. Cutter, "Judicial," 217.

59. Punishments requested by prosecutors included "pena ordinaria" (customary punishment, which appeared to be the death sentence in homicide cases), "pena del último suplicio" (death sentence), and "la mas grave pena" (the most severe penalty).

60. Tórrez mentions individual cases where each of these penalties was inflicted for murder. Tórrez, "Justice in New Mexico," 14–16.

61. Francisco Tomás Cabesa de Baca, defense of Juan Antonio Chaves, Peña Blanca, 25 February 1846, MANM, roll 41, frame 525.

62. Four rebels were decapitated on 24 January 1838 and rebel governor Gonzales was shot three days later, following the battle of Pojoaque. Lecompte, *Rebellion*, 70–74.

63. These figures are from research conducted by Robert Tórrez, "Justice in New Mexico," 2.

64. Taylor, *Drinking*, 102.

65. This description is found on the reverse side of a letter from Juan B. Vigil y Alarid to Francisco Ortiz y Delgado, 29 November 1838, MANM, roll 25, frames 259–60.

66. Barreiro, "Ojeada," 61.

67. Royal bando on prison reform from Alejo García Conde, Chihuahua, 20 June 1821, Spanish Archives of New Mexico (hereafter cited as SANM), roll 20, frame 697.

68. Proposals of Manuel Delgado, juez de paz of Real del Oro, for construction of jails, 27 March 1844, MANM, roll 37, frames 459–550.

69. Weber, *Mexican Frontier*, 38.

70. MANM, roll 33, frames 899–976.

71. Don Alejo García Conde, 22 June 1821, SANM, roll 20, frame 697.

72. This special legal status included only those natives living a sedentary life and accepting Spanish authority. The Pueblos made use of the Spanish legal system. This protected status did not apply to the indios bárbaros, who were semi-nomadic and did not accept Spanish authority or institutions. Charles R. Cutter, *Protector de Indios in Colonial New Mexico, 1659–1821* (Albuquerque: University of New Mexico Press, 1986), 61–62.

73. Cutter, *Protector*, 3, 98–99. On the effects of liberal legislation on Pueblo communal lands, see Hall and Weber, "Liberals and Indians," 5–22.

74. Gregg, *Commerce*, 165.

75. La leyenda negra was a phrase coined by the Spanish intellectual Julian Juderias in 1912 to explain anti-Spanish feelings in both Europe and America. This fear and dislike of Spain among European countries dated from the discovery of the Americas and Spain's growing power and influence in the New World. The Reformation and Spain's severe attempt to remain staunchly Catholic by instituting the Inquisition lent fuel to the legend. Fray Bartolomé de las Casas's "Brevísima Relación de la Destrucción de las Indias," written in 1540, was an attempt to reform Spanish laws regarding the treatment of Native Americans. Las Casas focused on the most negative aspects of the conquest and colonization, and his writings were widely circulated in Protestant countries of Europe, where they were used as propaganda against Spain. Spaniards were depicted as bigoted, lazy, brutal, and depraved. Over the centuries, the legend of Spanish cruelty was further embellished in the Americas through bigotry and propaganda, and has survived even into the twentieth century. On the "Black Legend," see Weber, *Foreigners*, 59–60, 68–71, and U.S. Department of the Interior, National Park Service, "The Spanish Black Legend, Origins of Anti-Hispanic Stereotypes," by Joseph P. Sánchez.

CHAPTER THREE

1. Unless otherwise noted this case is taken from the Sender Collection, roll 1, document 124, frames 725–51, Proceedings against Manuel Gallego for the murder of his wife, María Espíritu Santo Ruival, San Antonio del Rancho, 3 February to 22 April 1834.

2. Pearce, *Place Names*, 148–49.

3. A villa was considered larger than a pueblo and smaller than a ciudad. No New Mexico settlement ever reached the size or status of a ciudad. Generally in New Mexico only native villages were referred to as pueblos. However, some sources, such as the census of 1827, found in Carroll and Haggard, *Three Chronicles*, 88, refer not only to Indian pueblos, but also to some Spanish settlements as pueblos. Other communities that were smaller than villas included ranchos (households adjacent to farm lands), plazas (households grouped around a plaza for defense), *poblaciones* (populations, a grouping of scattered ranchos), and *lugares* (places). Often in the

documents, small communities or neighborhoods adjacent to larger communities might be called barrios. For a good description of different types of communities in New Mexico see, Marc Simmons, "Settlement Patterns and Village Plans in Colonial New Mexico," in *New Spain's Far Northern Frontier: Essays on Spain in the American West, 1540–1821*, ed. David J. Weber (Albuquerque: University of New Mexico Press, 1979).

4. Oakah L. Jones, Jr., *Los Paisanos: Spanish Settlers on the Northern Frontier of New Spain* (Norman: University of Oklahoma Press, 1970), 114–16; John L. Kessell, ed., *Remote beyond Compare: Letters of don Diego de Vargas to his Family from New Spain and New Mexico, 1675–1706* (Albuquerque: University of New Mexico Press, 1989), 62.

5. Fray Angélico Chávez, *Origins of New Mexico Families* (Santa Fe: William Gannon, 1975), 215–17.

6. Lecompte, *Rebellion*, 31.

7. Oddly, the alcalde noted in the auto cabeza de proseso that he counted out 344 steps to where the body lay, but he never suggested the significance of this revelation.

8. Robert Tórrez suggests that exile was a common punishment in colonial New Mexico for certain crimes that "disturbed public peace or offended public morality." He also cites specific cases where exile was the punishment meted out to convicted murderers. Tórrez, "Justice in New Mexico," 7, 15, 16. Banishment was still used as a punishment in Mexican times as evidenced by certain cases cited in Richard Salazar, comp., *Calendar to the Microfilm Edition of the Sender Collection, 1697–1884* (Santa Fe: Archives Division of the New Mexico State Records Center and Archives, 1988). For example see page 34; roll 2, document 292; where banishment is used as a punishment for adultery.

9. Francis Leon Swadesh defines cantor as a religious song leader, in *Los Primeros Pobladores*, xvi.

10. Cutter suggests that by the end of the judicial phase known as sumaria, the defendant was seriously disadvantaged. The sumaria was not an impartial investigation, rather it was geared to ferreting out evidence against the suspect. Cutter, "Judicial," 189–90.

11. "Pena ordinaria" literally translates as the customary penalty; however, in these cases it seems to refer to capital punishment, which is actually pena capital or pena del último suplicio. Perhaps the death penalty was the usual penalty for homicide, but it was almost never applied. See ibid., 217–19, for the colonial era.

12. Both of these entries are from the Sender Collection, roll 2, document 154, frames 11, 12.

13. The Rebellion of 1837, or the Chimayó Rebellion as it is often called, was prompted by general discontent in the Río Arriba. Constant Navajo attacks, poor conditions in the militia, neglect by the government, attempted reforms by the new governor, and new taxes were among the complaints of the northern rebels. Lecompte, *Rebellion*, 3–11. For the Battle at La Mesilla, see ibid., 21–32.

CHAPTER FOUR

1. Except where otherwise noted, the information for this case is taken from MANM, roll 32, frames 134–61, Proceedings against Rafael Montoya, Corrales, for murder of his wife, María Albina Gonzales, 22 December 1842 to 16 January 1844.

2. Marc Simmons, *Albuquerque: A Narrative History* (Albuquerque: University of New Mexico Press, 1982), 106.

3. Marc Simmons, "Hygiene, Sanitation, and Public Health in Hispanic New Mexico," *New Mexico Historical Review* 67 (July 1992): 221–22.

4. E. Boyd, *Popular Arts of Spanish New Mexico* (Santa Fe: Museum of New Mexico Press, 1974), 263.

5. Josiah Gregg, *Commerce*, 143; Carroll and Haggard, *Three Chronicles*, 94.

6. Marta Weigle and Peter White, *The Lore of New Mexico*, (Albuquerque: University of New Mexico Press, 1988), 406; Jones, *Los Paisanos*, 160.

7. Angélico Chávez, *Origins of Families*, 330, 331.

8. Barreiro, "Ojeada," in Carroll and Haggard, *Three Chronicles*, 53. The Franciscan missions in New Mexico had been declining since the late eighteenth century, and attempts to secularize them had not improved matters, since there were not enough secular priests to replace the Franciscans. At the onset of Mexican Independence there were twenty-three Franciscans and five secular priests administering to New Mexico, and by the end of the era there were eleven secular priests and one lone Franciscan. See Weber, *Mexican Frontier*, 57–60, 74; Bloom, "Mexican Administration," *Santa Fe* 1 (1913): 28.

9. Bandos were decrees or proclamations. This one on prison reform was issued on 20 June 1821, just prior to Independence, but it was probably still in effect during the Mexican Era. This bando makes a distinction between grillos and grilletes, allowing only the use of the second. Grillos are defined as irons, shackles, gyves, or fetters, whereas grilletes are defined as shackles or fetters. SANM, roll 20, frame 464, Decree of the Cortes, Madrid on prison reform, 12 October 1820.

10. Cutter, "Judicial," 180.

11. Not to be confused with the Cubero Grant west of Albuquerque near Laguna, which was granted in 1833. Pearce, *Place Names*, 43. Santa Rosa de Cubero was granted about 1805 and confirmed by the United States for 1,945 acres. William deBuys, *Enchantment and Exploitation: the Life and Hard Times of a New Mexico Mountain Range* (Albuquerque: University of New Mexico Press, 1985), 173, 323.

12. Agustín Durán is briefly mentioned as treasurer in Weber, *Taos Trappers*, 105, 129; as member of the Departmental Assembly in 1843 in Bloom, "Mexican Administration," *Santa Fe* 2 (1914): 159; as alcalde of Santa Fe during the Rebellion of 1837 in Lecompte, *Rebellion*, 32, 165; and involved in the plot against the Americans in late 1846, along with Diego Archuleta, the priest Gallegos, and Tomás Ortiz, in David Lavender, *Bent's Fort* (1954; reprint, Lincoln: University of Nebraska Press, Bison Books, 1972), 293, 296–98.

13. On Navajo raids, see Minge "Problems," 91–93. On the Texan aggression during this same time see Bloom, "Mexican Administration," *Santa Fe* 2 (1915): 153–55.

14. Fuero Juzgo, lib. 3, tít. 4, 1.4, taken from Susan Migden Socolow, "Women and Crime: Buenos Aires, 1757–1797," in *The Problem of Order in Changing Societies: Essays on Crime and Policing in Argentina and Uruguay, 1750–1940*, ed. Lyman L. Johnson (Albuquerque: University of New Mexico Press, 1990), 13.

15. In late-eighteenth-century Buenos Aires, Socolow found that married women were often victims of violent sexual attacks that were aimed at assailing the "manliness" of their husbands. Socolow, in Johnson, *Order in Changing Societies*, 7. Gutiérrez claims that in colonial New Mexico, "They [New Mexican men] judged honor by how well they resolved the contradictory imperatives of domination (protection of one's womenfolk from assault) and conquest (prowess gained through sullying the purity of other men's women)," Gutiérrez, *When Jesus Came*, 214.

CHAPTER FIVE

1. Except where otherwise indicated the following case is taken from MANM, roll 33, frames 978–1032, Proceedings involving the death of Juan José Montoya, resident of Algodones, Sandía, Juzgado 1, 30 August 1843 to 19 June 1844.

2. Punto de los Algodones translates as place of the cottonwood groves, Rubén Cobos, *A Dictionary of New Mexico and Southern Colorado Spanish* (Santa Fe: Museum of New Mexico Press, 1983), 8, 140.

3. Moorhead, *Royal Road*, 109.

4. Nostrand, "Hispano Expansion," 263–64.

5. "Cabresto," the term used in the documents, is defined in Cobos, *Dictionary*, 22, as a rope or horsehair rope. Modern dictionaries define a similar word, "*cabestro*," as a halter.

6. Servants were called sirvientes in the Río Abajo and criados in the Río Arriba. Oakah L. Jones, Jr., "Spanish Civil Communities and Settlers in Frontier New Mexico, 1790–1810," *Hispanic-American Essays in Honor of Max Leon Moorhead*, ed. William Coker (Pensacola: Perdido Bay Press, 1979), 52–53.

7. Not all captives were taken by indios bárbaros; the Spanish also raided for Indian slaves. Slave raids continued in New Mexico well into the nineteenth century, even after it became part of the United States. For a discussion of slave raiding in New Mexico, see Marc Simmons *Coronado's Land, Essays on Daily Life in Colonial New Mexico* (Albuquerque: University of New Mexico Press, 1991), 47–50; *The Little Lion of the Southwest*: A Life of Manuel Antonio Chaves (Chicago: Swallow Press Inc., 1973), 34–36.

8. See Magnaghi, in Vigil, Kaye, and Wunder, *Myths and Realities*, 114–30. For a good description of genízaro lifestyle and settlements in the Chama Valley, see Swadesh, *Primeros Pobladores*, 39–46. Swadesh also mentions how the term genízaro was sometimes used in a derogatory manner, 45. Swadesh's definition of genízaros

does not make the distinction that Magnaghi's does between indios sirvientes and indios genízaros, xviii.

9. Pearce, *Place Names*, 164. The grant was 12,801.46 square acres. Westphall, *Mercedes Reales*, 285.

10. Juan José the victim, and Barreras a witness, both called it a "*gueso*" (*hueso* is a bone). The juez de paz, when he examined the body, called it "*una estacada*" (*estaca* is a stick or stake). It seems more likely that Juan had driven a stick into his foot, although it could have been a splinter of an animal bone.

11. Lucero served at San Felipe Pueblo from September 1841 to August 1845, and up to the fall of 1844 he was also the priest at the nearby Santa Ana Pueblo. During his career, Lucero was the priest at several other parishes including Belén, Tomé, Taos, and Picurís. Fray Angélico Chávez, *Archives of the Archdiocese of Santa Fe, 1678–1900* (Washington D.C.: Academy of American Franciscan History, 1959), 259. Mariano de Jesús Lucero, while pastor of Arroyo Hondo in 1857, was one of the native clergy who, along with the better-known Taos priest Father Antonio José Martínez, was excommunicated by Archbishop Lamy. Paul Horgan, *Lamy of Santa Fe: a Biography* (New York: Farrar, Straus, and Giroux, 1980), 242–43.

12. Baxter, *Las Carneradas*, 86; Simmons, *Albuquerque*, 182. The Pereas were among the most wealthy New Mexican families. Two of don Pedro's sons, Juan and José, were listed as carrying over $25,000 worth of goods for trade to various Mexican cities in 1844. Moorhead, *Royal Road*, 195.

13. "Sin embargo del grande agravio que le havia hecho el agresor de su hijo, lo perdona de todo corazón, por que Dios muestro Señor le perdonase, y que a su consecuencia renunciaba todo derecho o acción que le competian para proceder contra el." MANM, roll 33, frame 1000, notificación a Juan Montoya y su respuesta.

14. The accuser would inform the justice of the crime of the delinquent, in order to take revenge on him, not only accusing, but asking that the culprit be punished. The accuser was responsible for proving his charges. Cutter said that in frontier society it was doubtful that a distinction was made between the accuser and the denouncer (*denunciante*), who simply reported the crime, without asking that the criminal be punished and without bearing the burden of proof. Cutter, "Judicial", 167–68.

15. It is unclear why Rael was asked to obtain proof of his baptism and was asked to verify his religion each time he was questioned. In other homicide cases, the religion of the defendant was never questioned. Was he suspected of being something other than a Christian? Perhaps he was thought to be a descendent of *conversos* (Jews that had converted to Christianity to avoid persecution and expulsion from Spain, also called New Christians). Many conversos had come to the New World hoping to escape the Inquisition in the sixteenth and seventeenth centuries. Colin M. MacLachlan and Jaime E. Rodriguez O., *The Forging of the Cosmic Race: a Reinterpretation of Colonial Mexico* (Berkeley and Los Angeles: University of California Press, 1980), 212–14.

16. A copy of volume 1 of *Practica Criminal* was found among Manuel Delgado's

possessions when his estate was settled in 1815. Delgado had the second largest private library in New Mexico. Gallegos, *Literacy*, 58–59. Regarding the procurador, see Cutter, "Judicial," 196.

17. MANM, roll 36, frame 298, February 1844; MANM, roll 39, frames 250–63, 27 May to 17 June 1845; MANM, roll 39, frames 264–69, 29 October 1845.

CHAPTER SIX

1. Except where otherwise indicated, this case is taken from the records in MANM, roll 41, frames 492–533, Proceedings against Juan Antonio Chaves for murder of his wife, 29 January 1845 to 5 August 1846.

2. Angélico Chávez, *Origins of Families*, 152–53; Cutter, *Protector*, 88–92; Malcolm Ebright, *Land Grants and Lawsuits in Northern New Mexico* (Albuquerque: University of New Mexico Press, 1994), 174–75.

3. Cutter, *Protector*, 99–100.

4. Marc Simmons gives this definition of teguas and says they were common footwear in New Mexican settlements, in *Coronado's Land*, 98. The term manta had been used to indicate a length of cloth, woven by the Indians in Mexico for tribute to the Spanish crown, following the conquest. Mantas were worn by Pueblo women, often over an undergarment, as described by Josiah Gregg (although he did not call them mantas), in *Commerce*, 194. See also Boyd, *Popular Arts*, 233–36.

5. Charles H. Lange, *Cochití: A New Mexico Pueblo, Past and Present* (Carbondale and Edwardsville: Southern Illinois University Press, Arcturus Books ed., 1968). On death and burial, 415–22; on the duties of the sacristan at Cochití, 216–17.

6. Gertrudis Barceló had only one known brother, called Trinidad, who was active in politics in Río Arriba. Fray Angélico Chávez, "New Names in New Mexico, 1820–1850," *El Palacio* 64 (October 1957) 295. Doña Tules, or La Tules as she was also called, was an intelligent, well-educated, and self-made woman. Although she did not grow up in a wealthy family, she became a good friend and confidante of Governor Manuel Armijo, and she made so much money dealing monte that she could afford to lend the United States Army money to pay off its troops in 1846. Janet Lecompte "The Independent Women of Hispanic New Mexico, 1821–1846," in *New Mexico Women: Intercultural Perspectives*, ed. Joan M. Jensen and Darlis A. Miller (Albuquerque: University of New Mexico Press, 1986). For a fictionalized biography of doña Tules see, Ruth Laughlin, *The Wind Leaves no Shadow* (Caldwell: The Caxton Printers, Ltd., 1986).

7. Don Pedro Bautista Pino, "Exposición," in Carroll and Haggard, *Three Chronicles*; Angélico Chávez, *Origins of Families*, 260. Manuel Doroteo Pino, mentioned in the Daily murder case, was the son of Miguel's half-brother Juan Esteban (son of Pedro Bautista and his second wife).

8. In homicide cases, the prosecution often called for the pena ordinaria (customary or indicated penalty). No one ever specified exactly what that punishment was. However, it seems safe to assume that it meant the death penalty since records show

that the defense would then always argue that the death penalty was too severe for his defendant. If capital punishment was the customary penalty for homicides, it is ironic that it was almost never used in New Mexico, nor in all of Mexico for that matter. Taylor, *Drinking*, 98. Furthermore, it appears that the authorities in New Mexico, including the governor himself, did not have the authority to hand down death sentences without having the approval of some superior authority. Cutter, "Judicial," 217–18.

9. Miguel E. Pino, promotor fiscal, to juez de primera instancia, 11 February 1846, MANM, roll 41, frame 515.

10. Angélico Chávez, *Origins of Families*, 152–54. Also see Cutter, *Protector*, 88–92, for information on the legal struggles between the Cabesa de Baca family and the Cochití and Santo Domingo Pueblos.

11. Francisco Tomás Cabesa de Baca, defensor, to juez de primera instancia, 25 February 1846, MANM, roll 41, frame 519.

12. Swadesh, *Primeros Pobladores*, xviii.

13. Moorhead, *Royal Road*, 162.

14. "Causa criminal seguida contra Juan Antonio Chabes [*sic*] por el [h]omicidio que cometio contra su muger [*sic*] María Angelina Herrera el dia 19 del precente mes de henero [sic] de 1846." MANM, roll 10, frame 496.

CHAPTER SEVEN

1. Lecompte, "Independent Women," 75.

2. Luis Martín, *Daughters of the Conquistadores: Women of the Viceroyalty of Peru* (Albuquerque: University of New Mexico Press, 1983), 3. On honor and patriarchal kinship see Ramón Gutiérrez, "Marriage, Sex, and Family: Social Change in Colonial New Mexico, 1690–1846" (Ph.D. diss., University of Wisconsin, 1980), 29.

3. Gutiérrez, *When Jesus Came*; on arranged marriages, see 227–78; on impediments to marriage and diligencias matrimoniales, see 243–48.

4. Janet Lecompte, "Independent Women," 78, 79.

5. Rosalind Rock found in her research on woman and the law in Spanish colonial New Mexico that reconciliation was the customary judgement in cases of abuse. Rosalind Rock, "Pido y Súplico: Women and the Law in Spanish New Mexico, 1697–1763," *New Mexico Historical Review* 65 (April 1990): 156.

6. Socolow, in Johnson, *Order in Changing Societies*, 6–7.

7. In Hispanic society of late-eighteenth-century Buenos Aires, Socolow noted that male relatives of victims of wife abuse sometimes reported the abuse, and that often women were too afraid to bring charges against their husbands. Socolow, in Johnson, *Order in Changing Societies*, 6. In the two areas of colonial Mexico studied by William Taylor, he noted a high proportion of victims of homicides were wives, even though in a society where wife beating is socially acceptable these often go unreported. Taylor, *Drinking*, 85.

8. MANM, roll 1, frame 1262; MANM, roll 2, frame 1296.

9. MANM, roll 2, frame 1288; MANM, roll 16, frame 1019.

10. MANM. roll 32, frame 103–9.

11. Lecompte, "Independent Women," 86. Gutiérrez discusses what it meant to be a slave in New Mexican society and mentions cases where slaves and servants sought help from the legal system against their masters' abuse. Gutiérrez, *When Jesus Came*, 180–90.

12. In Buenos Aires Socolow found the courts lenient when dealing with domestic violence. Socolow, in Johnson, *Order in Changing Societies*, 6. Likewise, Rock found that in New Mexico, although the law allowed for divorce in the event of abuse and violence, the courts attempted to reconcile couples even when abuse was evident. Rock, "Pido y Súplico," 156–57.

13. One woman in colonial New Mexico found redress from an unhappy marriage by murdering her husband. Ironically, she and her accomplice-mother were both rewarded by execution, giving them the distinction of being two of only four convicted murderers to suffer the death penalty in recorded New Mexico history, prior to U.S. takeover. Tórrez, "Justice in New Mexico," 13, 19–21.

14. Juan José Sánchez, 24 March 1843, the written prosecution of the case against Rafael Montoya. MANM, roll 32, frame 153. Lecompte also mentions this case in "Independent Women," 86. According to Spanish law a man could legally "punish" his wife and her paramour; homicide was defensible in these circumstances. Socolow, in Johnson, *Order in Changing Societies*, 13.

15. MANM, roll 32, frame 156.

16. MANM, roll 41, fame 510.

17. Lange, *Cochití*, 368, 369, 411.

18. Taylor suggests that motive is one of the most difficult topics to understand in homicide cases. The motives given are seldom the "real reasons" behind the violence; however, they are still valuable indicators of what people perceived as the proper way to react in certain situations. Taylor, *Drinking*, 90–91.

19. Regarding vergüenza, see Paul Kutsche and John R. Van Ness, *Cañones: Values, Crisis, and Survival in a Northern New Mexico Village* (Albuquerque: University of New Mexico Press, 1981), 136–29; Swadesh, *Primeros Pobladores*, xxiii; Facundo Valdez, "Vergüenza," *in The Survival of Spanish American Villages*, ed. Paul Kutsche (Colorado Springs: Colorado College Research Committee, 1979), 99–106; Gutiérrez, *When Jesus Came*, 177.

CHAPTER EIGHT

1. Except where otherwise indicated, the following case has been taken from MANM, roll 5, frames 1016–93, Proceedings against Andrés Márquez for murder of Juan Valdez, Santa Fe, 4 June 1826 to 17 July 1826.

2. Josiah Gregg, *Commerce*, 170.

3. Ibid., 170. Albert Pike also gives a lively if somewhat disdainful account of a fandango he attended in Taos in the early 1830s, in *Sketches*, 148.

4. Sunder, *Matt Field*, 204.

5. Webb claimed that he had heard of "disorders and serious brawls in fandangos, but it was almost invariably where Americans and whiskey were found in profusion." Webb, *Adventures*, 96, 97.

6. Olmsted, *Colonial Censuses*, 160.

7. According to church records, Cristóbal de Larrañaga had a son, José Mariano, born in 1780, who married at the age of twenty-eight in 1813. These figures don't add up, probably because Mariano was not sure of his exact age. He gave his age as forty-three years poco mas o menos in this statement in 1826. Assuming that the baptismal records were right, he was probably closer to forty-six. Angélico Chávez, *Origins of Families*, 204.

8. Marc Simmons, *Taos to Tomé: True Tales of Hispanic New Mexico* (Santa Fe: Ancient City Press, 1978), 13–15; Jones, *Los Paisanos*, 140.

9. Kate L. Gregg, ed., *The Road to Santa Fe: The Journal and Diaries of George Champlin Sibley* (Albuquerque: University of New Mexico Press, 1952), 135, 137–40. Sibley's journal also records the many instances of fandangos in Santa Fe, 134–35, 137.

10. Marc Simmons, "New Mexico's Spanish Exiles," *New Mexico Historical Review* 59 (January 1984): 67–76; MANM, roll 7, frame 296, Proceedings against the Spaniard, Atanasio de Bolíbar before José María Martínez, first alcalde of Santa Fe, 23–27 September 1827; Olmsted, *Colonial Censuses*, 140.

11. Josiah Gregg, *Commerce*, 184–85. At this time a Mexican peso was equivalent to a U.S. dollar; a real was worth one-eighth of a peso—making an expense of $1.25.

12. Connie Cortazar, "The Santa Visita of Agustín Fernández de San Vicente to New Mexico, 1826," *New Mexico Historical Review* 59 (January 1984): 31, 42–43.

13. MANM, roll 5, frame 1396 (10 December to 27 May 1827) and roll 7, frame 156 (3 January to 27 May 1827), Settlement of the estate of Cura Tomás Terrasas before José Francisco Baca, first alcalde of Santa Fe; Angélico Chávez, *Archives*, 214.

14. A good discussion of the revolt can be found in Lecompte, *Rebellion*.

15. Rafael Bracho was the defense attorney for the Cabeza de Baca family when the Cochití Pueblo brought suit against it over a land dispute in 1816. Cutter, *Protector*, 88–91.

16. MANM, roll 10, frames 3, 4, Proceedings before Alcalde Trujillo, Santa Fe, against Andrés Márquez for murder, 9 March 1829. Was this the same Andrés Márquez, soldier of the Santa Fe Company, who was charged with stealing property belonging to the deceased Captain Blas Hinojos six years later? MANM, roll 20, frames 546–54, 23 March 1835. This Andrés Márquez gave his age as thirty-two years, which if correct, indicates that they could not be the same person.

CHAPTER NINE

1. Except where otherwise indicated, the following case has been taken from MANM, roll 33, frames 899–976, Proceedings involving the murder of Antonio

Moya, resident of Tomé, Juzgado del Bado, 27 October 1843 to 28 February 1844. Modern spelling is "vado" (ford); for this work I will use the spelling found in the documents.

2. Drumm, *Magoffin*, 98.

3. Josiah Gregg, *Commerce*, 77.

4. J. W. Abert, *Report of Lieutenant J. W. Abert of His Examination of New Mexico in the Years 1846–1847*, seen in *Kiva, Cross, and Crown: The Pecos Indians and New Mexico, 1540–1840*, ed. John L. Kessell (1979; reprint, Albuquerque: University of New Mexico Press, 1987), 427.

5. Kessell, *Kiva, Cross, and Crown*, 415, 420.

6. Olmsted, *Colonial Censuses*, 262.

7. Marc Simmons and Joan Myers, photographer, *Along the Santa Fe Trail* (Albuquerque: University of New Mexico Press, 1986), 75; Josiah Gregg, *Commerce*, 77 n. 17.

8. For an overview of the military situation during the Mexican Era, see Weber, *Mexican Frontier*, 109–12. Regarding the numbers at the garrisons, Bloom mentions that in 1841 the "Permanent Co." of Taos consisted of only twenty-seven men, including officers. Bloom, "Mexican Administration," *Santa Fe* 2 (1914): 163 n. 548. The Santa Fe presidio had only 107 men in 1840. Charles R. McClure, "The Texan-Santa Fe Expedition of 1841," *New Mexico Historical Review* 48 (January 1973): 48. For further figures on military census see MANM, Military records.

9. In 1832 Licenciado Antonio Barreiro cited "the threats and attacks constantly attempted by the United States" and the "destructive hostility" of the "wild Indians" as obvious reasons to step up the military defense of New Mexico. "Ojeada," 74–77.

10. Lecompte, *Rebellion*, 9–11.

11. Bloom, "Mexican Administration," *Santa Fe* 2 (1914): 132–33, 152–53; Lecompte, *Rebellion*, 72–73.

12. The records of these National Companies can be found in MANM, roll 32, frames 378–439.

13. The term "alférez" has no exact equivalent in English. In Carroll and Haggard, *Three Chronicles*, 175 n. 125, the editors say that alférez was approximately equivalent to second lieutenant. Another definition of alférez, as field-grade officer in the Spanish army, similar to a colonel, is found in Kessell, *Remote*, 322.

14. Moorhead mentions the Chávez, Perea, Ortiz, and Otero families as being the ricos of New Mexico who were merchants as well as feudal lords. Antonio José Otero carried almost $5,000 worth of American goods south into Mexico in 1844. Moorhead, *Royal Road*, 194–95.

15. Myra Ellen Jenkins, *Calendar of the Microfilm Edition of the Mexican Archives of New Mexico (MANM) 1821–1846* (Santa Fe: State of New Mexico Records Center, 1970), 113, 120.

16. Bloom, "Mexican Administration," *Santa Fe* 2 (1914): 152.

17. Cortazar, "Santa Visita," 36–37.

18. MANM, roll 7, frame 174 (16 January 1827) Testimony of José de la O, Santa Fe, against Cura Francisco Leiba and others for gambling; Webb, *Adventures*, 76. For dates on Francisco Leyba see Angélico Chávez, *Archives*, 259.

19. On New Mexico dances, see Mela Sedillo, *Mexican and New Mexican Folk-dances* (Albuquerque: University of New Mexico Press, 1950), 25–31; Weigle and White, *Lore*, 188–92. Valse is the New Mexico Spanish spelling for waltz ("vals" in Castilian Spanish). Cobos, *Dictionary*, 173.

20. Mateo Marcellus Vittucci, *The Language of Spanish Dance* (Norman: University of Oklahoma Press, 1993), 142.

21. On drinking and fandangos see Davis, *El Gringo*, 263, 359; Webb, *Adventures*, 95 n. 138.

22 "Entro el difunto y se sento en el asiento de donde el que declara estaba sentado." This is not clear. Perhaps Moya actually sat on Lara, which might account for Lara's acute embarrassment. MANM, roll 33, frame 909.

23. The first district or prefecture was divided into two partidos. The first partido included Santa Fe, Bado, and San Ildefonso. The second partido included Cañada, Taos, Abiquiú, Ojo Caliente, San Juan, Chama, and Trampas. Tyler, *Sources*, 10. Juan Andrés Archuleta was the prefect of this first district.

24. McClure, "Expedition of 1841," 52; Davis, *El Gringo*, 336; George Wilkins Kendall, *Narrative of the Texan Santa Fe Expedition* (New York: Harper & Brothers, 1844).

25. According to all the previous records, the crime had clearly occurred on 27 October, yet Salazar repeatedly referred to 26 October while questioning the witnesses.

26. We don't know whether or not the host of this baile charged admission, but according to Bloom, licenses were required for every baile where admission was charged. Bloom, "Mexican Administration," *Santa Fe* 2 (1915): 240. One American, describing fandangos in Santa Fe in 1839, claimed that Mexicans never charged admission to their dances. He may have been misinformed. Webb, *Adventures*, 95.

27. Cutter, "Judicial," 199, 200.

28. The word "paisano" has various meanings, including countryman, peasant, and civilian. Like most expressions that are used to denote a certain class of individual, the word could be used in a derogatory sense.

29. Lecompte, *Rebellion*, 68.

CHAPTER TEN

1. Except where otherwise indicated, the following case has been taken from MANM, roll 36, frames 345–77, Proceedings against José María Sebada, Tomé, for murder of Pablo Salazar, 4 March to 9 September 1844.

2. For a season-by-season account of the workings of a New Mexico irrigation system, see Stanley Crawford, *Mayordomo: Chronicle of an Acequia in Northern New Mexico* (Albuquerque: University of New Mexico Press, 1988).

3. See the 1827 census taken by Colonel Don Antonio Narbona. Escudero, "Notícias," in Carroll and Haggard, *Three Chronicles*, 88.

4. On agriculture, see Josiah Gregg, *Commerce*, 107–12; Carroll and Haggard, *Three Chronicles*, 35–38.

5. One example of conflict over water rights and how the local judiciary functioned in civil cases can be found in Ebright, "Manuel Martínez's Ditch Dispute: A Study in Mexican Period Custom and Justice," chap. 3 in *Land Grants*, 73–83.

6. According to an 1827 census for New Mexico, Tomé had a population of 2,043. This census listed Isleta and Belén, but did not mention any other settlements along the river. It seems likely that villages such as Valencia and Peralta may have been counted in with Tomé. Carroll and Haggard, *Three Chronicles*, 88.

7. George Kubler, *The Religious Architecture of New Mexico in the Colonial Period and since the American Occupation* (Albuquerque: University of New Mexico Press, 1990), 126.

8. Angélico Chávez, *Origins of Families*, 330–31. Fernando Ortiz is mentioned in two other cases: the homicides of María Albina Gonzales and Juan José Montoya.

9. Priests regularly received offerings for performing baptisms, marriages, and funerals. In late-eighteenth-century Albuquerque, the extra fees for church burial ranged from four pesos at the back of the church up to sixteen pesos up front near the sanctuary steps. This is from Marc Simmons, *Albuquerque*, 122.

10. See Moorhead, *Royal Road*, 194–95; Baxter, *Las Carneradas*, 103.

11. Lecompte, *Rebellion*, 51–52; Bloom, "Mexican Administration," *Santa Fe* 2 (1914): 25–26, 134, 159.

12. For a description of Hispanic wakes, see Weigle and White, *Lore*, 387–89; Kutsche and Van Ness, *Cañones*, 131.

13. The name is spelled "Cebada" in Angélico Chávez, "New Names," 300.

14. Miguel Olona signed the previously mentioned Plan de Tomé. Lecompte, *Rebellion*, 52.

CHAPTER ELEVEN

1. Taylor, *Drinking*, 83–85.

2. Webb, *Adventures*, 97.

3. Ebright, *Land Grants*, 27, 68.

4. John Charles Chasteen, "Violence For Show: Knife Dueling on a Nineteenth-Century Cattle Frontier," in *Order in Changing Societies*, ed. Johnson, 54–55.

5. Ibid., 57.

CHAPTER TWELVE

1. Except where otherwise indicated, the information on this case is taken from MANM, roll 25, frames 72–212, Proceedings against Salvador Barela y Borrego and Diego Martín for the murder of Andrés Dayle, 1 March 1838 to 21 August 1843.

2. T. M. Pearce, *New Mexico Place Names*, 114.

3. Gregg, *Commerce of the Prairies*, 118.

4. John M. Townley, "El Placer: A New Mexico Mining Boom Before 1846," *Journal of the West* 10 (January 1971): 108–10, 113.

5. Baxter, *Las Carneradas*, 97, 117.

6. Colonel Francisco Perea recalled a Francisco Ortiz had a shop on the southeast corner of the plaza at this time. W. H. H. Allison, "Santa Fe as it Appeared during the Winter of the Years 1837 and 1838," *Old Santa Fe* 2 (1914): 181.

7. Josiah Gregg, *Commerce*, Moorhead's n. 12, 262. For this work I have chosen to use the spelling "Daily," as did U.S. Consul Manuel Alvarez in a letter to Powhatan Ellis, 14 December 1840, BR, Alvarez Letter Book, no. 9. Chávez mentions that in the Taos marriage register, a José Dayle, native of St. Louis, lived in San Carlos de Napeste and married María de la Cruz Suazo in October 1844. His parents were listed as Alejandro Dayle and Ana María Evans. Could these people have been any relation to Andrés Daily? Angélico Chávez "New Names," 304.

8. Townley, "El Placer," 108. Townley spelled his name with an "S" (Somohano). Regarding Manuel Delgado II, see Angélico Chávez, *Origins of Families*, 168–69; Baxter, *Las Carneradas*, 109.

9. Josiah Gregg, *Commerce*, 143.

10. Dr. Henry Masure died in March 1846 at Santa Ana. Drumm, *Magoffin*, 53 n. 17.

11. The place-name, Paraje de las Norias, still found on some modern maps in a shortened version (Las Norias) suggests that it was the location of wells that had been dug to supply water for the mining community. "Paraje" means place. In modern dictionaries the word "noria" is defined as the actual mechanism used to draw water from a well (i.e., a chain pump or draw wheel); however, in New Mexico the local people often use this term for a dug well. Pearce suggests that in New Mexico, from an early date, the term "noria" was used to signify a dug well. Pearce, *Names*, 110. Tyler defines a "poso [sic] de noria" as a dug well, and a well as either "pozo" or "noria." Daniel Tyler, "Underground Water in Hispanic New Mexico: A Brief Analysis of Laws, Customs, and Disputes," *New Mexico Historical Review* 66 (July 1991): 291, 297.

12. Josiah Gregg, *Commerce*, 214.

13. Townley, "El Placer," 104–05.

14. Manuel Armijo was governor three times during the Mexican Era (1827–29, 1837–44, 1845–46). For a good overview of Governor Armijo and his relations with foreigners, see Tyler, "Gringo Views."

15. The Mexican constitution abolished the old Spanish caste system. During colonial times official records, such as censuses, would have made note of the ethnic classification of the individual. The 1790 census distinguished between, españoles of pure Spanish blood, indios, of Indian blood, and various categories of castas or mixed bloods, including, mestizos, coyotes, lobos, color quebrado, genízaros, and mulatos. See Olmsted, *Colonial Censuses*, 1. For an explanation of the casta system in

New Mexico, see Adrian H. Bustamante, "Españoles, Castas, y Labradores, Santa Fe Society in the Eighteenth Century," in *Santa Fe: History of an Ancient City*, ed. David Grant Noble (Santa Fe: School of American Research Press, 1989), 70–74.

16. The suspect's full name was Salvador Barela y Borrego. At various times in the records he was called either Barela or Borrego. To avoid confusion here, he will be referred to by his full name or Barela.

17. A list of New Mexico settlements compiled by Manuel Armijo on 7 July 1840, listed two San Ildefonsos—one Indian and one Hispanic. The latter was designated as capital of partido one of the first district. Escudero, "Notícias," in Carroll and Haggard, *Three Chronicles*, 91.

18. Ibid., 91; on the same list, San Juan, in the same partido, is not designated as an Indian pueblo.

19. Juan Andrés Archuleta was the father of Diego Archuleta, who is best known for his part in the capture of the Texans in the Texas Santa Fe expedition. Drumm, *Magoffin*, 184–85 n. 78. New Mexico had become a department under the centralist constitution of 30 December 1836. It was divided into two districts or prefecturas. The northern prefectura (District 1) basically included everything from Santa Fe north, and the Bado area to the east. The northern prefectura was further divided into two partidos. Tyler, *Sources*, 10. Tyler's list differs somewhat from Armijo's list of 1840 taken from Escudero's "Noticias,". Escudero's list is more complete and places Cañada, San Juan and Abiquiú in the first rather than second partido of the first district. Escudero, "Notícias," in Carroll and Haggard, *Three Chronicles*, 91–93.

20. Boyd, *Popular Arts*, 181–214; Roland F. Dickey, *New Mexico Village Arts* (1949; reprint, Albuquerque: University of New Mexico Press, 1990), 104–24. Josiah Gregg, *Commerce*, 148.

21. There had been prohibitions against traveling without a permit since colonial days. Simmons mentions a royal order of 1784. Simmons, *Spanish in New Mexico*, 75.

22. David Lavender, *Bent's Fort* (1954; reprint, Lincoln: University of Nebraska Press, Bison Books, 1972), 206.

23. Subprefect José María Ortiz to jueces de paz, Sender Collection, roll 2, document 233. Comancheros were men who traveled out into the plains to trade with the Comanche or other nomadic tribes. Ciboleros were buffalo hunters who took similar risks beyond Hispanic settlements. Swadesh, *Primeros Pobladores*, xvi, xvii. For a look at the precarious lifestyle of the ciboleros, see Simmons, *Coronado's Land*, 97–102.

24. Manuel Alvarez to Powhatan Ellis, Santa Fe, 14 December 1840, BR, Alvarez Letter Book, no. 9.

25. Josiah Gregg, *Commerce*, 263. Lavender, *Bent's Fort*, 206.

26. Vigil's career did not end with the U.S. occupation; rather it flourished. He became acting governor of New Mexico when Charles Bent lost his life in the bloody Taos Revolt. Weber, *Arms*, xv to xvii.

27. Louis Robidoux, a French-American born in Missouri in 1796, settled in New

Mexico in the early 1820s with his brother Antoine. Robidoux hispanicized his name to Luis Robidú. Both brothers prospered in the fur trade, took common-law wives, and became naturalized Mexican citizens in 1829. Louis settled down with Guadalupe García from one of the old respected New Mexico families, and became active in politics in Santa Fe for at least ten years. He was the alcalde primero in Santa Fe when Matt Field arrived in New Mexico in 1839. In 1844 he moved his family to California. Craver, *Impact of Intimacy*, 30, 31; Sunder, *Matt Field*, 203 n. 90.

28. Manuel Alvarez (1794–1856) was a Spaniard who had lived in central Mexico since 1818. He traveled in the United States before moving to Santa Fe in 1824, where he opened a store on the plaza and became involved in the fur trade. Alvarez was well educated and fluent in Spanish, English, and French. In 1829, the Republic of Mexico ordered the expulsion of Spaniards from Mexico, and Alvarez was forced to leave New Mexico. Alvarez returned to New Mexico as U.S. consul and commercial agent in 1839. Thomas E. Chávez, *Manuel Alvarez, 1794–1856: A Southwestern Biography* (Niwot: University of Colorado Press, 1990).

29. Baxter, *Las Carneradas*, 102. Pedro Bautista Pino wrote the "Exposición" in 1812, one of the best sources of New Mexico history for the early nineteenth century. See Carroll and Haggard, *Three Chronicles*, for a translation of this work.

30. Josiah Gregg, *Commerce*, 266–67; Max L. Moorhead, "Spanish Transportation in the Southwest, 1540–1846," *New Mexico Historical Review* 35 (April 1957): 116–17.

31. Letter of 29 November 1838, MANM, roll 25, frames 259–60, describes the filthy condition of the Santa Fe jail.

32. Thomas Chávez, *Conflict*, 26; Westphall, *Mercedes Reales*, 45.

33. Domingo Fernández petitioned and actively fought for land of the abandoned San Cristóbal Pueblo and lands of the declining Pecos Pueblo. Emlen G. Hall, *Four Leagues of Pecos: A Legal History of the Pecos Grant, 1800–1933*, New Mexico Land Grant Series, ed. John R. Van Ness, vol. 2 (Albuquerque: University of New Mexico Press, 1984), 21, 31–66.

34. Minge, "Problems," 28 n. 46. Alvarez to Miranda, Santa Fe, 14 February 1840, BR, Alvarez Letter Book.

35. Felipe Sena was alcalde segundo of Santa Fe when he and other civilians and soldiers were captured at La Mesilla by the rebels in the uprising of 1837. Lecompte, *Rebellion*, 31–33. In 1844 Sena served as interim governor before Mariano Martínez de Lejanza took office. Bloom, "Mexican Administration," *Santa Fe* 2 (1914): 167.

36. Townley, "El Placer," 104, 105.

37. Ibid., 111.

38. Charles Bent, his brother William, and Ceran St. Vrain had formed a partnership in 1830 that grew to dominate the Indian trade in the southern Rocky Mountains. Their headquarters on the Arkansas River was known as Bent's Fort. Bent settled in Taos, married María Ignacia Jaramillo, sister of Kit Carson's wife,

and opened a store. He was appointed first U.S. governor by General Kearny and was assassinated in the 1847 Taos Revolt. For an interesting account of the Bents, see Lavender, *Bent's Fort.*

39. Bent to Alvarez, Taos, 1 December 1840, BR, no. 42.

40. Alvarez to Powhatan Ellis, Santa Fe, 14 December 1840, BR, Alvarez Letter Book, no. 9.

41. Bent to Alvarez, Taos, 10 December 1839, BR, no. 39.

42. Miranda to Alvarez, Santa Fe, 11 May 1841, BR, no. 208.

43. Albino Chacón (1808–1876) was second alcalde of Santa Fe during the 1837 Rebellion, which he witnessed first-hand and described in an unofficial account. He served off and on as Santa Fe alcalde until the American takeover in 1846, when he retired to Peñasco. Lecompte, *Rebellion*, 90. Albino Chacón's son, Rafael Chacón (1833–1925) wrote his autobiography. Jacqueline Dorgan Meketa, ed., *Legacy of Honor: The Life of Rafael Chacón, A Nineteenth-Century New Mexican* (Albuquerque: University of New Mexico Press, 1986).

44. Chacón to Alvarez, Santa Fe, 6 July 1841, BR, no. 116.

45. Alvarez to Albino Chacón, Santa Fe, 7 July 1841, BR, Alvarez Letter Book, no. 18.

46. Thomas Chávez, *Conflict*, 33–34.

47. McClure, "Expedition of 1841," 45, 47–48.

48. Lavander, *Bent's Fort*, 210, 215: Craver, *Impact of Intimacy*, 40–41.

49. McClure, "Expedition of 1841," 46–48.

50. Thomas Chávez, *Conflict*, 52–53.

51. Ibid., 55–56.

52. McClure, "Expedition of 1841," 51–53.

53. Ibid., 55; Kendall, *Narrative.*

54. By 1845 Juan Nepomuceno Urquidi had become the strongest buyer in the Chihuahua trade. In the summer of that year he purchased most of the fifteen thousand head of sheep that came across the Camino Real from New Mexican sheep men. Baxter, *Las Carneradas*, 109.

55. "Este es mi dictamen, mas U. resolvera' lo que crea justo." Licenciado Guerra to juez de la primera instancia, 21 August 1843, MANM, roll 25, frame 212.

56. Alvarez to Honorable Waddy Thompson, Santa Fe, 25 August 1842, BR, Alvarez Letter Book, no. 38.

57. Alvarez to Honorable Waddy Thompson, Santa Fe, 14 December 1842, BR, Alvarez Letter Book, no. 39.

CHAPTER THIRTEEN

1. Except where otherwise indicated, this case is taken from the records found in MANM, roll 29, frames 179–205, Proceedings involving the murder of Joseph Pulsiphur, 20 January 1841 to 14 February 1842.

2. Bent to Alvarez, Taos, 30 January 1841, BR, no. 46

3. A number of books describe the Santa Fe Trail and its history. See Marc Simmons, *Following the Santa Fe Trail: A Guide for Modern Travelers* (Santa Fe: Ancient City Press, 1984); Simmons and Myers, photographer, *Along the Trail*; Gregory M. Franswa, *Maps of the Santa Fe Trail* (St. Louis: The Patrice Press, 1989).

4. Simmons, *Following the Trail*, 173, 174.

5. Bieber claimed the Scolly Grant was made in 1843. Webb, *Adventures*, 74 n. 104. In *Mercedes Reales*, Westphall noted that the La Junta Grant was made to John Scolly in 1846. Westphall, *Mercedes Reales*, 153.

6. Bieber's note in Webb, *Adventures*, 74.

7. Craver, *Impact of Intimacy*, 9. Craver states that Bonney lived in Mora. Thomas Chávez, *Conflict*, 32 n. 9, wrote that "Bonney apparently lived around Las Vegas." Bonney's own letter to Consul Alvarez on 17 November 1840 in BR, no. 95, was written from Las Vegas and he wrote "I left the Vegas for the Mora on the 12," which indicates that Bonney was living in Las Vegas or near Las Vegas at this time.

8. Pearce, *Place Names*, 104.

9. Simmons, Following the *Trail*, 177.

10. Webb, *Adventures*, 76.

11. Drumm, *Magoffin*, 92, 93. Susan Magoffin was long considered to be the first Anglo-American to travel across the Santa Fe Trail; however, in 1987 historian Marian Meyer learned that Mary Donoho traversed the trail in 1833 with her trader husband and infant daughter. The couple set up a hotel on the same corner of the Santa Fe plaza where the La Fonda now stands. Marian Meyer, *Mary Donoho New First Lady of the Santa Fe Trail* (Santa Fe: Ancient City Press, 1991).

12. Thomas Chávez, *Conflict*, 31–33. Alvarez to Powhatan Ellis, Santa Fe, 14 December 1840, BR, Alvarez Letter Book, no.9.

13. This information is all contained in a letter from Bonney to Alvarez, Las Vegas, 17 November 1840, BR, no. 95. The reference to a Mr. Slover is curious. Could this have been Isaac Slover, the Taos trapper and mountain man who moved to California in 1837? If so, what was he doing back in Mora in 1840? Weber, *Taos Trappers*, 153.

14. Bonney to Alvarez, Las Vegas, 17 November 1840, BR, no. 95.

15. Ibid.

16. Ibid.

17. Ibid.

18. Ibid.

19. Bent to Alvarez, Taos, 1 December 1840, BR, no. 42.

20. Alvarez to Powhatan Ellis, Santa Fe, 14 December 1840, BR, Alvarez Letter Book, no. 9.

21. Miranda to Alvarez, Santa Fe, 21 January 1841, BR, no. 206.

22. Ibid.

23. Bent to Alvarez, Taos, 1 December 1840, BR, no.42.

24. Weber, *Mexican Frontier*, 83–93.

25. Thomas Chávez, *Conflict*, 33.

26. John Kessell, *Kiva, Cross, and Crown*, 455–58, 474; Hall discusses the decline of the Pecos Pueblo, putting the date of abandonment at 1837. Hall, *Four Leagues*, 60.

27. Thomas Chávez, *Conflict*, 32 n. 10; Angélico Chávez, *Origins of Families*, 318.

28. This quote is from Alvarez to the Honorable Waddy Thompson, Santa Fe, 25 August 1842, BR, Alvarez Letter Book, no. 38; the letter of 14 December 1842, BR, Alvarez Letter Book, no. 39, expressed the same sentiment.

29. Tomás Ortiz, Santa Fe, 6 July 1844, MANM , roll 37, frame 558.

CHAPTER FOURTEEN

1. Except where otherwise indicated, this case is taken from MANM, roll 36, frames 259–80, Proceedings against John D. Patten for murder, 25 April to 28 July 1844.

2. Benjamin M. Read, "In Santa Fe During the Mexican Regime," *New Mexico Historical Review* 2 (January 1927): 92. Planting trees on the plaza may have been one of Governor Martínez Lejanza's few good decisions. He was an outsider whose unpopular actions alienated New Mexicans, Indian people, and foreigners alike. His term lasted barely a year before he was recalled from office on 1 May 1845. Bloom, "Mexican Administration," *Santa Fe* 2 (1915): 223–35.

3. For descriptions of Santa Fe during the early nineteenth century, see Janet Lecompte, "When Santa Fe was a Mexican Town, 1821–1846," 79–82, and Wilson, "American Occupation," 101, 108, both in *Santa Fe*, ed. Noble; two articles by W. H. H. Allison, "Santa Fe as it Appeared during the Winter of the Years 1837 and 1838," *Santa Fe* 2 (1914): 170–83, and "Santa Fe in 1846," *Santa Fe* 2 (1915): 391–406; by Read, "In Santa Fe," 90–97.

4. Escudero, "Notícias," in Carroll and Haggard, *Three Chronicles*, 88–89.

5. Onzas de oro were gold coins that weighed approximately one ounce. Their worth varied, although an ounce of gold was worth sixteen silver Mexican pesos (a peso was worth one ounce of silver). Townley, "El Placer," 105.

6. Regarding the French in New Mexico, see Weber, *Taos Trappers*, 82–97. For French-Mexican marriages, see Craver, *Impact of Intimacy*, and for French names in New Mexico, see Angélico Chávez, "New Names," 291–318, 367–381.

7. Bloom, "Mexican Administration," *Santa Fe* 2 (1914): 161–69.

8. Martínez took over the office of governor from Felipe Sena, acting governor, on 29 April. His secretary, José Felix Zubia, was already acting as secretary of the government of the department by 25 April. He must have been acting under Felipe Sena on this date, since Martínez was not yet in office. Bloom, "Mexican Administration," *Santa Fe* 2 (1915): 168, 224.

9. Cutter discusses three different steps that might initiate a criminal case: *acusación*, where the injured party brought charges; *denuncia*, where a third party notified authorities; and *de oficio*, where the magistrate initiated the investigation. The difference between the acusación and denuncia was that the accuser had to prove his

charges, and the denouncer did not. Since the denunciante could also be the injured party, it was "safer" to use the denuncia approach than the acusación. Cutter, "Judicial," 167–68.

10. Webb, *Adventures*, 74 n. 104, 97, 98 n. 143. Bieber puts the date of the grant at 29 March 1843. Westphall gives the date as 1846, in *Mercedes Reales*, 153, 280, 286.

11. Craver, *Impact of Intimacy*, 55. James Giddings, born in 1812 in Kentucky, entered the Santa Fe trade in 1835. He settled in Santa Fe in 1840, and in 1853 he established a ranch on the Pecos River near present-day Fort Sumner, one of the first ranches in that part of the territory. Webb, *Adventures*, 97 n. 139. Both of these sources spell his name with an "S" (Giddings), although he signed his testimony Gidding. MANM, roll 36, frame 266.

12. The documents don't mention the actual date that John Patten was taken prisoner; however, his captor's testimony, taken in Santa Fe, was dated 28 April. Since the order for Patten's arrest did not go out until late on the 25th, it is doubtful that Constant could have made the trip (on horseback) from Santa Fe to Taos, captured the suspect, and returned him to Santa Fe in time to give testimony on the 28th. Travel between the towns probably took two long days in each direction. Patten did not give his testimony until 1 May. It seems likely that Constants's testimony was misdated; perhaps it was given the date when the actual capture took place in Taos. Andrew Constant and his marriage are mentioned in Craver, *Impact of Intimacy*, 54, and in Angélico Chávez, "New Names," 302.

13. Descriptions of travel between Santa Fe and Taos are found in Hafen, *Ruxton*, 188–89, and Pike, *Sketches*. Weber, *Taos Trappers*, 109, mentions Embudo and Jean B. Chalifoux.

14. Lecompte, *Rebellion*, 31.

15. Even more curious is the middle initial of his signature, which looks like a "D." MANM, roll 36, frame 272. A Juan S. Paton is listed as arriving in New Mexico in July 1827, and settling in Santa Fe. This Paton listed his place of origin as Kentucky and his occupation as carpenter. Perhaps there was some relationship. David Weber, *The Extranjeros: Selected Documents from the Mexican Side of the Santa Fe Trail, 1825–1828* (Santa Fe: Stagecoach Press, 1967), 41.

16. Typical of the elite families, Mariano was also active in New Mexico politics, like his father Francisco Xavier Chávez, who had been the first governor of New Mexico following Independence in 1822. Mariano served briefly in the Governor's office, in 1835 and for the first few months of 1844. Marc Simmons, *Murder on the Santa Fe Trail: An International Incident, 1843* (El Paso: Texas Western Press, 1987), 1–5. For a description of Chávez's home and property, see Drumm, *Magoffin*, 153–54; Simmons, *Little Lion*, 50. For an account of the most wealthy New Mexican merchants, see Moorhead, *Royal Road*, 195.

17. There was an alternate route that followed the west bank of the Río Grande between Socorro and San Felipe Pueblo. Moorhead, *Royal Road*, 106. Apparently George Frederick Ruxton, the Englishman, traversed part of the western bank when he traveled over the Chihuahua Trail in 1846. He describes camping in a pretty

valley under a bluff on the western bank of the Río Grande about two miles from San Felipe, in Hafen, *Ruxton*, 177.

18. Although he does not mention the name La Bajada, W. W. H. Davis gives a description of his journey from Santa Fe to Peña Blanca and the steep descent he had to negotiate on the way, in *Ruxton*, 338–39. This was not the main route of the Camino Real, but a separate descent used only by horsemen. Another route that Davis described wound six miles down the canyon of the Santa Fe River between two steep mesas (one was La Bajada) and across another mesa (La Majada), and then descended into the valley of the Río del Norte near the Santo Domingo Pueblo. *El Gringo*, 338–39, 347–48. In *Ruxton*, 177–79, Ruxton made no mention of La Bajada or a difficult descent or ascent, but he did describe traversing the bottomlands of the Galisteo Creek and the trials of a Yankee traveler climbing up out of that arroyo.

19. George Frederick Ruxton recounted his experiences while camped on the bluff above Galisteo Creek, in *Ruxton*, 177.

20. Drumm, *Magoffin*, in foreword by Howard Lamar, xix, xx.

21. Most accounts say that Mariano Chávez's home was at Hacienda de Padillas on the west side of the river, not Peralta, which was several miles downriver on the east bank. However, Chávez's extensive lands bordered both sides of the river, and he did apparently have a home on the east side as well.

22. El Placer refers to the placer mines south of Santa Fe. The old placers were located in the Ortiz Mountains, near the mining settlement of Dolores. The new placers were discovered in the San Pedro Mountains in 1839 by prospectors from Dolores. By 1845 the mining town of San Francisco de Tuerto at the new placers was prosperous enough to support a number of stores. John Townley, "El Placer," 114, 115. Fulton was probably heading for Tuerto, in the vicinity of present-day Golden. A direct route to the placers went east out of Albuquerque, through the (Tijeras) Canyon and north on the east side of the Sandía Mountains (Highway 14). This route is described in *Over the Chihuahua and Santa Fe Trails, 1847–1848: George Rutledge Gibson's Journal*, ed. Robert W. Frazer (Albuquerque: University of New Mexico Press, 1981), 36–38. Both old and new placers were mostly abandoned by the end of the Mexican Era.

23. The surname McDermot may be incorrect; the signature is difficult to decipher.

24. Drumm, *Magoffin*, xix.

CHAPTER FIFTEEN

1. Unless otherwise indicated, this case is taken from MANM, roll 39, frames 136–41, Proceedings against Extranjero Julian Colenes (Collins) for murder, 4 and 5 September 1845.

2. The Cañon de Pecos Grant, or part of it, would later become known as the Alexander Valle Grant. Kessell, *Kiva, Cross, and Crown*, 441–49. For a history of the

Pecos Pueblo, see Kessell, *Kiva, Cross, and Crown*. For a history of the Pecos Land Grant and the grants that encroached on it, read Hall, *Four Leagues*.

3. One of the original applicants for the grant, along with Juan de Dios Peña, was Juan Ortiz II. Ibid., 19.

4. Occasionally witnesses were disqualified due to close kinship ties. Cutter, "Judicial," 195.

5. Ibid., 186.

6. Although this was the only homicide found in the records of the Mexican Era where an extranjero was accused of murdering a New Mexican, there are recorded occurrences of violence directed against New Mexicans by extranjeros in the judicial records.

CHAPTER SIXTEEN

1. With total disregard for the Spanish decrees against trading with foreigners, a handful of Frenchmen made their way into New Mexico during the eighteenth century and managed to trade much-desired goods to local Mexicans. If captured, they faced arrest and imprisonment. This was the fate that befell the young American Lieutenant Zebulon Pike in 1806 while on an official expedition for the U.S. government. Pike wrote the first description of New Mexico by an American. Simmons, *Interpretive History*, 77–106.

2. For a good idea of the numbers and nationalities of foreigners that flocked to New Mexico between 1825 and 1828, see Weber, *Extranjeros*, 16–43.

3. Charles Bent and his brother William were in partnership with Ceran St. Vrain and his brother Marcellin. Together they built Bent's Fort in southern Colorado, which became the center of the fur trade. Lavender, *Bent's Fort*. On the Robidoux brothers and the fur trade, see Weber, *Taos Trappers*, 82–97. Milo Milton Quaife, ed., *Kit Carson's Autobiography* (1935; reprint, Lincoln: University of Nebraska Press, Bison Books, n.d.). See n. 7, this chapter, on Beaubien and Gervais Nolan.

4. Weber, *Taos Trappers*, 136, 219–22, 224.

5. Taos whiskey, also called aguardiente de Taos or Taos Lightning, was a popular alcoholic drink distilled from wheat and corn. Foreigners began brewing this lethal concoction as early as 1824 in the Taos area. It was illegal to trade whiskey to Indians, but the practice continued. Weber, *Taos Trappers*, 8, 72–73, 117–18, 225–26. A letter written by William Workman to his brother back in the States lists not only the articles he needed for his distillery but also items of clothing and food that were hard to get in Taos. David J. Weber, ed., "A Letter From Taos, 1826," *New Mexico Historical Review* 41 (April 1966): 158–61.

6. Weber, *Rare Imprints*, imprint no. 5 Antonio José Martínez's exposition to Santa Anna. This was printed on Martínez's own press. The only press in New Mexico during this time, it had been brought over the Santa Fe Trail by Josiah Gregg in 1834. Also see Weber, "American Westward Expansion and the Break-

down of Relations between Pobladores and "Indios Barbaros' on Mexico's Far Northern Frontier, 1821–1846," *New Mexico Historical Review* 56 (July 1981): 221–33. Donaciano Vigil also wrote about the problems caused by North American traders on the Mexican frontier, but, unlike Martínez, Vigil blamed Mexican policies rather than Americans. Weber, *Arms*, xi, xii.

7. The best known of these was the 1,714,765-acre tract that became known as the Maxwell Land Grant. It was granted in 1841 to Carlos Beaubien, a French-Canadian and naturalized Mexican citizen, and Guadalupe Miranda, Armijo's secretary of state. Narciso Beaubien, Carlos's young son, and Stephen Luis Lee, a Taos distiller, were awarded the adjoining 1,038,195-acre Sangre de Cristo Grant. Gervais Nolan, a one-time Taos fur trader who had immigrated to New Mexico with Carlos Beaubien in the mid- 1820s acquired two separate grants totaling over one and a half million acres. The largest grant of all was the sprawling 4,096,346-acre Las Animas Grant that bordered both the Maxwell and Sangre de Cristo Grants and one of Nolan's grants. This huge tract of land in present-day Colorado, was given to Ceran St. Vrain, a Taos merchant who staked fur traders, and Cornelio Vigil, juez de paz of Taos. Westphall, *Mercedes Reales*, 43–66.

8. Luis and Antoine Robidoux, French-Americans, both held the position of first alcalde of Santa Fe. Weber, *Mexican Frontier*, 235.

9. Weber, *Extranjeros*, 8, 9.

10. For a listing of works written by foreigners about New Mexico during the early to mid-nineteenth century, see n. 10, Introduction.

11. Hafen, *Ruxton*, 182–83.

12. Weber, *Foreigners*, 71–72.

13. Gregg, *Commerce*, 214.

14. Townley, "El Placer," 105 n. 9.

15. Bent to Alvarez, 10 December 1839, BR, no. 39; 1 December 1840, BR, no. 42; 30 January 1841, BR, no. 46; Thomas Chávez, *Manuel Alvarez*, 23–67.

16. Gregg, *Commerce*, 262–63. For a complete description of the Chávez murder, see Simmons, *Murder*.

17. Bent to Alvarez, Taos, 1 December 1840, BR, no. 42

18. Alvarez to Powhatan Ellis, Santa Fe, 14 December 1840, BR, Alvarez Letter Book, no. 9. No further information is given about these purported murders. Chávez mentions a Tomás Kennedy who asked to marry doña Luz Basan of Pajarito in 1832, and a Julian (William) Gordon, an Anglo-American who asked permission to marry Juana María Lucero in 1826. Angélico Chávez, "New Names," 307, 311. Could these have been the two murder victims mentioned by Alvarez?

19. Thomas Chávez, *Conflict*, 55–56.

20. MANM, roll 33, frames 1034–370, Proceedings involving the robbery of Amado Piérotin, 27 January to 3 March 1846; Minge, "Problems," 128–32, 228–32; Webb, *Adventures*, 97–98.

21. Thomas Chávez, *Manuel Alvarez*, 76.

22. MANM, roll 26, frames 745–64, Proceedings against Robert Beal for shooting of José María Guerrero, 27–30 September 1839.

23. MANM, roll 33, frames 882–97, Proceedings against the "extranjero" Maese for assault, 9–15 December 1843.

24. Craver, *Impact of Intimacy*, 41–45. Craver suggests that many extranjeros integrated peacefully into New Mexican society without conflict. New Mexicans turned against only a small portion of the foreigners who they felt were a threat to their lifestyle.

25. Craver, *Impact of Intimacy*, 41–45; Michael McNierney, ed., *Taos 1847: The Revolt in Contemporary Accounts* (Boulder: Johnson Publishing Co., 1980).

26. Counting only executions that were a result of due process and where it could be proven by primary evidence that an execution actually took place, state historian Robert Tórrez found that at least forty-nine (and possibly fifty-three) executions by hanging took place in New Mexico between 1849 and 1908. At least seven were hanged in Taos in April 1847, and six more in Santa Fe in August of that year, making at least thirteen executions (and possibly twenty) within a year of the American occupation. The estimate of sixty-two executions during the territorial years was arrived at by adding the more conservative figures (forty-nine plus thirteen). Tórrez, "Justice in New Mexico," 2, 3.

CONCLUSION

1. Haslip, "Crime," 166–70.

2. Barreiro, "Ojeada," in Carroll and Haggard, *Three Chronicles*, 60.

3. Weber, "Archives," 55–56.

4. Taylor, *Drinking*, 98.

5. Colin M. MacLachlan, *Criminal Justice in Eighteenth- Century Mexico: A Study of the Tribunal of the Acordada* (Berkeley: University of California Press, 1974), 79–80; Taylor, *Drinking*, 98–99; Haslip, "Crime," 194, 202–3.

6. Haslip, "Crime," 176–86.

7. A rúbrica was a special mark or flourish added to one's signature. Sometimes it stood alone without the signature.

Bibliography

ARCHIVAL SOURCES

Albuquerque, New Mexico. University of New Mexico. Zimmerman Library. Center for Southwest Research. Mexican Archives of New Mexico (MANM). Spanish Archives of New Mexico (SANM).

Jenkins, Myra Ellen. *Calendar of the Microfilm Edition of the Mexican Archives of New Mexico (MANM) 1821–1846*. Santa Fe: State of New Mexico Records Center, 1970.

Santa Fe, New Mexico. New Mexico State Archives and Records Center. Benjamin Read Collection (BR). Benjamin Read Collection/Manuel Alvarez Letter Book. Sender Collection.

Salazar, Richard J., comp. *Calendar to the Microfilm Edition of the Sender Collection, 1697–1884*. Santa Fe: Archives Division of the New Mexico Records Center and Archives, 1988.

PRINTED DOCUMENTS AND CONTEMPORARY WORKS

Becknell, Thomas. "The Journals of Capt. Thomas Becknell from Boone's Lick to Santa Fe, and from Santa Cruz to Green River." *Missouri Historical Review* 4 (January 1910): 65–84.

Carroll, H. Bailey, and J. Villasana Haggard, eds., trans. *Three New Mexico Chronicles: The "Exposición" of Don Pedro Bautista Pino 1812; the "Ojeada" of Lic. Antonio Barreiro 1832; and the additions by Don José Agustín de Escudero 1849*. Albuquerque: The Quivira Society, 1942.

Chávez, Fray Angélico. *Archives of the Archdiocese of Santa Fe 1678–1900*. Washington D.C.: Academy of American Franciscan History, 1959.

Chávez, Thomas E. *Conflict and Acculturation: Manuel Alvarez's 1842 Memorial*. Santa Fe: Museum of New Mexico Press, 1989.

Davis, W. W. H. *El Gringo, New Mexico and her People*. 1857. Reprint, Lincoln: University of Nebraska Press, Bison Books, 1982.

Drumm, Stella M., ed. *Down the Santa Fe Trail and into Mexico: The Diary of Susan Shelby Magoffin, 1846–1847*. 1962. Reprint, Lincoln: University of Nebraska Press, Bison Books, 1982.

Frazer, Robert W., ed. *Over the Chihuahua and Santa Fe Trails, 1847–1848: George Rutledge Gibson's Journal*. Albuquerque: University of New Mexico Press, 1981.

Garrard, Lewis, H. *Wah-To-Yah and the Taos Trail*. Edited by Ralph P. Bieber. 1938. Reprint, Philadelphia: Porcupine Press, 1974.

Gregg, Josiah. *Commerce of the Prairies*. Edited by Max L. Moorhead. Norman: University of Oklahoma Press, 1954.

Gregg, Kate L., ed. *The Road to Santa Fe: The Journal and Diaries of George Champlin Sibley*. Albuquerque: The University of New Mexico Press, 1952.

Hafen, LeRoy R. *Ruxton of the Rockies: Autobiographical Writings by the author of "Adventures in Mexico and the Rocky Mountains" and "Life in the Far West."* Norman: University of Oklahoma Press, 1950.

Kendall, George Wilkins. *Narrative of the Texan Santa Fe Expedition*. New York: Harper & Brothers, 1844.

McNierney, Michael, ed. *Taos 1847: The Revolt in Contemporary Accounts*. Boulder: Johnson Publishing Co., 1980.

Olmsted, Virginia Langham, G. R. S., trans., comp. *New Mexico Spanish and Mexican Colonial Censuses 1790, 1823, 1845*. Albuquerque: New Mexico Genealogical Society Inc., 1975.

Pike, Albert. *Prose Sketches and Poems, Written in the Western Country*. Edited by David J. Weber. Albuquerque: Calvin Horn Publishers, Inc., 1967.

Quaife, Milo Milton, ed. *Kit Carson's Autobiography*. 1935. Reprint, Lincoln: University of Nebraska Press, Bison Books, n.d.

Sunder, John E., ed. *Matt Field on the Santa Fe Trail*. Norman: University of Oklahoma Press, 1960.

Webb, James Josiah. *Adventures in the Santa Fe Trade, 1844–1847*. Edited by Ralph P. Bieber. 1931. Reprint, Philadelphia: Porcupine Press, 1974.

Weber, David J., ed. *Arms, Indians, and the Mismanagement of New Mexico: Donaciano Vigil, 1846*. Southwestern Studies Series, no. 77. El Paso: Texas Western Press, 1986.

——. *The Extranjeros: Selected Documents from the Mexican Side of the Santa Fe Trail, 1825–1828*. Santa Fe: Stagecoach Press, 1967.

——. *Northern Mexico on the Eve of the United States Invasion: Rare Imprints Concerning California, Arizona, New Mexico, and Texas, 1821–1846*. New York: Arno Press, 1976.

BOOKS

Baxter, John O. *Las Carneradas: Sheep Trade in New Mexico, 1700–1860*. Albuquerque: University of New Mexico Press, 1987.

Beachum, Larry M. *William Becknell, Father of the Santa Fe Trade*. El Paso: Texas Western Press, 1982.

Beck, Warren A., and Ynez D. Haase. *Historical Atlas of New Mexico*. Norman: University of Oklahoma Press, 1985.

Boyd, E. *Popular Arts of Spanish New Mexico*. Santa Fe: Museum of New Mexico Press, 1974.

Chávez, Fray Angélico. *Origins of New Mexico Families*. Santa Fe: William Gannon, 1975.

Chávez, Thomas E. *Manuel Alvarez, 1794–1856: A Southwestern Biography*. Niwot: University of Colorado Press, 1990.

Cobos, Rubén. *A Dictionary of New Mexico and Southern Colorado Spanish*. Santa Fe: Museum of New Mexico Press, 1983.

Craver, Rebecca McDowell. *The Impact of Intimacy: Mexican-Anglo Intermarriage in New Mexico, 1821–1846*. Southwestern Studies Series, no. 66. El Paso: Texas Western Press, 1982.

Crawford, Stanley. *Mayordomo: Chronicle of an Acequia in Northern New Mexico*. Albuquerque: University of New Mexico Press, 1988.

Cutter, Charles R. *Protector de Indios in Colonial New Mexico, 1659–1821*. Albuquerque: University of New Mexico Press, 1986.

deBuys, William. *Enchantment and Exploitation: the Life and Hard Times of a New Mexico Mountain Range*. Albuquerque: University of New Mexico Press, 1985.

Dickey, Roland, F. *New Mexico Village Arts*. 1949. Reprint, Albuquerque: University of New Mexico Press, 1990.

Ebright, Malcolm. *Land Grants and Lawsuits in Northern New Mexico*. New Mexico Land Grant Series, ed. John R. Van Ness, vol. 5. Albuquerque: University of New Mexico Press, 1994.

Franswa, Gregory M. *Maps of the Santa Fe Trail*. St. Louis: The Patrice Press, 1989.

Gallegos, Bernardo P. *Literacy, Education, and Society in New Mexico, 1693–1821*. Albuquerque: University of New Mexico Press, 1992.

Gutiérrez, Ramón A. *When Jesus Came, the Corn Mothers Went Away: Marriage, Sexuality, and Power in New Mexico, 1500–1846*. Stanford: Stanford University Press, 1991.

Hall, Emlen G. *Four Leagues of Pecos: A Legal History of the Pecos Grant, 1800–1933*. New Mexico Land Grant Series, ed. John R. Van Ness, vol. 2. Albuquerque: University of New Mexico Press, 1984.

Horgan, Paul. *Lamy of Santa Fe: a Biography*. New York: Farrar, Straus, and Giroux, 1980.

Johnson, Lyman L., ed. *The Problem of Order in Changing Societies: Essays on Crime and Policing in Argentina and Uruguay, 1750–1940*. Albuquerque: University of New Mexico Press, 1990.

Jones, Oakah L., Jr. *Los Paisanos: Spanish Settlers on the Northern Frontier of New Spain*. Norman: University of Oklahoma Press, 1970.

Kessell, John L., ed. *Kiva, Cross, and Crown: The Pecos Indians and New Mexico, 1540–1840.* 1979. Reprint, Albuquerque: University of New Mexico Press, 1987.

——, ed. *Remote Beyond Compare: Letters of don Diego de Vargas to his Family from New Spain and New Mexico, 1675–1706.* Albuquerque: University of New Mexico Press, 1989.

Kubler, George. *The Religious Architecture of New Mexico in the Colonial Period and since the American Occupation.* Albuquerque: University of New Mexico Press, 1990.

Kutsche, Paul, and John R. Van Ness. *Cañones: Values, Crisis, and Survival in a Northern New Mexico Village.* Albuquerque: University of New Mexico Press, 1981.

Lange, Charles H. *Cochití: A New Mexico Pueblo, Past and Present.* Carbondale and Edwardsville: Southern Illinois University Press, Arcturus Books ed., 1968.

Laughlin, Ruth. *The Wind Leaves no Shadow.* Caldwell: The Caxton Printers, Ltd., 1986.

Lavender, David. *Bent's Fort.* 1954. Reprint, Lincoln: University of Nebraska Press, Bison Books, 1972.

Lecompte, Janet. *Rebellion in Río Arriba, 1837.* Albuquerque: University of New Mexico Press, 1985.

MacLachlan, Colin M. *Criminal Justice in Eighteenth-Century Mexico: A Study of the Tribunal of the Acordada.* Berkeley: University of California Press, 1974.

MacLachlan, Colin M., and Jaime E. Rodriguez O. *The Forging of the Cosmic Race: a Reinterpretation of Colonial Mexico.* Berkeley and Los Angeles: University of California Press, 1980.

Martín, Luis. *Daughters of the Conquistadores: Women of the Viceroyalty of Peru.* Albuquerque: University of New Mexico Press, 1983.

Meketa, Jacqueline Dorgan, ed. *Legacy of Honor: The Life of Rafael Chacón, A Nineteenth-Century New Mexican.* Albuquerque: University of New Mexico Press, 1986.

Meyer, Marian. *Mary Donoho New First Lady of the Santa Fe Trail.* Santa Fe: Ancient City Press, 1991.

Moorhead, Max L. *New Mexico's Royal Road: Trade and Travel on the Chihuahua Trail.* Norman: University of Oklahoma Press, 1959.

Noble, David Grant, ed. *Santa Fe: History of an Ancient City.* Santa Fe: School of American Research Press, 1989.

Pearce, T. M., ed. *New Mexico Place Names: A Geographical Dictionary.* Albuquerque: University of New Mexico Press, 1965.

Sedillo, Mela. *Mexican and New Mexican Folkdances.* Albuquerque: University of New Mexico Press, 1950.

Simmons, Marc. *Albuquerque, A Narrative History.* Albuquerque: University of New Mexico Press, 1982.

——. *Coronado's Land, Essays on Daily Life in Colonial New Mexico*. Albuquerque: University of New Mexico Press, 1991.

——. *Following the Santa Fe Trail: A Guide For Modern Travelers*. Santa Fe: Ancient City Press, 1984.

——. *The Little Lion of the Southwest: A Life of Manuel Antonio Chaves*. Chicago: Swallow Press Inc., 1973.

——. *Murder on the Santa Fe Trail: An International Incident, 1843*. El Paso: Texas Western Press, 1987.

——. *New Mexico: An Interpretive History*. 1977. Reprint, Albuquerque: University of New Mexico Press, 1988.

——. *Spanish Government in New Mexico*. Albuquerque: University of New Mexico Press, 1968.

——. *Taos to Tomé: True Tales of Hispanic New Mexico*. Santa Fe: Ancient City Press, 1978.

Simmons, Marc, and Joan Myers, photographer. *Along The Santa Fe Trail*. Albuquerque: University of New Mexico Press, 1986.

Swadesh, Frances Leon. *Los Primeros Pobladores: Hispanic Americans of the Ute Frontier*. Notre Dame: University of Notre Dame Press, 1974.

Taylor, William, B. *Drinking, Homicide, and Rebellion in Colonial Mexican Villages*. Stanford: Stanford University Press, 1979.

Tyler, Daniel. *Sources for New Mexican History, 1821–1848*. Santa Fe: Museum of New Mexico Press, 1984.

Vásquez, Josefina Zoraida, and Lorenzo Meyer. *The United States and Mexico*. Chicago: University of Chicago Press, 1985.

Vigil, Ralph H., Francis W. Kaye, and John R. Wunder, eds. *Spain and the Plains: Myths and Realities of Spanish Exploration and Settlement on the Great Plains*. Niwot: University of Colorado Press, 1994.

Vittucci, Mateo Marcellus. *The Language of Spanish Dance*. 1990. Paperback ed., Norman: University of Oklahoma Press, 1993.

Weber, David J. *The Mexican Frontier, 1821–1846: The American Southwest Under Mexico*. Albuquerque: University of New Mexico Press, 1982.

——. *The Taos Trappers: The Fur Trade in the Far Southwest, 1540–1846*. Norman: University of Oklahoma Press, 1970.

——, ed. *Foreigners in their Native Land: Historical Roots of the Mexican Americans*. Albuquerque: University of New Mexico Press, 1987.

——.

Weigle, Marta. *Brothers of Light, Brothers of Blood: The Penitentes of the Southwest*. Santa Fe: Ancient City Press, 1976.

Weigle, Marta, and Peter White. *The Lore of New Mexico*. Albuquerque: University of New Mexico Press, 1988.

Westphall, Victor. *Mercedes Reales: Hispanic Land Grants of the Upper Río Grande Region*. New Mexico Land Grant Series, ed. John R. Van Ness, vol. 1. Albuquerque: University of New Mexico Press, 1983.

ARTICLES AND ESSAYS

Allison, W. H. H. "Santa Fe as it Appeared during the Winter of the Years 1837 and 1838." *Old Santa Fe* 2 (October 1914): 170–83.

———. "Santa Fe in 1846." *Old Santa Fe* 2 (April 1915): 391–406.

Bloom, Lansing Bartlett. "The Death of Jacques D'Eglise." *New Mexico Historical Review* 2 (October 1927): 369–79.

———. "New Mexico Under Mexican Administration, 1821–1846." *Old Santa Fe* 1 (July 1913): 3–49; (October 1913): 131–75; (January 1914): 235–87; (April 1914): 347–68. *Old Santa Fe* 2 (July 1914): 3–56; (October 1914): 119–69; (January 1915): 223–77; (April 1915): 351–80.

Chávez, Fray Angélico. "New Names in New Mexico, 1820–1850." *El Palacio* 64 (September, October 1957): 291–318; (November, December 1957): 367–80.

———. "The Penitents of New Mexico." *New Mexico Historical Review* 29 (April 1954): 97–123.

Cortazar, Connie. "The Santa Visita of Agustín Fernández de San Vicente to New Mexico, 1826." *New Mexico Historical Review* 59 (January 1984): 33–48.

de Aragon, Ray John. "Padre Antonio José Martínez: the Man and the Myth." In *Padre Martínez: New Perspectives From Taos*. Taos: Millicent Rogers Museum, 1988.

Hall, G. Emlen, and David J. Weber. "Mexican Liberals and the Pueblo Indians, 1821–1829." *New Mexico Historical Review* 59 (January 1984): 5–32.

Jones, Oakah, L, Jr. "Spanish Civil Communities and Settlers in Frontier New Mexico, 1790–1810." In *Hispanic–American Essays in Honor of Max Leon Moorhead*, edited by William Coker, 37–60. Pensacola: Perdido Bay Press, 1979.

Lecompte, Janet. "The Independent Women of Hispanic New Mexico, 1821–1846." In *New Mexico Women: Intercultural Perspectives*, edited by Joan M. Jensen and Darlis A. Miller. Albuquerque: University of New Mexico Press, 1986.

———. "Manuel Armijo's Family History." *New Mexico Historical Review* 48 (July 1973): 251–56.

McClure, Charles R. "The Texan-Santa Fe Expedition of 1841." *New Mexico Historical Review* 48 (January 1973): 45–56.

Moorhead, Max L. "Spanish Transportation in the Southwest, 1540–1846." *New Mexico Historical Review* 35 (April 1957): 107–22.

Nostrand, Richard L. "The Century of Hispano Expansion." *New Mexico Historical Review* 62 (October 1987): 361–86.

Oczon, Annabelle. "Bilingual and Spanish-Language Newspapers in Territorial New Mexico." Calvin Horn Essay. *New Mexico Historical Review* 54 (January 1979): 45–52.

Perrigo, Lynn. "New Mexico in the Mexican Period, as revealed in the Torres Documents." *New Mexico Historical Review* 29 (January 1954): 28–40.

Read, Benjamin M. "In Santa Fe During the Mexican Regime." *New Mexico Historical Review* 2 (January 1927): 90–97.

Rock, Rosalind. "Pido y Súplico: Women and the Law in Spanish New Mexico, 1697–1763." *New Mexico Historical Review* 65 (April 1990): 145–59.

Simmons, Marc. "Hygiene, Sanitation, and Public Health in Hispanic New Mexico." *New Mexico Historical Review* 67 (July 1992): 205–25.

———. "New Mexico's Spanish Exiles." *New Mexico Historical Review* 59 (January 84): 67–79.

———. "Settlement Patterns and Village Plans in Colonial New Mexico." In *New Spain's Far Northern Frontier: Essays on Spain in the American West*, 1540–1821, edited by David J. Weber, 99–115. Albuquerque: University of New Mexico Press, 1979.

Tjarks, Alicia V. "Demographic, Ethnic and Occupational Structure of New Mexico, 1790." *The Americas* 35 (July 1978): 45–88.

Townley, John M. "El Placer: A New Mexico Mining Boom Before 1846." *Journal of the West* 10 (January 1971): 102–15.

Tyler, Daniel. "Gringo Views of Manuel Armijo." *New Mexico Historical Review* 45 (January 1970): 23–46.

———. "Underground Water in Hispanic New Mexico: A Brief Analysis of Laws, Customs, and Disputes." *New Mexico Historical Review* 66 (July 1991): 287–301.

U.S. Department of the Interior. National Park Service. "The Spanish Black Legend: Origins of Anti-Hispanic Stereotypes," by Joseph P. Sánchez. N.p., n.d.

Valdez, Facundo. "Vergüenza." In *The Survival of Spanish American Villages*, edited by Paul Kutsche. Colorado Springs: Colorado College Research Committee, 1979.

Wagner, Henry R. "New Mexico Spanish Press." *New Mexico Historical Review* 12 (January 1987): 1–40.

Weber, David J. "American Westward Expansion and the Breakdown of Relations between Pobladores and 'Indios Bárbaros' on Mexico's Far Northern Frontier, 1821–1846." *New Mexico Historical Review* 56 (July 1981): 221–38.

———, ed. "A Letter From Taos, 1826." *New Mexico Historical Review* 41 (April 1966): 155–64.

———. "The New Mexico Archives in 1827." *New Mexico Historical Review* 61 (January 1986): 53–61.

UNPUBLISHED MATERIALS

Cutter, Charles Ross. "Judicial Practice in Northern New Spain, 1700–1810." Ph.D. diss., University of New Mexico, 1989.

Gutiérrez, Ramón A. "Marriage, Sex and Family: Social Change in Colonial New Mexico, 1690–1846." Ph.D. diss., University of Wisconsin, 1980.

Haslip, Gabriel James. "Crime and the Administration of Justice in Colonial Mexico City, 1696–1810." Ph.D. diss., Columbia University, 1980.

Minge, Ward Alan. "Frontier Problems in New Mexico Preceding the Mexican War, 1840–1846." Ph.D. diss. University of New Mexico, 1965.

Tórrez, Robert J. "Justice in Spanish Colonial and Territorial New Mexico: A Comparative Perspective." Lecture, 1989.

Index